MAIN TRENDS IN
SOCIAL AND
CULTURAL ANTHROPOLOGY

In the same series:

MAIN TRENDS IN HISTORY
MAIN TRENDS IN AESTHETICS AND THE SCIENCES OF ART
MAIN TRENDS IN PHILOSOPHY

MAIN TRENDS
IN SOCIAL AND
CULTURAL
ANTHROPOLOGY

Maurice Freedman

HOLMES & MEIER PUBLISHERS, INC.

NEW YORK • LONDON

Published in the United States of America 1979 by
HOLMES & MEIER PUBLISHERS, INC.
30 Irving Place, New York, N.Y. 10003

Reprinted from MAIN TRENDS OF RESEARCH IN THE SOCIAL AND
HUMAN SCIENCES—Part II

Copyright © Unesco 1978

ALL RIGHTS RESERVED

Library of Congress Cataloging in Publication Data

Freedman, Maurice.
    Main trends in social and cultural anthropology.

    (Main trends in the social and human sciences ;
1)
    Originally published as chapter 1 of Main trends
of research in the social and human sciences, pt. 2.
    Bibliography: p.
    1. Ethnology.   I. Title.   II. Series:
Main trends of research in the social and human
sciences. Selections ; 1.
GN316.F73   1979   301.2   79-12927

ISBN 0-8419-0504-5

MANUFACTURED IN THE UNITED STATES OF AMERICA

Contents

INTRODUCTION

If this chapter had been written according to the original plan (but not by
me), it would have appeared in the volume on the Social Sciences that pre-
ceded this one and with it makes a pair.[1] It would then have taken its place
quite naturally in a family of chapters on sister sciences. By the accident that
the chapter falls in this volume, social and cultural anthropology now takes up
position within the less organized group of the humanities, and it is possible that some practitioners of the subject may regret the apparent re-
alignment. I should like to suggest, therefore, that we do not repine at the
unplanned reclassification, and that, instead, we consider the possibility that
social and cultural anthropology, undoubtedly a social science, has as many
important links with the humanities as it has with those subjects which conventionally stand immediately around it. It is inconceivable – or at least, it
ought not to be conceived – that our discipline should find law, history, archaeology, or art more alien to it than, say, economics or political science.
Alternatively, it might be argued that the fortuitous transfer of the chapter
from the first to the second volume in the series quite accidentally underlines
one of the very 'main trends' to be detected in the present life of the subject,
at least as it is lived in some important centres of its development: a movement away from a preoccupation with a narrow range of problems and forms
of society, towards a wider conception of humanistic learning and contemplation.

'Main trends': one finds them by experience and judgment, and not by
some pseudo-scientific scrutiny of all the works written on social/cultural
anthropology, ethnology, and ethnography in whatever language. The experience and judgment are obviously those of the rapporteur and his five associate rapporteurs – based in England, France, India, Uganda, the U.S.A.,
and the U.S.S.R. – and of, to a lesser degree, the other scholars who, as
consultants on particular topics and regions, have been associated with the
enterprise. These men and women have done their best, within the very tight
time-schedule imposed on them by the reclassification of the chapter to
which reference was made in the last paragraph, to present a fair account of
what is now of significance in the subject. But the word 'significance' is being
used in a special sense: significance in relation to the present and the near
future. We do not, except incidentally, look back to the past of the discipline,
and, however unwillingly, we present an unhistorical account of our subject.
We are forced to neglect even some of its recent history by the overriding
need to fasten our attention on what seems now to be lively, promising, and,
in some cases, threatening. So that there is not only a large risk of distortion
involved in the attempt to survey what has been done in the last few years;
we have deliberately increased the chance of our displeasing our colleagues

1. *Main Trends of Research in the Social and Human Sciences, Part I: Social
Sciences* (1970). (Full bibliographical details of each work cited will be found in
the List of Works Cited at the end of the chapter, pp. 138-176.)

the world over by venturing to refer to the immediate future and what may or ought to be achieved in it. To have discussed trends which stopped dead on the last day of 1970 [2] would have been not to discuss them at all, for by their nature they move on into the time which lies just ahead of us. A normative element therefore creeps into our work: to prophesy is in some measure to dictate. It cannot be helped. On the other hand, no reader is likely to be so imprudent as to attach a strictly scientific value to our forecasts or so gullible as to think himself bound by any prescriptions we state or imply.

Nor will the careful reader overlook the fact that our treatment of social and cultural anthropology rests upon a framework which, precisely because it is a framework, breaks up reality in an arbitrary fashion: discontinuities may perhaps be seen where none ought to be discernible, and, more serious, topics and approaches which another framework might have brought clearly into view are here blurred or even neglected. Indeed, it would be a fascinating exercise to match this survey with one planned and carried out by a quite different set of anthropologists around the world.

To define the field covered by the title of the chapter is in fact one of the chief tasks of the chapter itself; it cannot be done at the outset except at the risk of oversimplifying. The reader will (I hope) see why that is so as the chapter unfolds. At this preliminary stage it is necessary only to say, under the head of definition, that the words 'social and cultural anthropology' (and 'anthropology' as a convenient abbreviation) will be used to cover the activities and writings of scholars who variously describe themselves as social or cultural anthropologists, ethnologists, or ethnographers. 'Ethnography' will normally be used in the restricted sense of 'descriptive account' or 'the facts of description'.

A further preliminary point needs to be made. This is not a bibliographical survey and the references to published work will be selective in the interest of brevity.

ACKNOWLEDGEMENTS

While I take full responsibility for the views expressed in and the defects of the chapter, I should like to underline the fact that it rests upon the labours of scholars in many parts of the world. I have found in the forbearance and helpfulness of my numerous colleagues good grounds for believing that, if it does not exist, a world republic of letters could be brought closer to being born. I do not make little of the differences in interests and points of view that have had, however unsuccessfully in the event, to be reconciled; it is the good nature of the co-operators that has impressed me.

I count myself very fortunate in having been guided and helped through

2. It has been impossible to resist the temptation to refer to work published up to mid-1971 (when the chapter was put into its final form), and even in a few cases to work appearing later than that.

the task by the general rapporteur of the volume, M. Jacques Havet, and whatever success has been achieved must in the first place be set down to him. Before I came to work with him I did not think it possible that a scholar could combine and put to use such vast resources of knowledge, erudition, tact, tolerance, and administrative efficiency. I am profoundly in his debt.

Among my fellow anthropologists in the enterprise I must mention first the associate rapporteurs, who have acted as my benign censors from start to finish: Dr. Ju. P. Averkieva, of Moscow; Professor Fred Eggan, of Chicago; Professor Jean Poirier, of Nice; Professor M. N. Srinivas, then of Delhi; and Dr. Victor C. Uchendu, then of Kampala. I have not felt myself a stranger in their midst, and I pay tribute to their kindliness and receptivity.

In writing about anthropology around the world I quickly exhausted my own knowledge and I have relied heavily upon, first, a body of documents already accumulated by Unesco before I entered the scene,[3] and, second, a series of regional reports commissioned and prepared for me at very short notice. Those reports are: on North America, by Professor Fred Eggan; on Latin America, by Professor Sutti de Ortiz (Mrs. S. Koch), of Cleveland, Ohio; on the U.S.S.R., by Dr. Ju. P. Averkieva; on Hungary and other Socialist countries of Europe, by Dr. Vilmos Voigt, of Budapest; on the German-speaking countries (other than the G.D.R.), by Professor Andreas Kronenberg, of Frankfurt am Main; on the Middle East, by Professor Fuad I. Khuri, of Beirut; on English-speaking Africa, by Dr. Victor C. Uchendu; on French-speaking Africa, by Dr. Yahia Wane, of Dakar; on India and Pakistan, by Dr. R. K. Jain, of Oxford; on Sri Lanka, by Dr. S. J. Tambiah, then of Cambridge; on Japan, by Professor Chie Nakane, of Tokyo; and on Australia and New Zealand, by Dr. L. R. Hiatt, of Sydney. Alas, I have been able to use in this chapter only a small part of the material so placed at my disposal.

Special reports were also produced on topics on which I thought my knowledge to be particularly defective: on visual art, by Mr. Anthony Forge, then of London; on music, by Professor Bruno Nettl, of Urbana, Illinois; on literature, by Dr. R. G. Lienhardt, of Oxford; on technology, by Mr. M. McLeod, then of Cambridge; on linguistics, by Professor Dell H. Hymes, of Philadelphia; on psychology, by Professor Otto Klineberg, of Paris; on ethology, by Mrs. Hilary Callan, of Birmingham; on social and cultural change, by Professor Jean Poirier; on applied anthropology, by Professor Sol Tax, of Chicago; on statistical methods in field work, by Dr. G. K. Garbett, of Manchester; and on mathematics and computers, by Professor Eugene A. Hammel, of Berkeley, California. Although he did not write a report, I have in the same category to thank Dr. William C. Sturtevant, of Washington, D.C., for the material he sent me on ethnohistory.

3. Of those documents the following are in published form in *The Social Sciences, Problems and Orientations* (1968): BARBUT, 'Anthropologie et mathématiques'; GERBRANDS, 'The study of art in anthropology'; de HEUSCH, 'Les points de vue structuralistes en anthropologie ...'; KULA, 'On the typology of economic systems'; KUNSTADTER, 'Applications of simulation techniques in social and cultural anthropology'; LIVINGSTONE, 'Physical anthropology and cultural evolution'; and MOORE, F. W., 'Current trends in cross-cultural research'.

Both the first and second drafts of the chapter were read and criticized not only by the five associate rapporteurs but also by many of the writers of the special reports, and, in addition, by Dr. William C. Sturtevant and Professor Pierre Alexandre, of Paris. The first draft was commented on by Professor Meyer Fortes, of Cambridge, the second by some of the authors of other chapters in this volume and by a number of scholars not associated with the enterprise, among whom I should like especially to thank Dr. John Beattie, of Oxford (now of Leiden), Dr. Audrey Colson, of Oxford, Dr. A. S. Diamond, of London, Professor Lucy Mair, of Durham (now of London), and Dr. Peter Rivière, of Cambridge (now of Oxford). It will be seen that my obligations are fittingly far-flung.

I thank my wife, without whose help I could not have written this chapter.

M.F.

A. CO-ORDINATES OF STUDY IN TIME AND SPACE

If anthropology were the study of Society and societies and of Culture and cultures, without qualification, it would be grotesquely encyclopaedic, and no men could be found to practise it. Even to suggest that it might tend towards realizing so englobing a plan would be to raise the flag of an intolerable scholastic imperialism. (It is not that the historians, sociologists, and so on, would cower; they would merely laugh. Or rather, most of them would; for there are a few among them who might react with jealousy: the possibility always remains that Kroeber-like aims [4] may once more be striven after by anthropologists with universalist pretensions.) Social and cultural anthropology is for the vast majority of its adherents a practicable subject because it is limited in scope − although few, if any, scholars can practise all of it. But it is a problem to decide by what criteria that limitation is brought about,

4. Cf. KROEBER, *Configurations of Culture Growth* (1969, first published 1944). And see MARKARJAN, *Očerki teorii kul'tury* (= Essays on Theory of Culture) (1969). *Current Anthropology. A World Journal of the Sciences of Man* (which lists social anthropology, physical anthropology, prehistory, archæology, linguistics, folklore, and ethnology in the device on its cover) may certainly give rise to the idea that Anthropology deals with everything human; and social and cultural anthropology within that broad setting may appear very ambitious. But in some circumstances the attribution of universalist aims comes from outside the discipline. The professionals are likely to be surprised by the following definition of 'anthropological research': '... investigation or research of a physical anthropological, social anthropological, cultural anthropological, sociological, physiological, group psychological, linguistic, ethnological, ethnographical, or ethno-historical nature and includes research into the human geography and human ecology of any area'. It is the definition used in 'An Act to Regulate Anthropological Research' enacted by the Parliament of Botswana in 1967; and in that context the definition makes sense. If anthropologists are to be subject to restriction in their work − the Act will repay close study − they may be made more cheerful by the knowledge that they are not being singled out.

to discriminate among the criteria, and to assess their mutual compatibility.

There was once – it still survives in some form in institutional arrangements, in universities and elsewhere – a unified discipline called Anthropology *tout court*; it comprised prehistoric archaeology, physical anthropology, ethnology, and linguistics. When it first developed in the nineteenth century and for the first period of its history, that subject could operate with a barely analysed notion of the 'primitive', for 'early', 'archaic', and 'simple' fitted together in an uncomplicated evolutionary frame. The unity of Anthropology has in many places long since disappeared. (That is not to say, however, that its divisions have lost intellectual touch with one another: but their contacts are now of a different kind.) Yet social and cultural anthropology has clearly inherited from the Anthropology from which it sprang a legacy with which it has difficulties in coming to terms.[5] In recent times it has been common enough for anthropologists to class themselves as specialists in (some would say, sociologists of) primitive society, that form of society being in turn defined as non-literate, small in scale, and based upon a simple technology. (Some would add a fourth criterion: absence of money.)

There appears to be an unwarranted evolutionary assumption behind this separation out of a special class of society: such primitive societies are on the road to large-scale, literate, and technologically developed societies and may be studied while they struggle along towards the destiny that will eventually take them beyond the anthropologist's ken. It can be denied by our saying that it is only a matter of convenience that we concentrate on them: their nature calls for a distinct method of study. Sociology and the specialized social sciences have enough to do tackling the study of developed societies; to us the primitive. But (the argument proceeds) primitive societies not only demand our peculiar skills; they also offer us, because they are small and relatively undifferentiated, the opportunity to make a special contribution to the social sciences by investigating and analysing total social and cultural systems. It is in this light that we must see the accent put on the ideal field method of social and cultural anthropology as it has developed, especially in western European and American scholarship and especially since the second decade of the present century. That field method requires that the investigator observe a society intensively over a long period (say, one or two years), using the language of the people under study. We shall need to come back to this matter later on.

The insistence on method of field study as the distinguishing mark of the anthropologist's profession can then be tortuously used to overcome several

---

5. Cf. MONTAGU (ed.), *The Concept of the Primitive* (1968). Nobody nowadays likes the condescension apparently conveyed by the word 'primitive', and one recognizes that the people to whom it is applied are justified in resenting many of its implications – and that they may come as a result to deny that anthropology has anything to do with them. (Cf. OKOT p'BITEK, *African Religions in Western Scholarship* [1971?], pp. vii sqq., 6, and 43 sqq.) But it is not always possible both to avoid using the term and to remain true to the literature of the discipline under review.

difficulties arising from the notion of 'primitive' which gave birth to (or justified) the method in the first place. To begin with, 'primitive societies' do not form a homogeneous class; some indeed are very small, others large; some lack centralized forms of government, others have state forms; some have very simple technologies, others quite complicated ones. It is field method that is often made to define the class, overriding these differences: 'primitive societies' are those studied by the method. Second, when societies acquire writing, and so escape the net of one definition of 'primitive', they can continue to be studied by the same method. Third, the method is still applied when the societies previously allocated to the anthropologists become of interest to the practitioners of other social sciences.

At the same time, the anthropologist's field method grows ambitious and spills over the boundary laid down by 'primitive', and it is enabled to do so by a twist in the significance of what was originally intended, by a kind of methodological play on words. The classical field method was framed to encompass the totality of a small society; it may therefore be called 'micro-sociology'; micro-sociology, the intensive study of the small, may then be applied to other small entities – but now small communities within large societies. Hence the anthropological study, nowadays very common and destined to expand still further, of villages and other communities and small groups within agricultural and industrial societies. In that formula 'totality' has gone.

In one central tradition of anthropology the main method of study entails a preoccupation with societies and cultures as they are now because they exist to be investigated at first hand. But this indirect consequence of a legacy from Anthropology is paradoxical, for it conflicts with the orientation to time which is part and parcel of that older and wider subject. That Anthropology was about the evolution from their first forms of, among other things, societies and cultures. A large part of anthropology has in the past cut itself off from the older vision of human development over great stretches of time. Yet this latter legacy from Anthropology now reasserts itself, and anthropologists find themselves reverting to some of the preoccupations of their forbears. An example can be given briefly.

It is a perhaps rather odd feature of contemporary anthropology that, for all its attachment to the study of the 'primitive', most of its researches neglect the purest examples: the tiny societies which live by hunting and gathering. But the smaller part of the profession that does concern itself with this variety of social life has been engaged in recent times in the discussion of the relevance of its findings for the understanding of society and culture before they were overtaken (some might argue, disastrously) by the neolithic revolution. The life of men before they domesticate animals and cultivate the soil is not only radically different from what, in thoughtless moods, we take to be typical of our lot; it is also in reality the mode of human life characteristic of the greater part of our total history. The results of the study of hunters and gatherers as they persist in the contemporary world are brought to bear upon the debate on what society and culture were during some nearly two million years, a period that accounts for all but a minute fraction of our past. That debate is vividly exemplified in *Man the Hunter*,[6] which, on its dust jacket, describes itself as 'the first intensive survey of a single, crucial stage of human development – man's once universal way of life'. The conference upon which the book rests is made the more significant for our present purposes by the fact that it brought together scholars from every major region of the world where anthropology is practised. The work underlines a growing rapprochement between, on the one hand, social and cultural anthropologists and, on the other, prehistoric archaeologists and physical anthropologists. There is no implication in this coming together that the divisions of an erstwhile Anthropology are once more about to coalesce into a unified discipline: it is enough that the intellectual bonds between the divisions, for long grown slack, are now being tightened.

Naturally enough, the scholars who took part in this conference differed among themselves about the extent to which evidence drawn from the study of present-day hunters and gatherers might be legitimately employed for the reconstruction of prehistoric life, and much caution was recommended. But that is in a way a subsidiary problem, for what seems important from the point of view of anthropology is the attempt to enter into a vision of human life that, by its wide angle, may counter two illusions liable to be produced by the professional deformation of some kinds of our subject: first, that, because primitive societies, and the hunters and gatherers above all, seem to be doomed to annihilation or 'development', they can be looked upon as negligible phenomena; and second, that because the corpus of ethnographic writings preponderantly treats primitive societies as though they existed in a timeless void, they are history-less and immobile.

As matters may appear to stand, then, much of anthropology operates at two ends of the human time-span: at the pre-neolithic (where 'primitive' equals early) and at the present (where 'primitive' means in some sense 'unsophisticated' – non-literate and technologically simple).[7] If the time dimension were to be more rigorously used, anthropology would need to venture into the fields largely abandoned to the archaeologists and historians, who between them account for the history of mankind from the neolithic to the recent past. We shall see later on that in fact interventions of that kind are being made,[8] and one must come to the conclusion that the concept – one

6. Edited by LEE & DeVORE (1968). And see DAMAS (ed.), *Contributions to Anthropology: Band Societies* (1969).

7. Cf. VOIGT, 'A néprajztudomány elméleti-terminológiai kérdései' (= Theoretical and methodological problems in recent East European ethnology, ethnography, and folklore) (1965).

8. And have for a long time been made within both Soviet and American anthropology, which, because of their close association with archaeology, have always been concerned with change over long spans of time. The reasons for and consequences of the integration of archaeology into American anthropology are discussed most informatively in EHRICH, 'Current archaeological trends in Europe and America, similarities and differences' (1970). And cf. in this volume the chap-

might more wisely say concepts – of the 'primitive' is/are of low power in the definition of the subject matter of the discipline.

By means of its typical field method (we have argued), and for several reasons (one of which is the increase in the number of its practitioners), anthropology has crossed over the boundary between 'primitive' and 'advanced', and introduced historicizing methods into our studies – literate societies have records and their past is historically obvious. But at the same time the shift to the civilized greatly expands the geographical range of the subject. An ethnographic map of the world dated some forty or so years ago would have shown vast areas of white, and it would have seemed natural enough that it did so. Now that the civilizations are accepted as proper subjects of study, that map, brought up to date, would be crowded.

Many implications of this shift in interest will be touched on at different points in the chapter. One of the implications must be dealt with now. When anthropology was about primitive societies, the primitives were the subject matter and Western civilized men were the students. The fact that anthropologists and their 'objects' were mutually exotic and, in the normal course of events, often separated by great physical distances, was a strength to the discipline. It could promote one kind of objectivity: the observer was totally from outside and unencumbered by the presuppositions of those under study. (One might add that the ethnographer did not then have to face the possibility that the people he described would read what he wrote about them.) Participant observation (as the major form of field work is known) pushed participation in an exotic society to the point at which understanding might be achieved without projecting it over the border beyond which it might degenerate into a desensitizing overfamiliarity and partisanship. The study of the exotic could serve to differentiate anthropology from its close neighbour sociology, that latter discipline being concerned above all (but not of course exclusively) with the societies from which the social sciences had sprung. Anthropologists were marked off from their subject matter by political privilege, geographical distance, and detachment.

The relative position of the student and the studied could of course be maintained. Indian and African scholars, for example, might return the compliment the West has long paid them by sending their field workers into European and North American communities. But that is not usually how things work out. A method devised for the study of the exotic is transmuted into a method of self-contemplation. The anthropologists in the countries where the discipline is new usually study themselves.

That is, of course, an oversimplification: 'themselves' calls for some analysis. The distancing between the observer and the observed in the 'classical'

---

ter on archaeology and prehistory by S. J. De Laet, pp. 182, 202-206 and 210-211. The integration is well brought out in SMITH & FISCHER (eds.), *Anthropology* (1970). In that book the first example offered of 'The concerns of anthropology' is the origins of New World civilization (pp. 6 sqq.). For the Soviet case see, e.g., the references cited p. 17, n. 20 below.

mode of field study is up to a point reproduced in the relationship between the 'new' anthropologist and the people he studies, even though he and they are members of one society; Africa, India, and some countries in Latin America provide very good examples because of their ethnic heterogeneity. Moreover, social scientists are not peasants or workers and are rarely drawn from their ranks. Indeed, it is probably the case that the bourgeois or member of the elite often sees in anthropology a way of seizing the reality of the, to him, strange life lived by the mass of his fellow countrymen.

On the other hand, the 'new' anthropologist is more than merely a member of his society; he is likely to be committed to the attempt to solve the practical problems that beset his country, and his status as a large and precious element of the intellectual capital of that country cannot so easily leave him to relish the disinterest with which his colleagues in the 'developed' countries feel free to conduct their professional lives. (In the view of many, that disinterest is in any case spurious.) He is impelled in some way to make himself obviously useful – and utility begins at home. The result is that few of the 'new' anthropologists are either inclined or, if inclined, enabled to venture for research beyond their own borders.[9] It may be argued that the few ought to be cherished, encouraged, and helped in the perhaps unrealistic expectation that their numbers will increase, for if they do not, then a large part of anthropology may perhaps sink from being a discipline of scholarship into the status of a mere technique for attempting to solve down-to-earth practical problems.[10]

But that is only part of the story of the risk to the study of the exotic. A threat comes, more unexpectedly, from the very quarter that brought the study of the exotic to birth. It is but a small step from the proposition that, despite its concentration on 'abroad', anthropology has a message for all mankind, to the proposition that anthropology, because by implication it is about all mankind, ought to be applied to the study of Western society by its own members. The process of involution takes place under the pressure of several factors. In the first place, the special skills developed within the discipline, both in field method and in the handling of particular topics (above all, that of kinship) seem themselves to push anthropologists in the West towards the study of what is immediately around them; they think they are able to supplement the work done by the sociologists. Second, the sense of commitment to social welfare, on the same principle that keeps the 'new' anthropologists at home, anchors a few Western practitioners to their own countries. The third factor arises from the very success of the discipline. As the numbers of practitioners grow they outpace the financial resources for

9. Cf. KOENTJARANINGRAT, 'Anthropology and non-Euro-American anthropologists. The situation in Indonesia' (1964), especially p. 295.

10. Of course, it is never argued that anthropologists should refrain from studying their own societies. They may do so with great profit, especially if they have the background acquired by working in foreign societies. For an interesting example of the self-realization induced by research abroad see NAKANE, *Japanese Society* (1970).

their field work abroad, and some of them have *faute de mieux* to apply their talents locally.[11] Finally, we come to the facts of international politics. Field work in foreign countries may be made impossible by the governments of those countries; visas may not be granted, and when granted lead only to limited access to the field; under such conditions some anthropologists stay and work at home. Of course, while one may deplore the actions of governments in preventing the free movement of anthropologists in their countries, there are obviously sometimes conditions which make that prevention prudent. The barrier set up to foreign anthropologists which would make them more angry than any other would be that which was inspired by the feeling on the part of scholars in the closed-off countries that the living material around them was their national property and not to be opened up to anyone from abroad;[12] for that attitude spells death to international scholarship.[13] The doubt remains in the minds of many whether self-study is the right path for anthropology to follow. For it could be argued as an absorbing paradox that the internationalism and transcultural nature of anthropology lie precisely in its plurality of national viewpoints. For many practitioners of the subject it is, to use the title of an influential textbook in the United Kingdom, the study of 'other cultures'[14] and not, therefore, the study of all cultures from, as it were, a neutral base; for a case could be made for saying that such a neutral base is chimerical. But the argument does not rest on that point alone: it can be based on the benefit accruing to the education of the foreign observer and of his fellow countrymen with whom he communicates. There is a sense in which to be cultured a man must know and esteem other cultures; he does not by that commit himself to a dubious relativism. If anthropology were truly cross-national in this manner – all national anthropologies studying all other societies, no two of them in consequence studying the same range – we should reach a remarkable peak of knowledge. But in fact, as we have seen, there is a fearful asymmetry. The study of the 'other' has been largely an occupation of Europe in its enhanced political and economic mobility about the face of the earth (for which the rude name is imperialism); and the imbalance persists.

It may very well be asked – and we must pose the question to stand on the debit side of our account of the current scene – whether there is not a se-

11. These remarks apply particularly to North America, Britain, and Australia. The German-speaking countries form a striking exception, partly perhaps because of the traditional split between *Völkerkunde* and *Volkskunde* (roughly, ethnology and folklore): there appears to be no tendency for ethnologists to undertake intensive field studies at home.

12. A similar restriction is, alas, to be expected among some minority groups in, e.g., the U.S.A.

13. There is a further reason, easily overlooked, why many anthropologists prefer to conduct their researches at home: in some countries, women, unless they are married to anthropologists (in which case husband-and-wife team research is often the result) are more reluctant than men to commit themselves to ethnography in faraway places.

14. BEATTIE, *Other Cultures* (1964).

rious risk that the establishment of more national anthropologies in a world of tormenting national barriers may lead to there being increasingly less work across frontiers, and to a growing preoccupation with national and ethnic issues. If, to add to the gloom, we note that growing nationalism sometimes takes the form of emphasizing the 'inside' view of culture and social institutions and of rejecting the validity of the 'outside' view, we may possibly conclude that we are at the beginning of a wholly depressing 'main trend': the study of the 'other', and with it the truly international character of anthropology, could die in a welter of national particularism and self-absorption.

But that is only one possible view of the present and the near future. The rise of new independent states and the correlative decline of colonial dominance (at least in its classical form) have brought with them an intellectual mood in which a, so to say, self-applied anthropology is argued to produce epistemological and scientific benefits. And one cannot fail to be impressed by the enthusiasm and energy with which anthropology has been put to work in the 'new' countries by its 'new' practitioners, sometimes at the cost of great personal sacrifice and in the face of grave practical difficulties.

It is sometimes said in favour of self-applied anthropology that it contributes to scientific understanding by cutting out a particular monopoly hitherto enjoyed by Western civilization. Until now, anthropology has been a process by which the cultures of the world have been ordered and analysed by Western categories, and therefore translated into a 'language' which has illegitimately been elevated to scientific pre-eminence. The need now is to destroy that monopoly. It is a good argument to the extent that a critique of any set of categories is a first duty in intellectual work. But it may have very bad consequences if for a set of categories used generally by international scholarship it substitutes a multiplicity of sets such that communication among anthropologists in different countries becomes impossible. The intellectual revolt against the West (to overdramatize) may produce anarchy not redress. The task of the next generation is to reconcile the many 'inside' views of cultures with the need (logically entailed in the notion of culture) for a language which all anthropologists can speak and understand. Fortunately, despite the powerful trend for the 'new' anthropologists to confine their researches to their own countries, great numbers of them travel abroad; many are trained in foreign universities; they receive their colleagues from other countries; and they argue within the common traditions established by internationally important learned journals. It may therefore be that, from this point of view, much is to be gained and little lost by 'involution'.

And on the credit side must be added the scientific and educational productivity that results from an economic use of anthropological resources. By staying at home, the 'new' anthropologists play a very important rôle in their universities, they exercise a continuous influence upon public opinion and official policy, and they can make the best use of the 'field' on their doorstep. Moreover, their very conditions of work and the tasks they assume in contributing to the public benefit lead them to experiment and innovate in anthropological method and to become receptive intellectually to the other disciplines with which they find themselves closely associated. Certainly, there are many parts of the Third World where the anthropologists have turned their back on the old division between their subject and sociology, and in operating as both anthropologists and sociologists have achieved a satisfying view of what research needs to be done to make a complex society intelligible. The move in that direction blurs even more the distinction between anthropology and sociology (to the embarrassment of university administrators and textbook writers), but it is a very small price to pay if it leads to intellectual advances.[15]

But as anthropology in the 'new' countries adjusts itself in this manner it begins (especially when it is disguised as sociology) to appear to some Western eyes as though it had ceased to be anthropology. Those who believe that anthropology is essentially the study of the 'other' may, however, adopt one or other of two quite different stances when they confront 'involution'. They may deplore the lack of mutual anthropologizing and hope that somehow it may be remedied in order that the subject may survive. Or they may take the view that anthropology is, after all, a product of the domination of the world by the West and not therefore capable of being exported. Of this latter view there are both radical and mild versions. A somewhat mild one is to be found in a statement by Lévi-Strauss: having condemned the formula of mutual anthropologizing as 'naïve and unworkable', he goes on to say:

Anthropology itself must undergo a deep transformation in order to carry on its work among these cultures for whose study it was intended because they lack a written record of their history. .... Anthropology will survive in a changing world by allowing itself to perish in order to be born again under a new guise. Wherever native cultures, though disappearing physically, have remained to some extent morally intact, anthropological research should be carried on along traditional lines. .... And wherever populations have remained physically strong while their culture rapidly veers towards our own, anthropology, progressively taken over by local scholars, should adopt aims and methods similar to those which, from the Renaissance on, have proved fruitful for the study of our own culture.[16]

But the practicality of that view is itself very much open to doubt . . . The debate is bound to continue.[17]

15. India furnishes a particularly interesting and important case of the adaptation of anthropology to both the intellectual and practical needs of a newly independent country. See, e.g., SRINIVAS, *Social Change in Modern India* (1966), Chap. 5 ('Some thoughts on the study of one's own society') and 'Sociology and sociologists in India today' (1970); MADAN, 'Political pressures and ethical constraints upon Indian sociologists' (1967); and UBEROI, 'Science and Swaraj' (1968). For a parallel view from French-speaking Africa, see WANE, 'Réflexions sur la recherche sociologique en milieu africain' (1970). A view from English-speaking Africa may be got from UCHENDU, 'Priority issues for social anthropological research in Africa in the next two decades' (1969).
16. LÉVI-STRAUSS, 'Anthropology. Its achievements and future' (1969), p. 126.
17. Cf. HOFER, 'Anthropologists and native ethnographers in Central European villages: Comparative notes on the professional personality of two disciplines' (1968). One line of argument, while stressing the difficulty in getting, say, African

The rôle of the exotic in the definition of anthropology is rejected in the Socialist countries, but unfortunately the debate between the anthropologies of the 'West' and those of Eastern Europe and the Soviet Union has hardly begun. For both political and linguistic reasons the two chief branches of the subject do not to any great extent communicate, and any attempt, such as is made in this chapter, to consider them together can achieve at most a modest success. And the best reward for the effort would undoubtedly be that it stimulated a more fruitful one . . .[18] The fact is that while the 'ethnography' of Eastern Europe and the Soviet Union is as wide-ranging as the anthropology of the 'West', and contains the same ingredients, it quite differently weights its elements. In the first place, it ascribes a relatively minor rôle to the field study in depth of foreign cultures, largely concentrating upon the cultural variety within its own frontiers so far as field research is concerned. Second, it is more thoroughly historical in its attitude, for, while it defines itself as more than a mere historical discipline to the extent that it calls upon linguistics, art, geography, and so on, it looks upon itself as first and foremost a kind of history – but a kind, of course, that assumes a regular course of human development. There is a further difficulty: to match the anthropology of the West one has to seek beyond the boundaries of 'Eastern ethnography', for much that is recognizably anthropological goes on within the folklore and literary studies conducted in Eastern Europe and the Soviet Union.[19] Yet if one allows for these differences and for those springing from the particular Marxist framework within which 'Eastern' anthropology is composed, one may also come to the conclusion that there is enough correspondence between the problematics and styles of the two great branches to justify our regarding them as members of the same discipline.[20] Certainly, all

---

anthropologists to carry out field studies in Europe (or indeed the relative unprofitability of such an enterprise), emphasizes the need for anthropologists to study neighbouring countries.

18. As far as my own reading goes, I should say that the fault lies mainly on the side of the 'West'. Scholars in Eastern Europe seem to be much better informed about the work done in 'Western' anthropology than are 'Western' scholars about 'Eastern' anthropology. Cf. MADAY, 'Hungarian anthropology. The problem of communication', and HOFER, 'Anthropologists and native ethnographers . . .' (1968). And see 'On Hungarian anthropology' (1970).

19. And the adjustment must be made for other parts of the world. Japan and the Scandinavian countries are good examples. Certainly, there are many countries in which the study of folklore includes, and sometimes exhausts, large areas of what in this chapter is considered to be anthropology.

20. A number of Soviet statements on the aims and achievements of 'ethnography' are, happily, available to the Western reader. See, e.g., BROMLEI (= BROMLEJ), 'Major trends in ethnographic research in the USSR' (1969); TOLSTOV & ZHDANKO (= ŽDANKO), 'Directions and problems of Soviet ethnography' (1964-65); TOKAREV, '50 Jahre sowjetische Ethnographie' (1969). See also VASILYEV (= VASIL'EV), 'Institute of Ethnography' (1970), and MONOGAROVA on the journal *Sovetskaja ètnografija* (1970). Two Hungarian publications provide an excellent opportunity to the 'Western' reader to follow work in progress in the Socialist countries: *Acta Ethnographica Academiae Scientiarum Hungaricae* and *Ethno-*

varieties of social and cultural anthropology have this in common: they assume one humanity realized in different cultural forms which are capable of being systematically studied wherever they are located in time and space. The programme is always impressive, even if it is only imperfectly put into practice.

B.   SOCIAL AND CULTURAL ANTHROPOLOGY BETWEEN OPPOSITE ATTRACTIONS

What has so far been said will have shown how difficult it is to define a precise field within which social and cultural anthropology operates. But the ambiguities are not yet exhausted; a number of them are discussed in this section as a series of tensions by which the discipline is held, in some cases more stably than in others, between opposite poles. One such tension was touched on in the last section: between the study of the 'other' and the study of 'self'.

1. *Culture and society*

Are social anthropology and cultural anthropology one and the same thing (as indeed the first pages of this chapter appear to assume)? In practice they may be, but the dual terminology is not insignificant. 'Culture' and 'society' are different concepts and may lead to different styles of analysis. It is natural enough that those different styles should by and large emerge in national anthropologies (but by no means exclusively), and there would be much to be learned (to take a striking example) from a systematic comparison between the two main anthropologies of the English-speaking world: the American and the British. They are tightly interconnected and intercommunicative, but – to borrow a *bon mot* – are often divided by their common language. The systematic comparison cannot be attempted here, but the case may be illuminating even if put briefly.

There is a very real sense in which, by a strange crossing of genealogical lines, American anthropology can be traced to E. B. Tylor, an Englishman, and British anthropology to L. H. Morgan, an American. The Tylorian heritage is enscapsulated in the famous definition of culture which, stated at the very beginning of *Primitive Culture* (1871), provides a charter for a cultural anthropology: 'Culture or Civilization, taken in its wide ethnographic sense, is that complex whole [those three words have assumed an incantatory air] which includes knowledge, belief, art, morals, law, custom, and any other capabilities and habits acquired by man as a member of society'. It will be seen that for Tylor *society* was at most a prerequisite for *culture*, and generations of American anthropologists have conceived of their work as being

---

graphia, both appearing in Budapest. For a 'Western', and earlier, survey of Soviet scholarship, see KRADER, 'Recent trends in Soviet anthropology' (1959).

directed to the study of 'that complex whole . . .',[21] *society* being relegated, so to say, to the status of a mere component. The Morganian heirloom in British anthropology is composed of the great American's contribution to (or, in the view of many, his foundation of) kinship studies; this inheritance is aptly illustrated by a recent work (1969) from the pen of a leader of the British school: Meyer Fortes, *Kinship and the Social Order. The Legacy of Lewis Henry Morgan.* For the British social anthropologists of the last generation *society* has been placed in the centre of the scene, *culture* being brought on stage from time to time to play a supporting rôle.

Now of course it will be seen that the modes by which men organize themselves (society) and the manner of their living and their thinking, their lives and world (culture), while being analytically distinct, are inseparable companions both in the concrete and in the studies, taken as a whole, of human society. But a particular work or class of work may, as in the generalized American case, range widely over actions, ideas, speech, and manufactured things, or confine itself, in the stereotyped British manner, to social institutions and groups. As a matter of fact, a marked narrowing of the gap between the American and British styles in, say, the last ten years can be noted; the narrowing moves at a growing pace, and is to be recorded as a 'main trend'. The academic bases of the sociology of anthropological knowledge are not to be ignored: in the United States and the countries it has influenced, social/cultural anthropology is still nearly always taught within the frame of Anthropology (that is, alongside prehistoric archaeology, physical anthropology, and often linguistics); in the British sphere, social anthropology has long since established itself as a quasi-independent teaching subject. The rapprochement between the two styles is reflected on the American side by the increased emphasis on the element of social/cultural anthropology, and on the British side by the widening of social anthropological curricula to take in linguistics and other 'cultural' aspects.

This summary comparison is intended to show that there have been genuine intellectual differences between two closely related national anthropologies, but the definition of the subject to which this chapter is devoted may not always rest on such respectable grounds. Labels may take their origin, or draw their significance, from academic politics, especially as they involve sociology, a discipline with which our subject has often had an uneasy relationship. '*Culture*' may be worn as a badge of difference from sociology, and in the confrontation between the two academically and professionally organized subjects an emphasis upon *culture*, even when very little is intellectually at stake – is it really possible to conceive of a sociology that did not substantively treat the facts of culture? – may serve as an emotional diacritic.

21. Cf. SINGER, 'The concept of culture' (1968), and WOLF, *Anthropology* (1964). From the fact that Tylor furnished a charter to later generations it does not follow that he intended what they took him to intend, a matter very well treated in STOCKING, 'Matthew Arnold, E. B. Tylor, and the uses of invention' (1963). The complexities in the genealogy of anthropological ideas are quite beyond the range of our present survey.

In the inverse case, a determination to lie academically and professionally alongside or within sociology (even sometimes perhaps to lie around and capture it) is well emblemed by *social* anthropology.[22]

In the countries where the terms *ethnology* and *ethnography* are used for our subject, the Anglo-American divergence may have little significance, but there is often in fact a tendency for the subject to be pulled to one or other of the poles of wide-ranging and narrow-ranging anthropology; and a preoccupation with social institutions and social structure, which is an obvious mode of restriction, is an analogue of social anthropology; cultural anthropology finds its counterpart in those versions of ethnology and ethnography which, without being attached to the tradition which the words enshrine, are devoted to 'that complex whole . . .'.[23]

2. *Antiquarianism and up-to-date-ness*

All anthropologists, not only those in the countries where the subject is new, are likely at some time to feel morally obliged as anthropologists to serve the needs of their respective countries (as they see those needs) and the interests (as they see those interests) of the people whom, in the process of studying, they have come to like and respect.[24]

These moral impulsions may lead specifically to works of applied anthropology, but they may more generally induce a frame of mind in which anthropology is made to seem above all a science of modern transformation, a study of the now and the near future. The past and all that which in the present represents the past (for it is either dead or must be helped to die, however painlessly) come to be undervalued. Simple societies brought under modern administration and subjected to agricultural discipline, peasants moved on to the fringes of the industrial world, all these are sometimes seen to be in need of the anthropologists' particular attention in order that the subject as

22. Some idea of the relationships between social anthropology and cultural anthropology may be got from the items grouped under 'Anthropology' (by GREENBERG, MANDELBAUM, and FIRTH) in SILLS (ed.), *International Encyclopedia of the Social Sciences* (1968), Vol. 1. And see DRIVER, 'Ethnology', *ibid.*, Vol. 5.

23. In the French-speaking countries, the division between *sociologie* and *ethnologie* to some extent corresponds with the difference between *society* and *culture, anthropologie sociale (et culturelle)* forming a bridge between them (in the view of many).

24. The emotions generated in the observer in the course of extended and intensive field work in an exotic society are complex; they are a moving aspect of the anthropological vocation, but not often discussed, perhaps partly for the reason that intellectuals prefer to discuss their own ideas and other people's emotions. In the literature that deals with the experience, as distinct from the technique, of field work, it may be worth mentioning: BOWEN, *Return to Laughter* (1954); READ, *The High Valley* (1965); MAYBURY-LEWIS, *The Savage and the Innocent* (1965); POWDERMAKER, *Stranger and Friend* (1966); and MALINOWSKI, *A Diary in the Strict Sense of the Term* (1967).

a whole may be taken to be in the midst for the forces making for rational change.

But the anthropologists' morals are more complex than that. In their attachment to, and respect for, the weaker societies that they study they may develop highly protective attitudes towards them, such that they spring to their defence when they are threatened with the upheavals (resettlement, the imposition of new rules of land tenure or taxes, labour recruitment, and so on) which are induced by the policies of often well-meaning governments, both colonial and independent.[25] At such a point anthropologists put themselves in the position of being accused, usually without justification, as enemies of progress in general, and hindrances to the work of national betterment in particular. In more violent forms of the prejudice so aroused, anthropologists are reproved for wanting to preserve ignorance and backwardness in order to maintain the open human zoos in which they may continue to practise their craft.

But in reality, the 'antiquarian' tendencies of anthropology lie elsewhere. It is a science dedicated to the study of human variety – whatever its aims ultimately to reduce that variety to uniform laws or bases. Its data are formed by the myriad communities which in the latter part of the twentieth century seem to be destined for extinction, or at least radical change, by industrialism or any other of the forces that go conveniently under the name of modernism. To many professionals, therefore, the main task to which the subject should devote its energies is that of studying and recording the small- and smaller-scale societies before they are pulled away out of reach.[26] One may easily make a debating point against people who hold this view by stating the true

25.   For an up-to-date version of this old attitude see JAULIN, *La paix blanche. Introduction à l'ethnocide* (1970).

26.   Since 1958 there has appeared an annual entitled *Bulletin of the International Committee on Urgent Anthropological and Ethnological Research* which owed its origin to the energy of Robert HEINE-GELDERN. See the *Bulletin*, Vol. 1 (1958), pp. 5 sqq. 'At the Fourth International Congress of Anthropological and Ethnological Sciences, Vienna, 1952, a special session was devoted to a symposium concerning the most urgent tasks of anthropological and linguistic research. The speakers pointed out that numerous tribes, cultures and languages which have never been investigated are fast disappearing and this constitutes an enormous and irreparable loss to science' (p. 5). The *Bulletin* is published with the financial help of Unesco, and one may conclude that the theme of urgent anthropology in this sense plays an important part in international thinking. Certainly, the need to record and collect data from the disappearing cultures and groups is a matter of importance for future scholarship. We cannot now conceive what the social sciences of the remote future will be like, but we can be reasonably sure that they will be grateful to have at their disposal the widest range of cultural materials we can collect for them ... But what is 'urgent'? It is highly instructive to examine an Indian report, VIDYARTHI, 'Conference on urgent social research in India', alongside the papers with which it appears, under the general heading 'Urgent anthropology', in *Current Anthropology* 10 (4), 1969. There is an 'antiquarian' 'urgent anthropology' – and a 'modernist', 'relevant' one. And cf. 'Urgent anthropology. Associates' views on the definition of 'urgency' (1970).

fact that the cry 'study primitive societies before it is too late' is as old as the subject; it is as integral a part of the history of the discipline as 'kinship' or 'culture'. But that would not be a genuine argument, for the tempo of 'annihilation' is increasing and the texture of human variety is certainly now being impoverished at a rate which calls for urgent anthropological action.

We are left with the fact that two options are open to anthropology: to concentrate either on that which precedes and fends off the industrial age or on the process by which industrialization scores its victories. Different anthropologists pick different options, and there is nothing to prevent one anthropologist choosing different options at different times; he often does. Anthropology is not necessarily about one kind of study to the exclusion of the other; it is in tension between the two. To move to one pole and stay there would be to flout the modern world and run the risk of angering the big battalions of development and progress. To move to the other pole and stay there would be to abandon what is distinctive of the subject and of its contribution to international culture. Despite appearances, there is no dilemma; anthropology can encompass a great range of the activities between the two poles, just as it succeeds in maintaining its integrity while oscillating between 'primitive' and 'advanced', between past and present, between 'other' and 'self'.

3. *Description and theory*

Ethnography, as the exercise of recording and description, accounts for a large part of the professional lives of anthropologists; ethnography, as the body of published descriptive work, makes up the bulk of the literature of anthropology. Yet description and theory are not easily to be disentangled, for it must be obvious that all ethnography is based upon some theory, however inarticulate, while all theory is about the facts of description and is founded in them. Modern anthropologists do not describe themselves as belonging exclusively to the ranks of the ethnographers or to those of the theorists; they are both; and 'ethnographer' is the name of a rôle that all anthropologists at some time assume. Despite the logical impossibility of a pure, that is, theory-free, ethnography, there was a time when some stay-at-home theorizers (Sir James Frazer was a notable example) allocated the rôle of pure recorder to others, a sort of research assistants who, unhampered by theoretical worries, could supply the theorist with the facts of which he stood in need. Few would take that view today.

The intermingling of ethnography and theory, each logically entailing the other, does not prevent the crystallization out of two rôles, either for the individual scholar, as we have seen, or for the profession as a whole. There are times and places where ethnography dominates theory, in the sense that the task of lengthy and meticulous recording is given priority over the development of the apparatus of theory. In such moods of the subject, theory may be looked upon as the necessary, but only regrettably necessary, spur to the desirable activity of fact-collecting, data in all their richness forming the glory of the subject. In the contrary mood, theory being placed in the forefront and accorded the honours, ethnography is subjected to demeaning glances cast from a peak of sophistication to a lowland of mere banausic skill.

Ethnography is typically the fruit of field work, but in fact anthropology has other descriptive methods. Nor is the importance attached to field work always accurately reflected in the research done by the professionals who teach and praise it as a method of prime value. In contraposition to the Sir James Frazers there are other stay-at-home anthropologists for whom the intellectual importance of field work is unquestioned. Marcel Mauss, in the France of the inter-war period, is a shining example.[27] The allure of field method lies in its capacity, when it is properly conducted – and the astonishing thing is that even scholars of less than great talent have shown themselves able by field work to draw out from live societies a thesaurus of data – to generate information that is both dense in its texture and comprehensive in the sense that it relates to the total nature of a society or culture. The tradition which, for example, the British trace to Malinowski and Radcliffe-Brown, and the French to Mauss, that emphasizes the wholeness and roundedness of the material that anthropology treats is both a cause and a consequence of the modern idea of what constitutes field work.

But field work is more than a technique for eliciting facts. If it were merely that, then it would never have come to occupy the position of eminence it enjoys. It is looked upon as a personal experience, a sensitizer of the observer, which must lie at the base of the individual anthropologist's life-work, however much in the event that work may move away from the treatment of personally gathered data. In the traditions of the anthropologies of the English- and French-speaking worlds it has by now become almost a *sine qua non* that the young scholar in the making spend part of his early professional years in the field engaged upon a first-hand study of a community. His reputation may come in the end to be only very tenuously related to what he achieved in that formative period, but his status as a professional rests in large measure on that experience, and his credibility as a theorist and analyst is in great part made a function of his exposure to the particular assault upon his sensibilities of the living material he has studied. A mystique may be added to a technique, and there is some truth in the assertions, first that greater academic value is often ascribed to field work than it merits, and second that the precise formula of that field work (long and 'lonely' residence in an exotic community, the one-man job) is less a method aimed at promoting efficient scholarship than a personal test of vocation. But the fuller implications of the matter must wait to be dealt with later in the chapter.

Individual scholars, the greatest among them, mix the two elements of

27. MAUSS, *Manuel d'ethnographie* (1967, 1st edn. 1947; the book is a compilation of Mauss's lectures, 1926-39), especially p. 13.

field work and study at home in very different proportions. For some, a satisfying and productive dialectic is set up between alternating periods of field research and writing and contemplation at home – but the periods are of necessity of unequal length, for merely to digest and write up what is gathered in the field occupies many more years than it takes to collect the material. Other professionals grow impatient of field work as they progress in their studies, or are kept away from it by practical considerations.

The prestige of field work in many traditions of the subject may inhibit other forms of ethnographic research. There is the ethnography of published evidence, of manuscript materials, of the objects collected in museums. These are not of light academic weight, but they run the risk of seeming second-best when attention is fastened on the splendour of field work. As a matter of fact, these alternative ethnographies are showing signs of reasserting themselves in the conditions of anthropology in the late twentieth century. The 'field' is not always accessible, for reasons we have touched on already, and other sources of data must be sought. A growing interest in the writing of anthropological history enhances the significance of documents. The widening of the definition of the range within which anthropology operates brings in the literate societies, whose records are as interesting as their living reality. And the modernization of erstwhile primitive societies lays down its own deposit of documents to distract attention from the classical mode of field research. Within the 'main trend' which is likely to carry field work wider and wider over the face of the earth and to increase its efficiency and precision, there lies another trend: to increase and make more subtle the use of less direct methods of description. The competition from this alternative mode may stimulate a closer interrogation of field work. Does its prime value lie in its function as a dredge of facts, as an instrument for the stimulation of thought, or as a sensitizer of young scholars? Is it, as a method should be, a handmaiden in the service of solving problems, or an overriding end in itself, forcing anthropology to serve it?

4. *Science and art*

The problem we have now to state lifts us from the realms of subject matter and technique of study to that of the status of anthropology within the total body of organized knowledge about men and their achievements. What kind of knowledge is anthropology, or, if that question cannot be answered, then what kind of knowledge ought it to be? There is perhaps a particular feature of the English language which, while not creating the problem of science *versus* art, brings that problem to the fore. The French *science* and the German *Wissenschaft* are, in English ears, tantalizingly ambiguous, for 'science' in English is more heavily loaded with the sense of 'natural science'. To place anthropology among the social sciences at once raises the question, are we or are we not like natural scientists? If our subject belongs entirely within the humanities (among which it now nestles in this volume), the matter does not arise. If (as is, however, undoubtedly the case) it occupies a secure place, whatever its affinities with the arts, in the social sciences, then it is not just organized knowledge, science, but of a special kind, 'science'.

The debate within anthropology of science *versus* art is not confined to the English-speaking traditions, but it tends there to be longer-lasting and sharper.[28] We may begin a short account of it by referring to a work – one cannot say from the pen of, for the book is the record of a discussion – by Radcliffe-Brown. The discussion was held in Chicago in 1937, at the end of Radcliffe-Brown's American period; because of the man's widespread influence throughout the English-speaking world, the statement may be taken as a key document in both the American and British traditions. *A Natural Science of Society* says at the beginning (pp. 3 sq.):

The problem with which we are to be concerned is that of the possibility of a natural science of human societies, that is, of applying to the phenomena of the social life of mankind – its moral, religious, juridical, political, and economic institutions, and the arts and sciences, and language – the same logical methods that are applied in the physical and biological sciences, and by that means to attain to scientifically exact formulations of significant and probable generalizations ... The theses to be maintained here are that a theoretical science of human society is possible; that there can be only one such science, although certain of the fields within the science may be capable of relatively separate treatment, as, for example, language; that it must be just as distinct from psychology as physiology is from chemistry; that such a science does not yet exist in its elementary beginnings; that the method it must pursue is that of the systematic comparison of societies of diverse types; and that the development of the science therefore depends at this time on the gradual improvement of the comparative method and its refinement as an instrument of analysis. This will require: (a) the continuous improvement of our methods of observing and describing societies; (b) the elaboration and exact definition of the fundamental concepts required for the description, classification and analysis of social phenomena; and (c) the development of a systematic classification of types of societies.

Now it will be clear that while pointing social anthropology to a scientific goal – for social anthropology was itself if possible to be that englobing and unified social science – Radcliffe-Brown was resting his case on a view of natural science that we should now be less likely to accept. So that we are faced by uncertainty at two levels: at the level of the model of natural science,

28. A French view of the matter, which in the present context has the additional value of referring to the Radcliffe-Brownian approach, will be found in LÉVI-STRAUSS's *Leçon inaugurale* (Chaire d'Anthropologie sociale) at the Collège de France, 5 January 1960, pp. 26 sq. (English translation, *The Scope of Anthropology* (1967), pp. 30 sq.). Social anthropology is said there to 'se nourrir d'un rêve secret: elle appartient aux sciences humaines ...; mais, si elle se résigne à faire son purgatoire auprès des sciences sociales, c'est qu'elle ne désespère pas de se réveiller parmi les sciences naturelles, à l'heure du jugement dernier' (p. 27) [(...) 'to harbour a secret dream ... of awakening among the natural sciences when the last trumpet sounds', having resigned itself 'to a period of purgatory beside the social sciences' (English translation, p. 31)]. For some of Lévi-Strauss's later reflections on the same subject, see his 'Criteria of science in the social and human disciplines' (1964), which also has the virtue of expressing grave doubts about the basis and utility of precisely the exercise in which this chapter is engaged.

and at the level of the model of a social science assimilated to that of a natural science. Science may need classification (not always) but it is not characterized by that activity. The typing and induction to which Radcliffe-Brown attached primary importance look alien against the background of a view of science in which the first status is given to the deduction and testing of hypotheses. Radcliffe-Brown wanted 'laws' and he thought we should discover them by refined inspection and classification.

His successors have for the most part either accepted his model of science and found anthropology in principle wanting, or rejected the model. Few have put forward a clear scientific model of a different kind and declared it to be the ideal towards which anthropology should strive, even though a loose adherence to the aims and methodology of natural science is sometimes expressed.[29] The most direct rejection of Radcliffe-Brown's proposals comes, perhaps paradoxically, from his most direct successor, Sir Edward Evans-Pritchard, who during the last quarter of a century has championed the cause of social anthropology as a discipline with close intellectual affinities with history.[30]

The champions of the scientific status of the subject still exist: G. P. Murdock in the United States, to take an obvious example, thinks (or at least thought when he wrote *Social Structure*, 1949) there to be enough evidence for suggesting that 'a high degree of precision and predictability is possible in the social sciences, and that allegations of indeterminacy, complaints about undue complexity, and special pleading for intuitive methods are as unwarranted in anthropology, psychology, and sociology as they are in physics, chemistry, and biology'. Most anthropologists in the English-speaking traditions would be reluctant to commit themselves to such views; they waver between a whole-hearted historiography and a half-hearted scientism.

It is obvious that one must have a clear idea of what natural science is before attempting to assess the degree to which social and cultural anthropology is or could be scientific. Very few anthropologists have that clear idea, and for the great majority the pole of science to which they sometimes veer is really an ideal of rigour and objectivity in method and a faith in the ultimate orderliness of what they have chosen to study. Much the same could be said of scholars, both in and out of anthropology, who would in no sense look to science for their canons or models. The oscillation in anthropology between the poles of science and art is, therefore, largely an illusion, even though its practitioners may feel themselves pulled to one or other of the extremes.

29. An exception to the general run of less than determined attempts to formulate an articulate scientific programme is to be found in NADEL, *The Foundations of Social Anthropology* (1951), a work of dogged and intelligent devotion to a science of social anthropology. See especially pp. 191-194. Later shifts in thinking about the methodology of the social sciences, especially as it has been affected by the success of structural linguistics, are illustrated in ARDENER, 'The new anthropology and its critics' (1971).

30. See, e.g., his two lectures 'Social anthropology: past and present' (1950) and The comparative method in social anthropology' (1963).

5. *Comparison and particularism*

Great store is set by comparison in anthropology, in both the 'scientific' and anti-scientific wings (exception being made of the structuralists, for whom a different mode of handling entities is prescribed). This is not to say that all anthropologists mean the same thing by 'comparison' or that they have the same degree of faith in its power to generate important conclusions.

There is a sense, of course, in which the activities of anthropology could not be other than comparative, for no social or cultural statement can be made against a blank background. The real arguments about comparison rest on the methodological and technical questions of establishing precisely what things are to be compared and how. We shall come to that matter later on.

There is a common view of history which, stated in the abstract and out of the context of what historians do, makes that activity seem to be concerned with the unique. And a firm wedge is then driven between history and the kind of work done by anthropologists, even if the latter is not then called 'science'. But the so-called uniqueness of the historian's facts and events is better described as particularity,[31] because the historian is no freer of the need to compare than is his colleague in anthropology; what in principle distinguishes the two men is the former's preference for, so to say, the originality and special character of the things he seizes upon, and the latter's attachment to the general properties of his chosen subject matter. But historians and anthropologists can, and often do, change places: one systematically compares and generalizes, the other weds himself to particularity. But it should be noted that when the anthropologist gives priority to particularity he is, unlike the historian, often preoccupied with the wholeness of a society or culture, a wholeness which endows all its lesser particularities with their character.

We are in reality back to the matter of ethnography, in its double sense. Describers observe and record particular things, and their constructs from these things are sometimes presented in their particularity. This is the tradition, in which all anthropologists share to some degree, by which communities or societies are monographically described with the minimum of attention to generality. Some men may be driven to lavish the most scrupulous attention upon the myriads of small facts that go to make up what, perhaps thoughtlessly, they offer as a complete account. The strength of this mode lies in its richness of detail and in the apparent immediacy to the reader of what is described. And although one may brand so-called 'raw ethnography' as naive, for it is always processed by the theories, however rudimentary, of the man who compiled it, yet there is an important service rendered to anthropology by the 'complete' account. The facts are established and made public from which other constructions may be made, upon which other interpretations may be placed. Nobody who has examined the uses to which Malinowski's ethnography of the Trobriands has been put by a generation of

31. Cf. ELTON, *The Practice of History* (1969), pp. 21, 23 sqq. And cf. in this volume the chapter on history by Geoffrey Barraclough, pp. 276 sqq.

British, American, and French scholarship – from Mauss's 'Essai sur le don' (1923-24) to S. J. Tambiah's 'The magical power of words' (1969) – can be in any doubt about the value of detailed ethnography.[32]

There is a snobbery of 'theory' and generality: facts are pushed into the servants' quarters. There is a snobbery of 'ethnography' and particularity: the artisan's craft is raised above that of the parasitic intellectual. Among themselves anthropologists are victims of both forms of prejudice, as subjects and objects; as objects they are pulled both ways by the demands of the wider reading public. Great generalizations and powerful theories are demanded of them, but they are also reproved for alienating their readers from the complexities and richness of real life.

The determination to compare across societies [33] requires that categories be set up (wet-rice agriculture, ancestors, matriliny, warfare, and so on) and concrete facts allocated to them. To this enterprise two related objections may be made. First, two or more facts may be arbitrarily assigned to the same category or box; matriliny in society A is not really the same as that in B. Second, even if they are from a restricted point of view more or less the same thing, then they cannot be taken out of the total social and cultural contexts within which they have their natural being. A Malinowskian devotion to the interconnectedness of everything develops a delicate (some might say finicky) sense of the whole formed by a social or cultural system, which is offended by the apparent brutality of a comparative method that rips institutions and customs out of their context. The comparativists, on their side, call for a more robust sense of relevance. The tug-of-war goes on, often between two scholars, sometimes between two persons within the same scholar – he will be attentive to every nuance as ethnographer and ride roughshod over the terrain of comparative studies. It can certainly be said in favour of field work, or of some other mode of painstaking analysis of a body of data from one society, that it protects the scholar from an insensitive attitude to particularity.

The difficulties in the way of achieving large-scale comparison seem to some professionals to be insuperable; more modest programmes are sketched out for comparison among closely similar societies (to reduce the number of variables in play), among different areas of the same society, and within the same society of different points in time. The merits of these proposals need not be discussed here; their significance at the moment is that they show the continuing strength of the tradition by which one major task set for itself by anthropology is generalization, comparison being its servant. Another major task is full and contextual analysis; its method is ethnography. All-round and deep ethnography competes for devotion with the mastery of significant differences.

32. The tradition of publishing very full ethnographic information seems to survive most fully in the German-speaking countries, precisely because the data are thought to be important for later studies.

33. On the general problem see GOODENOUGH, *Description and Comparison in Cultural Anthropology* (1970), pp. 98-130.

6. *Structure and history*

It will by now have become clear, if it was not to begin with, that the various tensions to which this section of the chapter is devoted are closely inter-related, although not equally so. The pole of history, when its opposite is structure, may represent the kind of anthropology in which emphasis is given to the particular, the descriptive, and the humanistic. Structure then stands for the more scientific and abstract, for the more generalized and systematic. But there is, or there may be, a further dimension of the difference between the two poles: time. Structure may be the result or the foundation of the study of systems as they stand at one point in time; history then occupies a similar position in relation to systems through time.

The opposition between synchrony and diachrony is, on the other hand, ambiguous.[34] It may imply either that structures exist in (may be postulated for) one time or over time, or that structure can be found only in synchrony, never in diachrony. In this latter formulation, history becomes a flow of events whose significance can never be seen until, the button which arrests movement being pressed, it freezes into a motionless state – and then ceases to be history; at that point analysis begins, to produce structure. There can be few, if any, anthropologists who would adopt this view of the matter, for even when they ignore time and perform their operations on social and cultural systems as they are at one point, they do not legislate for the sup-pression of a different kind of structure across time. An earlier generation of British social anthropologists may appear to have been doing precisely that, but a mere careful reading of their work will show that what they were ruling out was a spurious history of primitive societies based upon no or little evidence. The primitive societies they chose to study being history-less in the sense of record-less (as they saw it), there was only the present to examine and in which to find structure. Radcliffe-Brown, one of the two great leaders of that generation, and responsible for imposing the notion of structure on the school he created, was at the same time a follower of Herbert Spencer's evolutionary creed, and he could not have been so if he had thought the past to be made up of chaos.

The Radcliffe-Brownian structure is social structure, which may be trans-lated as the continuing network of social relationships in a society. It runs through time until, in the process of evolution or by the action of historical causes which distort the evolutionary path, it changes into another structure. While it exists to be studied (either embodied in a living reality or in reliable historical records) it can be treated as timeless, for it is by definition uniform in a given period of time. On this view, which in some form is still potent in

34. As is the word 'synchrony'. Drifting from Saussurean linguistics into the social sciences, it has there failed to expand its meaning in accordance with post-Saussurean usage. See GREIMAS, 'Structure et histoire', p. 819 in POUILLON *et al.*, *Problèmes du structuralisme* (1966) or p. 107 in GREIMAS, *Du sens. Essais sémio-tiques* (1970): 'La structure d'un langage quelconque ne comporte [pour les théories du langage post-saussuriennes] aucune référence temporelle, et le terme de syn-chronie n'y est conservé que par tradition.'

Anglo-American anthropology, we may study the structure of a society as it is now or as it once was; we may study the manner in which one structure changes into another; or we may study a different kind of structure, which, running through time, is the form of the process by which societies grow more diverse and more complex. Only the fourth and last alternative, the evolutionary, has been dropped from the Radcliffe-Brownian heritage. The third alternative involves, not the study of structure as such, but the historical process by which it develops. The rôle of this last kind of study is now much larger than it was and is likely to grow, as we shall see later on; the same holds true for the second alternative (the study of past structures); structure and history are interwoven.

But to say 'structure' in a world-wide context is today to evoke a different sense: the 'structure' of structuralism, a doctrine which, ramifying in the kingdom of knowledge, has a branch in anthropology to which the name of Lévi-Strauss is attached. What is relevant in it at the moment is its attitude to, and implications for, time and history.

The matter is extraordinarily complex. Lévi-Strauss would not wish the historical dimension to be put away from anthropology; far from it: 'Scorning the historical dimension on the pretext that we have insufficient means to evaluate it, except approximately, will result in our being satisfied with an impoverished sociology, in which phenomena are set loose, as it were, from their foundations.' [35] Moreover, structure is admitted to, or inserted into, historians' history,[36] and modern structuralism is recorded as having diverged from the Saussurean interpretation of the dichotomy between synchronic and diachronic.[37] Yet, while these and other pronouncements [38] appear to establish a place for history in or alongside anthropology, there is another aspect of Lévi-Straussian structuralism that throws the matter into doubt, at least as far as the study of primitive societies is concerned. These societies exist in history; they have a history; yet they 'seem to have elaborated or retained a particular wisdom which incites them to resist desperately any structural modification which would afford history a point of entry into their lives'.[39] True, the distinction being made between 'cold' primitive so-

---

35. 'Dédaigner la dimension historique, sous prétexte que les moyens sont insuffisants pour l'évaluer, sinon de façon approximative, conduit à se satisfaire d'une sociologie raréfiée, où les phénomènes sont comme décollés de leur support.' *Leçon inaugurale*, p. 20; English translation, *The Scope of Anthropology*, p. 23.
36. *Ibid.*, p. 23; English translation, p. 27.
37. *Ibid.*, pp. 24 sqq.; English translation, pp. 27 sqq.
38. See Chapter 1 in *Anthropologie structurale* (1958) (*Structural Anthropology*, 1963), where history and social anthropology are bracketed together as organizing, respectively, the conscious and unconscious expressions of social life: p. 25 (English transl., p. 18). The same book, pp. 313 sq. (English transl., pp. 285 sq.) places social anthropology (*ethnologie*) in opposition to history in respect of their treatment of time: the first is concerned with reversible and non-cumulative time; the second with directed and irreversible time.
39. Elles 'semblent avoir élaboré, ou retenu, une sagesse particulière, qui les incite à résister désespérément à toute modification de leur structure, qui permettrait à l'histoire de faire irruption dans leur sein.' *Leçon inaugurale*, p. 41; English

cieties and 'hot' developed ones is mainly theoretical,[40] but we may well wonder whether, if primitive men can be said to have obstinately resisted history,[41] the category history has any great relevance to anthropology.

But there is a deeper reason for questioning the receptivity of structuralism to a recognizable historical method. A structure is worked out only by the study of transformations. When we come later on to deal with structuralism as a separate topic we shall see that, at least in the Lévi-Straussian version, these transformations may range over (that is, may be located everywhere in) time, in such a manner that time becomes irrelevant because neutral. So that while in the versions of anthropology which are still willing to deal with cause, change, and sequence a lively school of historiography can emerge, a structuralist anthropology may bow to history but be incapable of extending a hand to it.[42]

7. *Evolutionism and functionalism*

The contrast between evolutionary and functionalist approaches can be made only in isolation from structuralism, for as soon as that third term is introduced the first two can be seen to merge to take up a joint opposition to it. It may prove a disconcerting experience for most evolutionists and functionalists to find themselves in the same barracks; they may think that they have fought enough battles to justify their separate encampment. In fact, two indications of their common heritage have already in part been alluded to: that a leading British structural-functionalist, Fortes, can trace his descent to Morgan, from whom also springs a line of American evolutionists, is one marker; that Radcliffe-Brown, the arch-priest of anthropological structural-functionalism (and one of Fortes's nearer ancestors), can be shown to have been a Spencerian evolutionist is another and more telling one. Evolutionary and functionalist attractions are not mutually exclusive, although they usually appear to be so; they form two poles between which many anthropologists may move backwards and forwards.

The structuralist's solidifying war on both ends of the continuum is motivated by his view of time and development on the one hand, and his explanatory system on the other. He cannot avoid conceiving of human time as beginning with the mysterious emergence of man from non-man and stretching in a homogeneous form from that origin to all living men; but he refuses to see time acting on all men in the same way. The neolithic revolution has

---

translation, pp. 46 sq.

40. *Ibid.*, p. 42; English translation, p. 47.

41. *Ibid.*, p. 44; English translation, p. 50.

42. See GREIMAS, 'Structure et histoire', pp. 825 sq. in POUILLON *et al., Problèmes du structuralisme* (1966) or pp. 113 sq. in GREIMAS, *Du sens* (1970) for a contrary point of view. And cf. DE IPOLA, 'Ethnologie et histoire' (1970). Now see BURGUIÈRE *et al., Histoire et structure* (1971), especially BURGUIÈRE's 'Présentation' at pp. i-vii.

not touched all societies; the industrial even fewer. Societies may grow (in any sense of the verb) and diminish. Most important of all, a class of 'cold' societies, stubborn in their sage simplicity, brushes aside the flow of development that carries other societies forward. Evolution then becomes meaningless, for it implies a steady progression, even if all runners in the race do not move at the same speed. To explain, structuralism has its transforming structure; a doctrine (functionalism) which rests on the assumption that a society consists of a multitude of interlocking parts such that everything in it has significance only in relation to all the others is recalcitrant to its demands. Structuralism can tease both evolutionism and functionalism; it can insult the latter by pointing out that its theory was invented by historians.[43] (The correlated attack on diffusionism need not detain us.)[44]

It may be doubted whether the structuralist case against evolutionary and functionalist theories has been fully made out. At any rate, they live. And their concerns and methods belong to the present and the immediate future. Each will be dealt with separately in a later section as an example of current styles. For the moment we need say little more than that both names are fairly loose descriptions of the things to which they are applied, one of them being preoccupied with the mutation of social and cultural forms (and by both shifts in stage of development and processes of divergence), the other with the close examination of how a particular society aggregates and orders its parts.

At once, then, we can see that they are not of necessity antagonistic and guess how it can be that they form alternative, not mutually exclusive, enterprises. Functionalists do not in reality assert that because the parts of a system are closely integrated it cannot change (even though some may have written their analyses as if they thought so); the literature of functionalist anthropology is littered with speculations about how things came to be and about how they may develop. The theory is more of a method, especially of field work, and leaves its practitioners free to be pulled towards the kind of endeavour for which evolutionism is the name. There are trends of development, mutations of type, divergences from common origins: at one point in time an anthropologist may think and write on them and is then an evolutionist. On his side the evolutionist (that is, the man for whom the preoccupation with evolution is overwhelming) may turn to the analysis of particular systems in a fashion which turns him into a functionalist, even when he denies the name. We shall be able to see when we deal more fully with functionalism and evolutionism in section D that they not only interpenetrate but form along with structuralism a complex system of interacting styles.

43. See LÉVI-STRAUSS, *Anthropologie structurale*, pp. 5 sq., 16 sqq., and 22 (English translation, pp. 3 sq., 11 sqq., and 16).
44. For a general statement see HEINE-GELDERN, 'Cultural diffusion' (1968).

C. THE MAIN FIELDS OF STUDY

The first five fields to be discussed are not in principle specialisms, although in practice they may be. On the other hand, whatever the extent of *de facto* specialization, it is highly unlikely that any anthropologist in one of the central traditions will not at some time have done research on some aspect of those five broad topics (kinship, politics, law, economics, and religion). It will at once be noticed that there is no mention of what is called social structure or social organization. There was a time when social structure as a concept would have merited a full discussion; but not now.[45] In a sense, the greater part of anthropology is about this subject, and many of its aspects are touched on throughout the chapter. But not every topic of social structure/ organization is dealt with. Space does not allow.

The second group of fields (art, music, literature, and technology) are seen by the great majority of anthropologists as specialisms, although in the view of many they ought not to be. Other fields might have been added to the list, but encyclopaedism is out of the question. Language might well have qualified for entry; it is in fact dealt with in Section D.

1. *Kinship and marriage*

The priority given to this topic is likely to go unquestioned by the mass of anthropologists, for, coming at its problems from many angles, they converge to raise it jointly to the peak of their science. In view of that eminence, it would be surpising if the topic were not to be one where 'main trends' were found in large measure and for which an interesting future was predictable. Not all the trends converge, but many of them are complementary.

The study of kinship and marriage is above all that of relations between the generations and the sexes. In the large specialist vocabulary we find the following terms: descent, filiation, alliance, incest, exogamy, and kinship terminology (nomenclature). They will do as a short list to generate a number of current problems. It might be possible to conceive of a society where members born within it were not generally ascribed to the women who bore them; but we know of none. The human infant is first his mother's responsibility and remains bound to her by a set of mutual rights, which may extend beyond life. We have, then, one kind of filiation. We have another in regard to fathers, but the matter is now more complex. We assume, at least outside the realm of possibilities opened up by second-stage industrial society, that women and their children are dependent on men. Husbands may well be fathers to the women's children in the sense in which, *mutatis mutandis*, the women are their mothers, but they may not be. My mother's husband may or may not be the man to whom I am attached by the main ligature that binds me through a male to the generation that stands above me. That man may be my mother's brother.

45. Cf., e.g., FIRTH, *Essays on Social Organization and Values* (1964), Pt. 1.

In either case, my father is the brother-in-law of my mother's brother. Those two men are bound by alliance, and I am connected to both terms of it. If my society places me in one descent group (patrilineal, where descent is traced exclusively through males) with my father, then my mother and her brother are – but there are exceptions – members of another such group. If I am in a matrilineal descent group (in which descent is traced exclusively through females) with my mother and her brother, my father is in another such group. In both cases my father is at once linked to me through parenthood and affinity (that is, marriage); in matrilineal systems the affinal link is direct, for my father and I are members of two different groups linked in marriage; in a patrilineal system it is indirect. One of the great and continuing debates in the literature is between those who view kinship in terms of descent, in which case marriage is seen as a set of bonds between kinship groups, and those for whom the key concept is alliance, when marriage is viewed as structuring the system. Whether these opposing views severally apply to different systems or whether they truly compete in the interpretation of all systems is part of the argument.

To come back to the obvious: father and mother's brother are different men because brothers and sisters do not marry. The brother-sister unit is exogamous, but restrictions on marriage are usually much wider, and by casting the marriage net far afield, they may bring large aggregates into systematic relations with one another. Whatever else it may be, marriage is a union implying continuity of relationships. But, needless to stress, there are other sexual relations between men and women; they are prohibited between specified kinsmen by the rules of incest. And we are now in the middle of an interesting debate. The range of people covered by the rules prohibiting marriage is not always exactly the same as that of the people included within the bar on incest. What then is the relationship between exogamy and rules of incest? We might say that there is no relation between them: they are one and the same, despite a few incongruities. The prohibition of incest is seen as the driving force behind marriage and the making of alliance. For many theorists, the two things are different; priority is assigned to one of them, such that its explanation would lead to an explanation of the other by virtue of its dependence; or the two things are put into different explanatory frameworks. For example, exogamy being accounted for by the need to form relations among families, the prohibition of incest is then seen as a means to enhance order within families.

'Descent' calls for more comment. In ordinary language, I am descended from any ancestor I care to name, and I may be linked to him through males and females indifferently – cognatically. That usage spills over into anthropology, but many theorists will not allow the term to be used beyond the context of unilineally constituted groups. Systems of patrilineal and matrilineal kinship have traditionally stood at the centre of attention, and an elaborate literature analyses them and relates them to other institutions of society.

Unilineal systems are common and can count on continuing to be given a prominent place in research. Non-unilineal systems, although common enough in parts of the world (e.g., South-East Asia and Europe) and present too in areas where unilineal systems predominate (as in Black Africa), have had to wait until fairly recent years to be accorded the analytical attention they deserve. Some of the recent work addresses itself to what may morphologically be thought of as systems intermediate between unilineal and non-unilineal systems, in that, lacking a unilineal principle, they yet recruit members to groups which in their social and genealogical arrangements closely resemble unilineally constituted groups.

The total range of systems is examined from structural and functional points of view, but anthropologists are also concerned with their evolution and mutation. One might generate an increasing number of possible systems by starting from a few basic assumptions and adding to them further assumptions until models 'accounting for' all known systems are formed. But it is left to historical study or the observation of changes now taking place to establish how mutations occur and whether any general pattern can be discerned in them. For example, most anthropologists do not expect to find elaborate descent groups in societies of hunters and gatherers; they are usually convinced that matrilineal systems withstand modern conditions less than do patrilineal; [46] they see in industrialization the end of unilineal grouping. Logical, experimental, and empirical forms of study along these lines all appear in current work and seem destined to grow in intensity and subtlety.[47]

The approach adopted in the U.S.S.R. and other Socialist countries re-

46. But see DOUGLAS, 'Is matriliny doomed in Africa?' (1969).

47. In the enormous literature we must confine ourselves to the following references: LÉVI-STRAUSS, *Les Structures élémentaires de la parenté* (1949; 2nd edn., rev., with new preface, 1967) (English translation, *The Elementary Structures of Kinship*, 1969); MURDOCK, *Social Structure* (1949); RADCLIFFE-BROWN & FORDE (eds.), *African Systems of Kinship and Marriage* (1950); HOMANS & SCHNEIDER, *Marriage, Authority, and Final Causes. A Study of Unilateral Cross-Cousin Marriage* (1955); EGGAN (ed.), *Social Anthropology of North American Tribes* (enl. edn., 1955); GOODY (ed.), *The Developmental Cycle in Domestic Groups* (1958); MURDOCK (ed.), *Social Structure in Southeast Asia* (1960); SCHNEIDER & GOUGH (eds.), *Matrilineal Kinship* (1961); LEACH, *Rethinking Anthropology* (1961); FORTES (ed.), *Marriage in Tribal Societies* (1962); NEEDHAM, *Structure and Sentiment. A Test Case in Social Anthropology* (1962); JOSSELIN DE JONG, 'A new approach to kinship studies' (1962); SCHAPERA (ed.), *Studies in Kinship and Marriage Dedicated to Brenda Z. Seligman on her 80th Birthday* (1963); SCHMITZ, *Grundformen der Verwandtschaft* (1964); SHAH, 'Basic terms and concepts in the study of family in India' (1964); FOX, *Kinship and Marriage* (1967); NAKANE, *Kinship and Economic Organization in Rural Japan* (1967); BOHANNAN & MIDDLETON (eds.), *Marriage, Family and Residence* (1968); GUIART, 'L'enquête d'ethnologie de la parenté' (1968); MERCIER, 'Anthropologie sociale et culturelle' (1968), pp. 931 sqq.; BUCHLER & SELBY, *Kinship and Social Organization. An Introduction to Theory and Method* (1968); FORTES, *Kinship and the Social Order* (1969); SMITH, R. T., 'Comparative structure [of the family]' (1968); EGGAN, 'Introduction [to kinship]' (1968); GOODY, 'Descent groups' (1968); ORANS, 'Social organization' (1970), pp. 145-165; GOODENOUGH, *Description and Comparison in Cultural Anthropology* (1970); NEEDHAM (ed.), *Rethinking Kinship and Marriage* (1971); MAIR, *Marriage* (1971); BARNES, *Three Styles in the Study of Kinship* (1971); DUMONT, *Introduction à deux théories*

mains more faithful to the tradition established by Lewis H. Morgan, or rather, Engels's interpretation of his work. In this tradition the history of society is made to rest on a sequence of stages with which particular forms of kinship structure are associated. Apart from recording institutions of kinship, family, and marriage as they are found now, chiefly in the U.S.S.R. itself, Soviet scholarship has devoted much of its energy to refining the Morgan-Engels schema. The current view of 'the overwhelming majority of Soviet investigators' is that

the primitive herd was transformed directly into the gens . . . that the appearance of the first form of marriage coincides with the appearance of exogamy and the gens. Marital relations originated as relations not between individuals, but between collectives, gentes. The form in which these relationships existed was dual-gentile organization . . . the primitive gens could only be matrilineal . . . After the epoch of the primitive herd is singled out as a special stage in primitive history, a period remains embracing the time from the first appearance of the gens to the appearance of class society.

But while Soviet scholars agree with Morgan and Engels that the primitive gens was matrilineal,

they take account of the fact that whereas the decay of collective property and the appearance of private property necessarily gave rise to a tendency for matrilineal filiation to be replaced by patrilineal, the effectuation of this depends upon specific historical conditions.[48]

It will be seen that Soviet scholars enjoy a more confident vision than do

---

d'anthropologie sociale (1971); Müller, *Der Begriff 'Verwandtschaft' in der modernen Ethnosoziologie* (in press — 1973). For the parallel literature from the Soviet Union and Eastern Europe, see below, note 48.

48. SEMENOV, 'The doctrine of Morgan, Marxism and contemporary ethnography' (1965), pp. 12 sq. See also bibliography to PERŠIC, A. I. & ČEBOKSAROV, 'Polveka sovetskoj ètnografii' (= Half a century of Soviet ethnography) (1967); KISLJAKOV, 'Problemy sem'i i braka v rabotah sovetskih ètnografov' (= Problems of marriage and the family in the works of Soviet ethnographers) (1967); VINNIKOV, 'Novoe v semejnom bytu kolhoznikov Turkmenistana' (= New aspects of the family life of collective-farm workers in Turkmenistan) (1967); PANJAN, 'Izmenenija v strukture i čislennosti sel'skoj sem'i u armjan za gody sovetskoj vlasti' (= Changes in the structure and size of the Armenian rural family in the years of Soviet rule) (1968); *Razloženie rodovogo obščestva i formirovanie klassovogo obščestva* (= The Break-up of the Patrimonial System and the Formation of Class Society) (1968); *Leninskie idei v izučenii istorii pervobytnogo obščestva, rabovladenija i feodalizma* (= Leninist Ideas on the Study of the History of Primitive Society, Slavery, and Feudalism) (1970); OL'DEROGGE, 'Osnovnye čerty razvitija sistem rodstva' (= Main evolutionary features of kinship systems) (1960) and 'Several problems in the study of kinship systems' (1961); GURVIČ & DOLGIH (eds.), *Obščestvennyj stroj u narodov Severnoj Sibiri* (= Social Structure of North Siberian Peoples) (1970). For work elsewhere in Socialist Europe see, e.g., SELLNOW, I., *Grundprinzipien einer Periodisierung der Urgeschichte* (1961); SELLNOW, W., *Gesellschaft – Staat – Recht* (1963). For reappraisals of Morgan's work see PERSHITZ (= PERŠIC), A. I. (ed.), 'Symposium: La théorie de L. H. Morgan de périodisation de l'histoire de la société primitive et l'ethnographie moderne' (1970); and by a 'Western' Marxist, TERRAY, 'Morgan et l'anthropologie contemporaine' (1969) (English translation, 'Morgan and contemporary anthropology', 1972).

their 'Western' colleagues of the origins and development of forms of kinship.

The most apparent feature of kinship, its terminology, gives us the impression of being able to grasp a system, but as time has gone on anthropologists have learned to avoid some of the traps laid by the 'obviousness' of the data. There may be no one vocabulary in the system; a set of terms of address and one of reference may be accompanied by others (e.g., in relationship to the dead). There is great variability in the extent to which a kinship vocabulary overlaps with other lexical sets in its language. The same word (lexeme) may function both in and out of the context of kinship (cf. English 'father') such that a decision by the analyst to assign it primarily to the kinship set, and to describe other usage(s) as derived or secondary, becomes arbitrary. A consequence of the overlap is that the range of connotation of a term must be brought into the analysis of what it means when it is being used to denote. The use of personal names for kinsmen is a fact of kinship. Finally, there is unlikely to be an invariant set of terms such that, in denoting a kinsman, the speaker is always free of the obligation to make a choice; he may select from a range which enables him to express the momentary state of relations between him and the addressee/referee, the expectations he places upon the latter's response, and his hopes for the future state of their relations. (Cf. English 'father/dad/daddy/papa'.)

The meaning of kinship terms is therefore a complex meaning, and no simple formula can be produced for relating a terminology to the social system within which it is used. Kinship terminologies do not specify individually each and every position on a genealogical tree. Nor, when, as is often the case, they group terminologically, under one term, several such positions (cf. English 'uncle'), does each term *necessarily* reflect a uniform set of rights and duties and affectivity between the speaker and each of the addressees/ referees. The language of kinship, like all language, is a system that works independently, is not a mere reflection, of another level of social life, and yet affects and is affected by it.

The problem has been to try to come to grips with the fact that kinship terminologies (if we may set aside some of the cautions already expressed) do show some fit with the arrangements and ordering of kinship systems, and the correspondence is often striking. So much so that field workers are surprised if they discover, for example, that a form of terminology associated in the literature with matrilineal descent is in use among speakers whose kinship system lacks a principle of matriliny.[49] 'Types' of kinship terminology are inscribed in the literature; the theorists have been striving to break their grip. One mode of attack has been developed by the adoption of techniques of

49. Discrepancies of this sort have in the past been the material from which speculative 'histories' have been written: a society with kinship system of type A but using a terminology of type B must have been, and therefore was, formerly of system B. As a matter of fact, the speculation may sometimes have merit, but the interesting thing is that it contradicts the thesis upon which it is based, for if·system and terminology are inevitably linked, then a change in one should produce a corresponding change in the other, and terminological residues should not be found.

analysis taken from linguistics; it is in origin an American enterprise. Componential analysis [50] starts from the assumption (not in itself new) that a set of kinship terms can be made to reveal their interrelated meaning by being submitted to a dissection that extracts their semantic components. A term X may be shown to contain components for distance in generation from the speaker; difference of sex in relation to the speaker; kinship (cognation as opposed to affinity) with the speaker; and so on. Further, by transformational analyses,[51] particular systems of terminology are shown to have embodied in them rules which, so to say, convert one relationship into another, to produce the observed pattern. The formal elegance of these exercises is obvious, but they have excited some hostility on the grounds that they do not explain but merely restate, or that they explain only up to a point. It must be said, therefore, that the formal analysts usually present their technique as one mode of attack and their results as contributory to a wider enterprise. But the full import of the work cannot be seen outside the context of linguistic anthropology.[52]

Much of what has been said rests on thin ice. The anthropological world knows passionate controversies (kinship is/is not biological; patriliny and matriliny are true/false categories; and so on) which make any brief statement perilous. We must move on to the trend by which anthropologists expand their kinship studies to include data drawn from complex societies; and in doing so find themselves, by a paradox, engaging in 'purer' kinship studies than were formerly made. The reason is this. In small-scale societies, kinship is a framework within which a vast repertory of behaviour is performed, for it is there also economic, political, legal, and religious life. In a large-scale society the investigator interested above all in kinship finds it less weighed down by an institutional load. To be sure, a study of family and kinship in, say, North America or Western Europe must tease out their economic, political, legal, and religious components, but the centre of gravity of these institutional complexes lies elsewhere, in the specific arrangements of a differentiated society. In the Americas, Europe, Asia, Africa, and Australia, anthropologists at an increasing tempo are examining the kinship lives of people in both old and new complex societies, using their traditional skill in kinship study to do what scholars from other disciplines are not inspired to do.

And once they venture into this newer branch of their studies, the work of anthropologists comes more fully to the attention of other scholars, who are content to leave primitive societies to anthropology but are sensitive to what is now being done in their midst. It would be too much to say that kinship study to do what scholars from other disciplines are not inspired to do.

50. See BUCHLER & SELBY, *Kinship and Social Organization* (1968), and Parts 3 and 4 of TYLER (ed.), *Cognitive Anthropology* (1969), a book of readings.
51. They might more appropriately be called 'generative' – and sometimes are.
52. See p. 88 below (D. 5) and pp. 114-117 below (E. 4). For a Soviet example of the modern study of kinship terminology, see LEVIN, Ju. I., 'Ob opisanii sistemy terminov rodstva' (= Kinship nomenclature) (1970). See ORANS, *Social Organization* (1970), pp. 157-162, for a review of the recent arguments about the analysis of kinship terminology.

upon the thinking of the historians, political scientists, and so on, but there are signs that the effect is growing.[53]

2. *Politics and government*

The fact that in a small-scale society many institutional activities, as we view them by our categories, go on simultaneously at the same loci did not inhibit the early emergence of the specialized study of particular institutional forms. But when we come to the more recent literature we see that the specialization is carried a stage further: we have now (although many dislike the terms) a political anthropology, an economic anthropology, a legal anthropology, and a religious anthropology. A fate of separatism has overtaken the science of the total. Three interconnected shifts account for the change: the growth in the scale of the profession itself, such that a division of labour is encouraged; an increased sensitivity to the arguments generated within the specialized social sciences; and the drift to the study of complex societies, where institutional crystallization is a fact of life. If in the study of kinship, anthropology can teach the world, it has a great deal to learn from the other social sciences when it comes to politics and the rest.[54]

Two monitors of Anglo-American anthropology are able to say and carry conviction that 'Fortes and Evans-Pritchard, with *African Political Systems*, virtually established "political anthropology" '.[55] The Introduction to that pioneering work[56] has certain features which later scholarship has striven to eradicate or correct. It is typological, and shifts in anthropological vision

53. For an example of the penetration of anthropological categories into the historical writing on Europe, see BULLOUGH, 'Early medieval social groupings: The terminology of kinship' (1969). The author refers *inter alia* to the historical-anthropological study by LANCASTER, 'Kinship in Anglo-Saxon society' (1958). The following are some examples of recent kinship studies of the civilizations: SHAH, 'Basic terms and concepts . . .' (1964); NAKANE, *Kinship and Economic Organization* . . . (1967); SCHNEIDER, *American Kinship. A Cultural Account* (1968); FIRTH, HUBERT & FORGE, *Families and Their Relatives: Kinship in a Middle-Class Sector of London. An Anthropological Study* (1969); FREEDMAN (ed.), *Family and Kinship in Chinese Society* (1970); ROSTWOROSKI DE DÍEZ CANŞECO, 'Succession, co-öption to kingship and royal incest among the Inca' (1969); LOUNSBURY, 'The structure of the Latin kinship system and its relation to Roman social organization' (1967). See also CUISENIER, SEGALEN & VIRVILLE, 'Pour l'étude de la parenté dans les sociétés européennes: le programme d'ordinateur ARCHIV' (1970).
54. Not that the traffic is one-way, as we may see, e.g., in a chapter entitled 'Politics in tribal societies', in MACKENZIE, *Politics and Social Science* (1967), where (p. 192) it can be said that 'what is most characteristic of the social anthropologists at present [but the author has principally British social anthropologists in mind] is that they use "bow and arrow" techniques at a high level of sophistication', but the debt of modern political science to anthropology is made plain, and courteously. For another political scientist's view, see EASTON, 'Political anthropology' (1959).
55. GLUCKMAN & EGGAN, 'Introduction' [to BANTON (ed.), *Political Systems* . . .] (1965), p. xx.
56. FORTES & EVANS-PRITCHARD (eds.), *African Political Systems* (1940).

make some of its classifications now seem implausible. It is, naturally, tied to the African evidence. It views primitive political systems as relatively immobile and marvellously self-correcting. It takes for granted a background of colonial peace which blocks off perception of upheaval, warfare, and the turbulence of primitive 'international relations'. (But this last point is an exaggeration.) It is preoccupied with political structure to the detriment of political process . . . In the newer anthropology, 'process' and 'dynamics' become the watchwords, but they need to be eyed with caution, for they may be made to advance one proposition in the guise of another. All 'structures' have 'processes' to which they must be referred; they are all in a state of the endless movements of parts. It is another matter to say that the 'structures' must be eternally in change. They may or may not be. The stimulus given by the world around us to concentrate our attention on that which is changing in structure is not also an excuse for concealing the relative stability of some structures, past and present.

From *African Political Systems* flow many continuing arguments. One is the (not altogether nominal) discussion about the relation between 'politics' and 'government'. It was a major achievement of that book to establish a clear distinction in primitive societies between systems of order in which the key was centralized and delegated power and those where, in the absence of such power, the mechanism is a 'set of inter-segmentary relations . . . a balance of opposed local loyalties and of divergent lineage and ritual ties' (p. 13). The first class of systems have government, the second do not. But both obviously have politics in the sense that they know (and must know) competition and clashes of interest. On the other hand, there may be some intellectual difficulty in conceiving of a society that shows no form of government whatever, for elements of management and leadership must surely be universal. It is for that reason that one modern analyst prefers to write of 'minimal government' when she refers to the kinds of system placed in the second of the categories arising from the earlier study.[57] Of course, the units within which minimal government may be detected may be so small that political anthropology ceases at that point to share a common field with political science.

A second argument concerns the notion of territory and its place in political life. In states and state-like systems authority runs within fixed territorial boundaries. (Not that all hierarchically organized political communities are tied to territory: some international religious communities show the negative case.) Non-centralized primitive systems still exhibit the territorial principle at work, but in a different form. Groups of people occupy and exploit particular areas and are attached to them by bonds of sentiment (often ritualized). The argument has gone on to produce the assertion that in political life both kinship and locality 'serve everywhere to link people together . . .'.[58] But in fact in some societies the territorial limits to which society runs cannot be specified (the Tallensi described by Fortes are an example), or the territory

57. MAIR, *Primitive Government* (1962).
58. SCHAPERA, *Government and Politics in Tribal Societies* (1956), p. 5.

occupied by it is not thought of as being held exclusively against outsiders.[59]

The case of the Tallensi (Northern Territories of Ghana) in turn may serve as a reminder that the entities to which the word 'society' is attached are sometimes very vague. We speak of the world of men as though they were distributed neatly among a finite number of societies, and we proceed to compare one such society with others. We can hardly do otherwise, but it is necessary for anthropologists to remind themselves from time to time that their societies are artefacts of particular kinds of classification and that a real world of discrete political, cultural, and economic units is not at their disposal.

An aspect of this problem emerges when anthropologists confront, as they have done increasingly in recent years, the complex entities formed by or under the aegis of colonial or other dominant powers. In what sense is a political entity such as Malaysia a society? It is, to give a common sense answer (for which J. S. Furnivall, not an anthropologist, was primarily responsible),[60] a plural society. Composed of definable cultural elements, each of which has some political cohesion, the plural society is neither a mere juxtaposition of its elements nor a coalescence of them. Although that is a true statement it is not theoretically very interesting, and a debate begins in which anthropologists, treating societies of this kind, argue about pluralism to the point that some of the most fundamental questions of political and social cohesion are raised. And the argument is bound to go on.[61]

Meanwhile the more traditional political preoccupations of anthropology continue to exercise their force, and the literature expands with new data, the raising of fresh topics, the critique of typologies, the insertion of time as a dimension, the refinement of terminology, and the work of synthesis.[62] The

59. See, e.g., WOODBURN, 'Stability and flexibility in Hadza residential groupings' (1968), p. 105.

60. See, e.g., his *Netherlands India. A Study of Plural Economy* (1939). He in turn was inspired by Dutch economists concerned with what we now know as Indonesia.

61. See KUPER & SMITH, M. G. (eds.), *Pluralism in Africa* (1969), both for its arguments and its bibliography.

62. In addition to those already mentioned, the following works of a general character may be noted: BALANDIER, *Anthropologie politique* (1967) (English translation, *Political Anthropology*, 1970); GLUCKMAN, *Politics, Law and Ritual in Tribal Society* (1965); SWARTZ, TURNER, & TUDEN, *Political Anthropology* (1966); COHEN, R. & MIDDLETON (eds.), *Comparative Political Systems. Studies in the Politics of Pre-Industrial Societies* (1967); COLSON, 'The field [of political anthropology]' (1968); SMITH, M. G., 'Political organization' (1968); FRIED, *The Evolution of Political Society. An Essay in Political Anthropology* (1967); FRIED et al. (eds.), *War. The Anthropology of Armed Conflict and Aggression* (1967); COHEN, R., 'The political system' (1970); SIGRIST, *Regulierte Anarchie. Untersuchungen zum Fehlen und zur Entstehung politischer Herrschaft in segmentären Gesellschaften Afrikas* (1967); MERCIER, 'Anthropologie sociale ...' (1968), pp. 954 sqq.; LÉVY-BRUHL, H., 'L'ethnologie juridique' (1968), pp. 1127 sqq. The regional studies cannot be surveyed here, but it is worth drawing attention to the studies of caste in relation to politics; see, e.g., BÉTEILLE, *Caste, Class and Power. Changing Patterns of Stratification in a Tanjore Village* (1965).

'bow and arrow' techniques are still in use, but often supplemented with more sophisticated methods. The study of electoral behaviour by some anthropologists should establish their credit with some political scientists. It is more interesting that attempts have begun to infuse into the anthropological study of politics ideas about the nature of struggles for power, political 'entrepreneurship', and the process of decision-making.[63] In a large part of their political life, as in their economic life, men calculate their actions and their possible outcome; we are in the field of full awareness. And while it may be true, as the structuralists have it, that there are structures of the unconscious (which are to them the focus of interest), there are also structures of the willed and the foreseen. Game theory and its cognates have not yet lodged themselves fully within political anthropology, but the thing may yet happen.[64]

3. *Law in the context of social control*

A case could be made for saying that it is only the existence of an academic subject called law that justifies a legal anthropology. Without that external constraint anthropologists would treat law fully within their studies of politics and government. Order, conflict, compromise, adjudication, mediation, and command are members of both now analytically separated spheres. Indeed, the anthropological insistence on treating law as part of a wider field of social control might encourage a lesser allegiance to the academic tradition by which law is separated off from political science (to put the matter in an unhistorical way). Moreover, the anthropologist's law is not that of all lawyers, for some of whom law exists only when there is a state to enforce it.

The broad view taken in legal anthropology is that it has a double task: when judicial and legislative institutions exist, to study them within the larger systems of rules, expectations, and sanctions of which they are part; and when these institutions are absent to analyse how by other means rules are enforced and rights protected. The classical dilemma between applying a narrow definition of law to primitive societies to make many of them lawless, and taking the word in a very wide sense, when we are forced to speak of law in the absence of courts and judges, is perhaps best overcome by maintaining the obvious distinction between law as a body of binding norms, which every society has by definition, and law as judicial institutions, a privilege not universally enjoyed.

But the body of norms has to be further specified. We may say that the

63. See, e.g., BAILEY, *Stratagems and Spoils. A Social Anthropology of Politics* (1969).

64. For a survey of these questions see: Social Science Research Council, *Research in Social Anthropology* (1968), pp. 17-24, and for a wide-ranging review of the current work see WINCKLER. 'Political anthropology' (1970). For the relevance of game theory, decision-making. and 'transactions', see BARTH, 'Segmentary opposition and the theory of games' (1959), and *Models of Social Organization* (1966); and various anthropological contributions to BUCHLER & NUTINI (eds.), *Game Theory in the Behavioral Sciences* (1969).

relevant norms are those which relate to the conduct of men, singly or in collectivities, among themselves and to their reciprocal rights and duties. To enforce that conduct and uphold those rights there is an array of positive and negative sanctions, which are social (as opposed to ritual) when they are applied by men acting singly or in groups. Law in the second sense appears when some kind of adjudicative procedure comes before the application of negative sanctions.

As in the field of politics, so in the field of law, anthropologists have made a special point of indicating how order is producible in societies which lack centralized institutions; where on first principles one might expect chaos, there is to be found that 'ordered anarchy' delineated in Evans-Pritchard's now classic study of the Nuer of Sudan.[65] Legal and political anthropology stresses the rôle of reciprocity; it gives weight to alignments and coalitions, and to the tendency for cohesion and compromise to be generated by cross-cutting loyalties; it stresses the force of mobilized opinion. Tit-for-tat and the blood-feud have their rules. It is obvious that the principles and character of these unplanned mechanisms for the production of order bear a haunting resemblance, not to the political and legal properties of modern states, but to the nature of the transactions among them. 'It therefore becomes apparent why many modern writers, such as Kelsen, have argued that international law is closely analogous to primitive law as it constitutes a binding normative system relying for enforcement on self-help remedies, but lacks the centralized organs which are the features of developed law.' [66] One may easily take the analogy too far,[67] but in trade, war, treaty, alliance, and diplomacy the international order may be seen as the monstrous version of the minutely figured 'anarchy' of primitive societies. Men suffer in both, but then they suffer too in the regulated political and legal systems of complex societies.

But by no means all primitive societies are without centralized power and judicial mechanisms, and the legal anthropologists have there the opportunity to move from the study of the 'non-legal' law of ordered anarchy to that of the 'legal' law [68] of courts, judgment, and enforcement, although in doing so they must exercise caution in assimilating the institutions and procedures of foreign societies to those described by such English words as 'courts' and 'judgment'. It is true that they cannot observe so easily the analogues of legislation, for in the absence of writing willed changes of rules leave no or little deposit, and what norms are found at any point are made by those who adhere to them to appear to belong to endless time. The few studies which

65. EVANS-PRITCHARD, *The Nuer. A Description of the Modes of Livelihood and Political Institutions of a Nilotic People* (1940). And cf. SIGRIST, *Regulierte Anarchie* . . . (1967).

66. LLOYD, *The Idea of Law* (1964), p. 238. And see BARKUN, *Law without Sanctions. Order in Primitive Societies and the World Community* (1968).

67. And even tentative uses of the analogy excite opposition from some lawyers, who see in present-day international law evidence of supra-national jurisdiction.

68. Perhaps the most striking of such studies is GLUCKMAN, *The Judicial Process among the Barotse of Northern Rhodesia* (2nd edn., 1967).

are able to show the process of legislation in conditions still very close to those of the pre-literate past are the more precious for their rarity. Schapera's pioneering work on the Tswana, of what is now Botswana, is a model.[69]

We reach a third level of study, and the one in which the major trend will very soon lie, when we examine the work done by anthropologists fully within the context of modern state forms. It is composed of a number of styles. In one of them, the investigators concentrate on the operation of traditional adjudicative procedures constrained by the modern state. In another, they focus their attention on the modern court system itself. In a third, they are concerned with the genesis of new laws and their actual and potential relationships with the existing system of norms. All three styles have this in common, that they are fully sociological in their aims, and in this they differ from much of the corresponding work done by lawyers; they attempt to examine rules and procedures within the context of the full range of interests and relative positions of the parties to actions and of those involved in law-making. For the anthropologist, a suit brought in court is the culmination of a perhaps long and complex dispute or grievance; it is played out within an arena where more is involved than the application of rules to be found in writing; it may lead on to a sequel that no court interests itself in. In other words, the technical analysis of the law in action is conducted within the study of the political forces that shape the course of a judicial or legislative train of events. It is not to be wondered at that, having acquired the experience of such work in exotic societies, some anthropologists are ambitious of applying the same style of analysis to the legal phenomena about them. Here they meet the legal sociologists and with them must face the difficulties constituted by the laws of libel and the discretion and solidarity of incorporated legal personnel – which is not to imply that they do not sometimes encounter such obstacles in more traditional fields.

But we must go back to more classical pursuits to round off the discussion. Every ethnographer, legal anthropologist or not, records rules and regularities. When he publishes them they become part of a record upon which, sometimes to the dismay of the recorder, people may draw in support of a legal or political argument. The disconcerting effect of this kind of action is that it puts the ethnographer in the position of an unintended legislator or authority for tradition. Books about non-literate societies easily turn into manuals of conduct when reading becomes common, and a statement of fact about the year 1940 is transmuted into a rule meant to govern 1970. It was said of the great *adatrecht* (customary law) compilations made by the Dutch in their eastern empire that they acted to freeze into rigidity what should have been allowed to develop. Anthropologists do not want to find themselves accused of the same intervention in other people's lives.[70] (The terms on which,

69. SCHAPERA, *Tribal Legislation among the Tswana of the Bechuanaland Protectorate* (1943), and its revised version: *Tribal Innovators: Tswana Chiefs and Social Change 1795-1940* (1970).

70. The compilation and codification of 'customary law' still goes on. There is important activity along this line in Sub-Saharan Africa. One may note the work

as applied anthropologists, they may wish to intervene are different.) But it is as well that they take into account this dramatic evidence of the usually less marked fact that anthropologists in the field are men acting upon men and have to accept the burden as well as the privilege of dealing with their equals.[71]

4. *Economics*

A satirical history of the growth of the treatment of economic themes within anthropology might portray it as composed of three stages. In the first, scholars wrote descriptive accounts of the technology of production and discussed the effects of environment on it. In the second, they described the trinity of production, consumption, and exchange. And in the third, they lost themselves in economic theory. Unfair as it is, this characterization shows us at least two important things: that the term 'economic(s)' is near-fatally ambiguous, and that the trend of what is now called economic anthropology is towards a strenuous effort to bring its theory into relation with that of economic science, either by integration, adaptation, or flat rejection.

Nobody denies that all societies have economies in the sense that everywhere men produce and exchange goods and services, even if the production and exchange are based upon a rudimentary division of labour, individual and communal. (Not that a division of labour is anywhere the sole basis of exchange, for the latter's value may lie not in the complementarity of the things or services involved but in its nature as a transaction between parties who initiate or sustain a social relationship.) Different societies have different economies (if we may set aside for the sake of convenience the difficulty of drawing lines round either kind of entity). Some have market-places, others not. Some have media of exchange, others not. Some and not others

---

being done in Britain (from the School of Oriental and African Studies, University of London: The Restatement of African Law), in France (Département d'Anthropologie juridique, Faculté de Droit de Paris), and in Belgium (Centre d'Histoire et d'Ethnologie juridiques de Bruxelles).

71. The recent trends of development in legal anthropology may be traced in the following general works: KULCSÁR, *A jogszociológia problémái* (= Problems of Legal Sociology) (1960); GLUCKMAN, *Politics, Law and Ritual* (1965); POIRIER (ed.), *Etudes de droit africain et malgache* (1965); NADER (ed.), *The Ethnography of Law* (1965); BOHANNAN (ed.), *Law and Warfare. Studies in the Anthropology of Conflict* (1967); TÁRKÁNY-SZŰCS, 'Results and task of legal ethnology in Europe' (1967); POIRIER, Introduction à l'ethnologie de l'appareil juridique' (1968); LÉVY-BRUHL, H., 'L'ethnologie juridique' (1968); ALLIOT, 'L'acculturation juridique' (1968); POSPISIL, 'Law and order' (1968); NADER (ed.), *Law in Culture and Society* (1969); GLUCKMAN (ed.), *Ideas and Procedures in African Customary Law* (1969); MOORE, S. F., 'Law and anthropology' (1970); SCHOTT, 'Die Funktionen des Rechts in primitiven Gesellschaften' (1970); POIRIER, 'Situation actuelle et programme de travail de l'ethnologie juridique'/'The current state of legal ethnology and its future tasks' (1970). And see in this work the chapter on Legal Science by Viktor Knapp, pp. 1006-1007.

have sizeable non-physical markets and 'true' money such that supply and demand may interact finely on a considerable scale and the profitability of alternative actions be calculated with some precision.

That last point brings us to the heart of current controversies. One argument, put simply, says that the calculus of scarce resources in relation to alternative ends is made a criterion of economic science only because of the nature of the economic system from which that science has emerged. Many societies (it goes on), even when they have money, and more so when they do not, involve people and groups in acts of producing, consuming, and exchanging which, by the imposition of strict norms and fixed institutional procedures, prevent people from exercising a wide range of choice. They have economic obligations and rights, but they do not act as so many *homines economici*. The counter-arguments (again put very briefly) make two chief points. The first is that economic science is well aware of, and at least sometimes takes into account, the customary and institutional restraints upon the exercise of choice; moreover, it does not operate with a simple-minded notion of what constitutes an economic end or a value to be maximized. In principle, at any rate, and certainly in exercises in the economic analysis of particular sectors of real life, economics knows that people may balance off, say, higher earnings against loss of opportunity for leisure, lower profits against increased social standing and solidarity, or the payment of lower prices against the loss of prestige. The second general point is that choice always exists as part of the human condition. Resources are scarce and men always make more demands on them than they can satisfy. Somebody at some time must choose between taking one or other of several courses of action. It may be that, so to say, the community has, by setting standards and conventions, shut out many of the choices open in pure a-cultural theory to the individuals who compose it, but the norms so established still impose on men the need to manoeuvre within them and discriminate among options of different value – a gift to this kinsman and therefore not to that, a day's fishing and therefore a day's absence from chiefly pursuits, consumption of grain today and therefore not at tomorrow's feast.

But if anthropologists are persuaded by counter-arguments of that sort they are then faced by the problem of how to satisfy themselves that an economic calculus is at work in the absence of a measure of value called money. The allocation of scarce resources to the service of alternative ends calls for an idea of relative costs and gains. Ethnographically, there is no doubt whatever that people make these calculations, but how can they make them with precision? And if they do not so make them, there is no way of matching within anthropology some of the analyses and elegantly spare models constructed by economists. Economic anthropology has been born but it cannot yet be economics – although it may be seen to be not quite so far away from its ideal when we realize that economists are forced to interest themselves in some non-monetary transactions, as when they study the allocation of resources in large firms.

One of the most interesting, and in its way most intellectually encouraging, aspects of the wide-ranging debate is that the economists themselves have entered the lists, and there is pleasure to be got from a reading of the polemical literature that has grown up. It is to be noted that different economists take different sides, aligning themselves some with the 'economic anthropologists', some with their opponents. If there is a general lesson to be learned it is that, as in politics, so in economics, anthropology has at least potentially the data from which to construct theories of self-conscious behaviour and of self-aware rationality, a reason of men reasoning among themselves and forecasting the consequences of their actions.[72]

From one point of view, the anthropologist is a kind of economic historian of simple societies whether he fastens upon technology, the interaction with the environment, or the economic process itself: ethnography and analyses, in abundance, show how physical resources are extracted and put to use, how time is employed, how goods and services are pumped along the channels of institutions, how morality, aesthetics, and religious and political ideas

72. The current debates are well reflected in a number of contributions (including those by an economist) in FIRTH (ed.), *Themes in Economic Anthropology* (1967). See also the diverting polemic by KULA, 'On the typology of economic systems' (1968); Kula argues against GODELIER, 'Objet et méthodes de l'anthropologie économique' (1965; republished, in slightly augmented form, 1971). Among other recent works of general importance may be mentioned: various items in the series 'Economie, Ethnologie, Sociologie', ed. POIRIER (1959 to date); FIRTH & YAMEY (eds.), *Capital, Saving and Credit in Peasant Societies* (1964); NASH, 'Economic anthropology' (1965); FIRTH, *Primitive Polynesian Economy* (2nd edn., 1965); SERVICE, *The Hunters* (1966); WOLF, *Peasants* (1966); NASH, *Primitive and Peasant Economic Systems* (1966); BELSHAW, 'Theoretical problems in economic anthropology' (1967); POTTER, DIAZ & FOSTER (eds.), *Peasant Society. A Reader* (1967); LeCLAIR & SCHNEIDER (eds.), *Economic Anthropology. Readings in Theory and Analysis* (1968); POIRIER, 'Problèmes d'ethnologie économique' (1968); MERCIER, 'Anthropologie sociale ...' (1968), pp. 963 sqq.; LEE & DeVORE (eds.), *Man the Hunter* (1968); VAYDA (ed.), *Environment and Cultural Behavior. Ecological Studies in Cultural Anthropology* (1969); DALTON, 'Theoretical issues in economic anthropology' (1969); TERRAY, *Le marxisme devant les sociétés 'primitives'. Deux études* (1969) (English translation, *Marxism and 'Primitive' Societies. Two Studies*, 1972); SALISBURY, 'Economics' (1970); PANOFF, 'Ethnologie et économie' (1970); DALTON, 'The economic system' (1970); RÖPKE, *Primitive Wirtschaft, Kulturwandel und die Diffusion von Neuerungen* (1970). See also MEILLASSOUX, *Anthropologie économique des Gouro de Côte d'Ivoire* (1965). A somewhat earlier book in this field, POLANYI, ARENSBERG, & PEARSON, *Trade and Markets in the Early Empires* (1957), has led to some recent work along the same lines in Eastern Europe. For examples of work from Latin America, see: GARCÍA, 'Estructura de una hacienda señorial en la Sierra Ecuatoriana; análisis y proyecto de recolonización dentro de un esquema de reforma agraria' (1963); ORTIZ, 'Colombian rural market organization. An exploratory model' (1967). As one might have expected, India is producing work on economics which both pursues classical problems (e.g., SINHA, *Culture Change in an Inter-Tribal Market*, 1968) and shows the effect of contact with other disciplines (e.g., SHETH, *The Social Framework of an Indian Factory*, 1968). A recent study from Sri Lanka illustrates the continuing importance of studies of land tenure: OBEYESEKERE, *Land Tenure in Village Ceylon. A Sociological and Historical Study* (1967). As an example of the relevance of anthropology to economic development, see EPSTEIN, T. S., *Economic Development and Social Change in South India* (1962).

and practices enter into the determination of ends and means, how economic life is at once economic behaviour and the outcome of the interplay of all the analytically distinct forces of society. That approach has the advantage of functionalist completeness; it leaves us with an understanding of how systems work. It has the additional advantage that it lays down deposits of material upon which future scholars may draw for their exercises in the analysis of the weight to be given to this or that factor in economic development, for we cannot really grasp the relative significance of different factors in one society until time and comparison have entered to discriminate among them. The economies which have been well described and analysed by anthropologists differ greatly among themselves as total systems and the differences have to be dissected.

At the opposite pole from an economic anthropology striving after the sophistication of economics lies a modern version of what might be termed environmental economics, whose model is ecology. We are no longer in the world of choice made in the market, but in that of the dialogue between man and non-human nature. The argument is of course not concerned to revert to an outmoded geographical determinism, but rather, in the words of a spokesman, to make 'cultural behavior intelligible by relating it to the material world in which it develops or occurs'.[73] Anthropologists are often in an excellent position to observe and analyse the fine adjustments men make to their physical surroundings (although it is much more than a mere matter of economics), and a cultural ecology that takes its place among the other modes of studying social adaptation and change is an important member of economic studies in all their range.

However, some of the arguments which emerge in favour of the new ecology must be uncongenial to many other practitioners of economic analysis. The spokesman already quoted says elsewhere:

Attention to cultural ideas, values, or concepts cannot, however, be said to be a *sine qua non* of the analysis of ecosystems including man. One may choose rather to place emphasis upon the actual physical behavior or bodily movements through which man directly effects alterations in his environment ... Indeed, a possible approach, suggested by Simpson ... among others, is to regard human culture simply as the behavior or part of the behavior of a particular species of primates.[74]

It may be asked, how much must we fail to learn by pretending that as men we do not need to empathize with and see through the eyes of the men we study?

From the new ecology there is a shading off into what one of its champions terms cultural materialism. Marvin Harris makes his long and briskly argued history of anthropological theory a series of dialogues around the principle of techno-environmental and techno-economic determinism.

This principle holds that similar technologies applied to similar environments tend to produce similar arrangements of labor in production and distribution, and these

73. VAYDA, in VAYDA (ed.), *Environment and Cultural Behavior* ... (1969), p. xii. Cf. STEWARD, *Theory of Cultural Change* (1955), pp. 30 sqq.
74. VAYDA, 'Anthropologists and ecological problems' (1965), p. 4.

in turn call forth similar kinds of social groupings, which justify and coordinate their activities by means of similar systems of values and beliefs.[75]

We can see that the spectrum of the anthropology of economics is no narrower than that of social and cultural anthropology as a whole, an unsurprising conclusion, but one which will prevent our fastening upon 'economic anthropology' as the only trend to be watched with interest.

Like every other kind of anthropologist, the specialist in economic life is pushed on from the study of primitive societies to that of the complex, and the literature is (as the few bibliographical notes will have suggested) full of work on what are called peasant societies. The term is vague but is usually taken to mean those 'part-societies' living by agriculture which politically and economically are attached to larger and more differentiated entities. In this sense, of course, the agriculturalists of primitive societies soon become peasants, but clearly the name 'peasant' is being used to establish a middle category for anthropology, between primitive on the one hand and industrial on the other. The ambition to be observers and analysts of industrial society certainly exists, but the greater part of those leaving the traditional primitive field seem to find the peasant niche more comfortable. With money and modern forms of market-place to be added to the repertory of things to study, anthropology can grow more like some forms of economics and yet retain the style of work to which it is accustomed. It is not difficult to see why anthropologists, the economists of development, and the planners of development come increasingly together, or why, through its economic interests, our subject finds a direct route to practical applications.[76]

5. *Religion and ritual*

If the fields of politics and economics provide anthropology with its best opportunities to study the structure of human intentions and self-consciousness in behaviour, then it has in religion the complementary chance of concentrating on the unconscious. It is perhaps not an accident that structuralism has scored its successes more in the study of what men believe in a half-conscious way (myth and 'totemism') than in the realms of human reason acting more in the open. *La pensée sauvage* [77] is the very anatomy of mind (*esprit*) below the surface.

There have been times when some anthropologists have placed the accent on the pragmatic side of religious belief, to stress the support it may give to the arrangements of social life and to deprive it of its independence as a mode of experience and thought. In a narrow sociologism of religion the nuances and complexity of belief are lost to view, and the problem of striking deep into its roots does not present itself. In many areas of anthropology, the

---

75. *The Rise of Anthropological Theory. A History of Theories of Culture* (1968), p. 4.

76. Cf. DALTON (ed.), *Economic Development and Social Change* (1971).

77. LÉVI-STRAUSS, *La pensée sauvage* (1962) (English translation, *The Savage Mind*, 1966).

last decade and a half or so have marked a shift from religion as only an institution to religion as a way, however difficult of access, of knowing and apprehension. There has been a 'religious revival'.

There have been different routes to this more recent stage. One may be roughly called the 'theological' road, along which scholars travel when they set out to treat a primitive religion as a set of interrelated concepts only imperfectly connected with mundane social life. Another approach has been via the study of symbolism, yet another through that of modes of classification – the study of cognition and that of religion overlap. All these styles take religious ideas very seriously, but it is not to be supposed that because there has been a reaction in some quarters against the older and more sociologistic styles, the study of religion has there been cut adrift from that of society. On the contrary, the newer styles have, so to say, tried to do justice to ideas while maintaining the study of the interaction between them and the social arrangements of the men who hold them.

The history of the anthropology of religion begins with the establishment of categories which, as times go on, are added to and brought to the bar of interrogation. Yet they have a curious capacity to survive the ordeal. 'Religion' and 'magic' are constantly under attack as two separate 'things'. At a lower categorial level, 'ancestor worship', 'totemism', 'taboo', 'shamanism', 'witchcraft', and 'myth' have all been said to be labels for non-things or the names of disparate things. Yet the vocabulary is with us still. Even 'animism' and 'mana' are to be seen in the current literature as the names of definable and general entities. There is a trend for entities to disperse under attack and form up again under the same banners – an old trend that will continue.

It would be instructive to enquire what the word 'religion' itself now covers. Some anthropologists declare that it cannot be precisely defined any more than some other terms of art in the subject, such as 'kinship' and 'culture'; and that it functions merely as the vague delimiter of a field within which important problems may be formulated. And while anthropology may veer between, say, a study of beliefs and actions in relation to Tylorian spiritual beings and a study of the supernatural or the sacred, finding itself disenchanted with all solutions, in practice it maintains a more or less fixed roster of topics, including both rites and beliefs. In practice too 'religion' has often attached to it the study of morals, partly no doubt because of the old European linkage between ethics and theology, but mainly, one suspects, as a result of a tendency for anthropology to lump together in the category 'religion' all aspects of its work that pertain primarily to ideas. It is therefore worth recording that although by and large anthropologists write on ethics only in passing (and then from a philosophical point of view which is often confused), there has been a thin stream of important works in the English-speaking world on what might be termed the anthropology of moral philosophy. It has, happily, had the benefit of involving a dialogue between anthropologists and philosophers, as is best demonstrated in the collaborative study by the Edels.[78] There obviously ought to be a more sustained effort

78. EDEL & EDEL, *Anthropology and Ethics. The Quest for Moral Under-*

to perfect the analysis of moral systems as codes and of the relationship between those codes and the other systems to which anthropology more traditionally devotes itself.

From the study of morals we may move to that of classification, where the
investigation of cognitive structures [79] shades off into that of the conventionally religious themes of totemism, taboo, and myth, three topics which
have of late been raised within French- and English-speaking anthropology
to the height of subtle and prolonged debate. The arguments centre on a number of crucial issues: the necessity or positive undesirability of producing
analyses of systems of thought/ideas which somehow commend themselves
as valid to the thinkers (the informants); the methods by which the structures
are ascertained and the materials to be used for examination; the direct or
indirect relevance of the analyses made for the understanding of the social
arrangements within the framework of which men generate their ideas; the
possibility of arriving at structures which have universality in the sense that
they rest on mental properties native to all men (a point at which anthropology converges with the psychology of Piaget and the linguistics of Chom-
sky). In these arguments structuralism makes its points against functionalism
– as when it swings the study of myth away from the investigation of its
claim- and right-supporting functions to that of the logic of the thought in-
forming it; and when it rejects a utilitarian explanation of 'totemism' in favour of one which establishes it as a mode of classification. The functionalists and others resist, concede, and reassert their positions; and a great deal
more argument will need to go on before the debate can be properly assessed
and its consequences clearly seen. Yet we are obviously in the midst of an
argument that, once finished or at any rate put to one side, will have marked
a shift in anthropological thinking.[80]

Interesting results flow from the new work. One is the reshaping of the
influence that anthropology has for long had on the interpretations by classi-

---

standing (rev. edn., 1968). See also a somewhat older philosophical work, MAC-
BEATH, *Experiments in Living. A study of the Nature and Foundation of Ethics
or Morals in the Light of Recent Work in Social Anthropology* (1952), and the
following: GINSBERG, 'On the diversity of morals' (1956); BRANDT, *Hopi Ethics. A
Theoretical Analysis* (1954); LADD, *The Structure of a Moral Code. A Philosophical Analysis of Ethical Discourses Applied to the Ethics of the Navaho Indians*
(1957); and FÜRER-HAIMENDORF, *Morals and Merit. A Study of the Values and
Social Controls in South Asian Societies* (1957).

79. See, e.g., TYLER (ed.), *Cognitive Anthropology* (1969).

80. See especially LÉVI-STRAUSS, *Le totémisme aujourd'hui* (1962) (English
translation, *Totemism*, 1963) and *La pensée sauvage* (1962); DOUGLAS, *Purity and
Danger. An Analysis of Concepts of Pollution and Taboo* (1966) and *Natural Symbols. Explorations in Cosmology* (1970); LEACH (ed.), *The Structural Study of
Myth and Totemism* (1967); LEACH, *Genesis as Myth, and Other Essays* (1969);
MIDDLETON (ed.), *Myth and Cosmos. Readings in Mythology and Symbolism*
(1967); TYLER (ed.), *Cognitive Anthropology* (1969); BUCHLER & SELBY, *A Formal
Study of Myth* (1968); this last work is discussed in KUTUKDJIAN, 'A propos de
l'étude formelle du mythe' (1970). Cf. the symposium 'Le mythe aujourd'hui'
(1971).

cal scholars of their literary materials.[81] Another is that the anthropologists themselves apply the newer methods to the world religions, including their own. This latter is a further example of the way in which anthropologists are prone to make sudden forays into the non-primitive without assuming responsibility for its total study.

Of all the topics that figure in recent work and that show every sign of continuing to command interest – ancestor worship, spirit-mediumship and spirit possession, divination, cosmologies, *rites de passage*, symbolism, witchcraft, and millenarian movements – the last three at least call for some comment. The work on symbolism has demonstrated in a particularly striking fashion the virtues of a method that meticulously probes and dissects the configuration of ideas and sentiments clustering about a given symbol, the relationships among sets of symbols, and the connexion between symbols and the arrangements of society.[82] It is as though structuralist impulses had here made their impact without overthrowing a functionalist sense of the due proportions of ideas, actions, and social relationships.

The balance between ideas and social order is maintained within the quite amazingly fertile study of witchcraft. The most abundant literature comes from the Africanists (and is traced to the work of one of their leaders),[83] but the phenomenon itself has been studied elsewhere in the conventional ethnographic world,[84] while its European and American versions have been brought into the discussion. It can easily be seen how in the study of witchcraft, scholars are able to weave together moral ideas of good, evil, and responsibility; ideas of causality; rites of detection and redress; social control and the engendering of quarrels. It is (if the image be not too incongruous) an anthropologist's paradise.

Witchcraft is often studied in its most modern settings along with the anti-witchcraft movements that arise. The study of millenarian movements has an even tighter connexion with the study of modern conditions because although they are far from being merely a present-day phenomenon, they frequently appear and take on striking forms among peoples in a subordinate position, typically in a colonial system. The literature on Melanesian 'cargo cults' alone is now difficult to master.

But the study of the 'modern' is not just a matter of the study of the odd; the anthropology of religion spreads its net to encompass the systems which were once the preserve of the orientalists and students of comparative religion. Islam, Hinduism, Buddhism, and Christianity (the last, however, more usually when it is recently established) along with other complex systems are now firmly established in the anthropological literature. Clearly, it could hardy have been otherwise, and the forecaster of the future may speculate

81. See, e.g., FINLEY, *The World of Odysseus* (1956); KIRK, *Myth. Its Meaning and Functions in Ancient and Other Cultures* (1970).

82. See especially the work by TURNER, *The Forest of Symbols. Aspects of Ndembu Ritual* (1967) and *The Ritual Process. Structure and Anti-Structure* (1969); and DOUGLAS, *Purity and Danger* ... (1966) and *Natural Symbols* ... (1970).

83. EVANS-PRITCHARD, *Witchcraft, Oracles and Magic among the Azande* (1937).

84. As in another pioneering work: KLUCKHOHN, *Navaho Witchcraft* (1944).

on the extent to which the few hints now provided can be used to predict a rewriting of comparative religion on the basis of the new facts and vision that anthropology can bring to bear. Everything else aside, there is a special virtue in the painstaking description and analysis of how a religion is thought and lived by ordinary people in the ordinary round.[85]

The revival of anthropological interest in religion is also to be noted in the Soviet Union and, to some extent, in the other Socialist countries of Europe. There, however, a special problem is encountered in the research into contemporary religion, for what is still alive to be studied has sometimes to be reprobated. In the field of religion, as in all others, one can only regret the isolation from each other of two great branches of anthropology, the 'Eastern' and the 'Western'.[86]

85. Along with the works already cited, the following provide a guide to the work on religion in recent years (except for the work done in Socialist Europe which is cited in note 86): GEERTZ, 'Anthropological study [of religion]' (1968); LEACH (ed.), *Dialectic in Practical Religion* (1968); NATHHORST, *Formal or Structural Studies of Traditional Tales. The Usefulness of some Methodological Proposals Advanced by Vladimir Propp, Alan Dundes, Claude Lévi-Strauss, and Edmund Leach* (1969); MERCIER, 'Anthropologie sociale ...' (1968), pp. 972 sqq.; BASTIDE, 'La mythologie' (1968); Social Science Research Council, *Research in Social Anthropology* (1968), pp. 33-41; EVANS-PRITCHARD, *Theories of Primitive Religion* (1965); FORTES & DIETERLEN (eds.), *African Systems of Thought* (1965); WALLACE, *Religion. An Anthropological View* (1966); BANTON (ed.), *Anthropological Approaches to the Study of Religion* (1966); MIDDLETON (ed.), *Magic, Witchcraft and Curing* (1967) and *Gods and Rituals. Readings in Religious Beliefs and Practices* (1967); MAIR, *Witchcraft* (1969); MARWICK (ed.), *Witchcraft and Sorcery. Selected Readings* (1970); DOUGLAS (ed.), *Witchcraft Confessions and Accusations* (1970); GEERTZ, *Islam Observed, Religious Development in Morocco and Indonesia* (1968); LEWIS, *Ecstatic Religion* (1971); GRIAULE & DIETERLEN, *Le renard pâle*, Vol. 1, *Le mythe cosmogonique*, Fasc. 1, *La création du monde* (1965); KRONEN-BERG & KRONENBERG, 'Soziale Struktur und religiöse Antinomien' (1968-69); MÜHL-MANN (ed.), *Chiliasmus und Nativismus. Studien zur Psychologie, Soziologie, und historischen Kasuistik der Umsturzbewegungen* (1961); STANNER, *On Aboriginal Religion* (1964). As examples of work in Latin America, see: PEREIRA DE QUEIROZ, *O messianismo no Brasil e no mundo* (1965); REICHEL-DOLMATOFF, *Desana. Simbolismo de los Indios Tukano del Vaupés* (1968) (English translation by the author, *Amazonian Cosmos. The Sexual and Religious Symbolism of the Tukano Indians*, 1971). In India, anthropological studies of religion and ritual in their own right have shown a downward trend, but there has been a corresponding rise in work on religion in relation to economics and politics. See, e.g., SRINIVAS & SHAH, 'Hinduism' (1968).

86. The range of Soviet work on religion may be suggested by the following: PORSHNEV (= PORŠNEV), 'Attempts at synthesis in the field of the history of religion' (1968-69); TOKAREV, *Religija v istorii narodov mira* (= Religion in the History of the Peoples of the World) (1964), *Rannie formy religii i ih razvitie* (= Early Forms of Religion and Their Development) (1964), 'Probleme der Forschung der frühen Religionen' (1969) and 'The problem of totemism as seen by Soviet scholars' (1966); HAJTUN, *Totemism, ego suščnost' i proishoždenie* (= Totemism, Its Meaning and Origin) (1968); FRANCEV, *U istokov religii i svobodomyslija* (= Origins of Religion and Free Thinking) (1959); BASILOV, 'Nekotorye perežitki kul'ta predkov u Turkmen' (= Some survivals of ancestor workship among the Turkmens) (1968); KRYVELEV, 'K harakteristike suščnosti i značenija religioznogo provedenija' (= Features of the essence and meaning of religious behaviour) (1967) and *Religioznaja kartina mira i*

6. *Visual art*

At this point we make the transition from a narrowly delimited anthropology
to one which in its breadth is both characteristic of a number of national
styles and promises increasingly to exert its influence upon the more restricted versions. At the same time we begin in our survey to consider the
relevance of the museum, the storehouse, classifier, and potential distorter of
the things drawn trom ethnographic reality. The underlying concepts and the
techniques of the study of visual art clearly overlap with those of the study of
religion and ritual; it is the museum, the palace of the concrete and a machine
for decontextualization, that tends to drive a wedge between the two.

The field studies of primitive art by Boas and Haddon had their successors
in continental Europe, especially in the German-speaking areas; the evidence
of art was used in diffusionist studies, a tradition surviving in more sophisticated form in the work of Schmitz and of Fraser and his followers.[87] Just before and after the Second World War, art studies, while still being museum-
based, were once again more generally founded in field work, and largely
concentrated on the connected problems of style, the relationship between
styles, and the techniques employed by and the individuality and independence of the artist. The evidence was accumulated to document the generalization that primitive artists have personal styles and are far from being
slavish copiers of ancestral originals.[88]

---

ee bogoslovskaja modernizacija (= The Religious Picture of the World and Its
Theological Modernization) (1968); BAJALIEVA, *Doislamskie verovanija i ih perežitki u Kirgizov* (= Pre-Islamic Beliefs and Their Survivals among the Kirgiz)
(1969); ŠAREVSKAJA, *Starye i novye religii Tropičeskoj i Južnoj Afriki* (= Old and
New Religions in Tropical and South Africa) (1964); SNESAREV, *Relicty domusul'-
manskih verovanij i obrajadov u Uzbekov Horezma* (= Survivals of pre-Muslim
Beliefs and Rituals among the Uzbeks of Khoresm) (1969). See also the bibliography to PERŠIC, A. I. & ČEBOKSAROV, 'Polveka sovetskoj ètnografii' (1967). One
has also to look beyond Russian 'ethnography' to Russian folklore and literary
studies to find research which connects up with that done in the 'West'. Many
Soviet scholars have recently been busy with important studies (many of them in
a structuralist vein) of European and Oriental mythology. See, e.g., the most recent
work of MELETINSKIJ: 'Mif i skazka' (= Myth and folk tale) (1970); 'Klod Levi-
Stross i strukturnaja tipologija mifa' (1970) (in English, 'Claude Lévi-Strauss and
the structural typology of myth', 1970-71); 'Die Ehe im Zaubermärchen' (1970);
and 'Structural typological study of folklore' (1971).
    87. SCHMITZ, *Wantoat* (1963); FRASER *et al., Early Chinese Art and the Pacific
Basin* (1968).
    88. See, e.g., HIMMELHEBER, *Negerkünstler* (1935) and *Negerkunst und Neger-
künstler* (1960); FAGG, *Nigerian Images* (1963). GERBRANDS, 'The study of art in
anthropology' (1968) gives a summary of the most important work on this theme,
while his *Wow-ipits. Eight Asmat Woodcarvers of New Guinea* (1967) shows that
individual variation is not restricted to stratified and more complex societies. The
work done by scholars in the European Socialist countries may be exemplified by:
IVANOV, S. V., *Materialy po izobraziteľnomu iskusstvu narodov Sibiri XIX-
načala XX v.* (= Materials of the Art of Siberian Peoples, 19th and Early 20th
Centuries) (1954) and *Skuľptura narodov Severa Sibiri XIX-pervoj poloviny XX v.*
(= Sculptures of North Siberian Peoples in 1800-1950); VAJNŠTEJN, 'Ornament v

Still largely museum-based, this line of work extends into other problems, for example, the personality of the artist,[89] the stereotyped view held of the artist by his society,[90] and the attempt to quantify stylistic variation.[91] Yet all this detailed and precise work has failed to move to a new theoretical framework, being often concerned to reduce the material of primitive art to the categories of the art historians of European civilization. 'Sculpture', 'masks', 'painting', and so on are used as though they were necessarily the categories within which all artists must work, Moreover, the individuality of the primitive artist being now established, there is a tendency to ignore the relationship between individual and collective styles. Holm clearly shows the range of choice open to each artist within what is at first sight a very formal and rigidly controlled style, and documents stylistic change over time.[92]

By a strange inversion, the re-awakening of interest in art among anthropologists more generally has been in great measure linked with the very theme of standardization rejected by the museum men in their own studies. Since the Second World War there have been several lines of advance, from different starting-points. All these approaches owe something to the recent impact of linguistic theory, but they remain separate in the classes of material they examine and in their analytical aims. At this early stage of the new developments it is difficult to see how they could ever be reconciled, yet if we take them as a whole we can discern the outline of an analysis of a body of visual material as an independent system, and of the relationship between such a system and the other cultural systems with which it is associated.

One such approach may be put under the name 'iconics', even though it is difficult to establish any clear definition of the term, which may be taken to have a definite academic function if no precise denotation. In general, what is at stake is the study of, so to say, 'look-likeness', but the system of analysis used for the study of objects and graphic signs is that learnt from the method of componential, and to some extent transformational, analysis, as it has been applied in the United States to kinship terminology [93] and the study of 'folk

---

narodnom iskusstve tuvincev' (= Ornament in the folk art of the people of Tuva) (1967). And see bibliography to PERŠIC, A. I., 'Aktual'nye problemy sovetskoj ètnografii' (= Current problems of Soviet ethnography) (1964). Naturally, a great part of the research in Socialist Europe is concerned with folk art, of which the 'iconological' study appears to be most highly developed in Poland. See especially the journal *Polska Sztuka Ludowa*, published by the Art Institute of the Polish Academy of Sciences, Warsaw, and BIAŁOSTOCKI, *Stil und Ikonographie. Studien zur Kunstwissenschaft* (1966).

89. See FISCHER, 'Künstler der Dan: die Bildhauer Tame, Si, Tompieme und Sõn – ihr Wesen und ihr Werk' (1962).

90. See AZEVEDO, *The Artist Archetype in Gola Culture* (1966), and 'Mask makers and myth in Western Liberia' (1973).

91. SCHEFOLD, *Versuch einer Stilanalyse der Aufhängehaken vom Mittleren Sepik in Neu-Guinea* (1966).

92. HOLM, *Northwest Coast Indian. An Analysis of Form* (1965). The variation within stylistic limits is also treated in FORGE, 'The Abelam artist' (1967).

93. See above C. 1, pp. 37-38.

classification'.[94] The analysis aims at establishing a 'grammar', often presented in the form of a flow chart, which provides complete instructions on how to produce (generate) the class of objects being treated. There is an analogy with sentence production in a language. Sturtevant and others have shown that this method can furnish an orderly description of change by the introduction of new stages and by reordering the relationship between stages. Yet most of these models remain descriptive, not semantic. The demonstration by iconics that classes of artefacts can be shown to be systematic has in turn aroused interest among archaeologists and others concerned with the study of material culture. A recent review article surveys the present position over the whole field of material culture including many classes of objects certainly ranking as art.[95] But not only is meaning lost but also aesthetic power, and the group of iconists seem to display a somewhat puritanical style. Eventually this problem will have to be faced. Watt, although not concerned with aesthetics, is embarked on a large study of the translation between a visual system (cattle brands) and language,[96] the issues raised and the question of correspondence between the two systems being directly relevant to any system of graphic signs. In any system such as that of cattle brands, it is obvious that the system can function only if ambiguity is reduced; and attempts to use iconics in the study of art, such as those by Munn,[97] reveal very clearly the importance of ambiguity in art systems, especially when the art is also ritual. Munn's work raises some problems forcefully. How do people learn such a system? How does it communicate, and what? How can an outside observer discover what is communicated? We need to turn to other modes of dealing with them.

In the last decade or so the study of ritual has seen a remarkable development of the idea that its content, upon analysis, can be shown to be structured and to have complex meaning for its performers and witnesses. The source of many symbols seems to be the human body itself, and we must reckon with the possibility that there exists a trans-cultural symbolism with a more prosaic basis than that postulated by, for example, Jung. Certainly, the analysis of ritual acts and their verbal accompaniments has been taken further than that of their visual components, but such evidence as there is suggests that visual systems involved in ritual contexts are not merely illustrations of what is being said and done, but are self-contained orders of communication acting directly upon the beholder.[98] They appear to work independently of,

---

94. One of its main figures is STURTEVANT. See his 'Seminole men's clothing' (1967); other work by this author is in preparation. See also FRIEDRICH, 'Design structure and social interaction. Archeological implications of an ethnographic analysis' (1970).

95. HYMES, 'Linguistic models in archaeology' (1970).

96. WATT, *Morphology of the Nevada Cattlebrands and their Blasons*, Pts. 1 and 2 (1966; 1967). There is to be a third part.

97. MUNN, 'Walbiri graphic signs. An analysis' (1962) and 'The spatial representation of cosmic order in Walbiri iconography' (1973).

98. MUNN, 'Walbiri graphic signs ...' (1962); AZEVEDO, 'Mask makers ...' (1973), and FORGE, 'Art and environment in the Sepik' (1966).

but in combination with, speech (including myth) and acts.

Moreover, it has come to be realized that in the study of non-European art the decoration and adornment of the human body and many forms of ephemeral constructions may well be essential parts of the visual system that also includes works of art in more narrowly defined terms. Indeed, some cultures devoid of art in the sense of sculpture and painting possess visual systems of great aesthetic power, as in body-painting and head-dress.[99]

The extended vision of what constitutes art and of its meaning entails two changes. First, the corpus of material to be studied expands, and includes natural objects when these are part of the set of which artefacts are members. Second, the search for meaning is no longer a matter of straightforward translation, each object standing for one thing. In primitive art, art objects are rarely representations *of* anything; they seem to be *about* relationships. Even single figures or masks have attributes, some in themselves ambiguous, whose interrelationship provides meaning additional to that of the object itself.[100] In some art systems, it would appear that communications are being made which cannot be made verbally and may not indeed be totally conscious.[101] The newer approach involves the analysis of a body of art into its basic elements of form, and the discovery of the rules for their combination and apposition, rather in the manner of iconics, but meaning is registered for each element and each combination. It seems common for these elements to be given alternative meanings without an order of priority among them. Both simple and complex arrangements of elements may have alternative meanings. Ambiguity is thus fundamental to the system – an ambiguity closer to that of poetic language than to the ambiguity of bad prose. On this view, art becomes a system of multiple reference, not only relating disparate things, but increasing the supernatural power of the focus of a rite by invoking in visual terms the other occasions when the same elements are employed in different combinations.

How people internalize and are affected by these systems has hardly been tackled, one of the exceptions being Munn's work which shows that the meanings of graphic elements are learnt by Walbiri children as they watch their mothers illustrating stories by drawing in the sand.[102] But how are the systems to become accessible to the outsider?

There is, in a restricted sense of the term, a structuralist approach. Lévi-Strauss himself has published a paper on split representation,[103] but it does not seem to have been followed up. In his analysis of western European cave

99. See, e.g., STRATHERN & STRATHERN, *Self-Decoration in Mount Hagen* (1970).

100. For example, AZEVEDO, 'Mask makers . . .' (1973) and THOMPSON,' 'Àbátàn: a master potter of the Ègbádò Yorùba' (1969).

101. See FORGE, 'Art and environment' (1966).

102. MUNN, 'Walbiri graphic signs . . .' (1962). See also FORGE, 'Learning to see in New Guinea' (1970).

103. 'Le dédoublement de la représentation dans les arts de l'Asie et de l'Amérique' (1944-45, 1958) / 'Split representation in the art of Asia and America' (1963).

art Leroi-Gourhan has used a basically structuralist method in which arrays of paintings are analysed and the spatial relationships of the various elements in each array are considered to portray basic oppositions which constitute the meaning.[104] The same method does not appear to have been used in the study of primitive art. One of the difficulties involved in the use of structuralist methods of any kind (although their proponents might well not concede the point) is that they rely in some sense on sequence, in time or space. Most primitive art has neither beginning nor end. The viewer is given no scanning instructions; his eye does not begin at one point and move in a orderly manner to a conclusion. Communication is achieved all at once.

A structuralist treatment of art in eastern Europe can be traced back to the 'functional-structural' method propounded by P. G. Bogatyrev between the two World Wars; this man's work is now receiving attention among students of semiotics and has influenced recent studies of folk art.[105]

One final topic may be briefly mentioned: the basis of indigenous aesthetic judgment. Little is known about the preferences of non-artists in primitive societies, but what is known suggests that they are exercised not simply on the basis of beauty but on the power of art objects in ritual contexts. Indeed, one of the functions of art in primitive society seems to be that of concentrating supernatural power by the use of ancestrally sanctioned and beautiful productions.

The impact of the new work in the study of primitive art upon that of the art of more developed cultures remains to be seen. Within anthropology itself some trends are fairly clear. The alienation of the museum from anthropology, strongest in Britain perhaps but found elsewhere, continues, but it seems likely that the newest functionalist and structuralist exercises by anthropologists will increasingly reach the museums.[106] There is a growing number of specialist students of primitive art, especially in the United States, and the work accumulates fast. In the next decade it will be surprising if the study of art has failed to make an important place for itself within anthropology; and

104. Leroi-Gourhan, *Préhistoire de l'art occidental* (1965). It needs to be mentioned that important research on the earliest forms of art has been published in the Socialist countries. See, e.g., Abramova, *Izobraženija čeloveka v paleolitičeskom iskusstve Evrazii* (= The Image of Man in Eurasian Palaeolithic Art (1966); Okladnikov, *Utro iskusstva* (= The Dawn of Art) (1967); László, *Az ősember művészete* (= The Art of Ancient Man) (1968).

105. See his collected papers: Bogatyrev, *Voprosy teorii narodnogo iskusstva* (= Theoretical Problems of Folk Art (1971). The English reader can now consult Bogatyrev, *The Functions of Folk Costume in Moravian Slovakia* (1971, originally published in Czech in 1937). For recent work in this vein see Václavík, *Výroční obyčeje a lidové uměni* (= Calendar Customs and Folk Art) (1959); Reinfuss, *Malarstvo ludowe* (= Folk Painting) (1962); Fél & Hofer, *Saints, Soldiers, Shepherds: The Human Figure in Hungarian Folk Art* (1966).

106. There is now emerging in the U.S.A. a new attempt, sponsored by the American Anthropological Association and the Wenner-Gren Foundation for Anthropological Research, to encourage social and cultural research on museum collections. In some countries, e.g. France, there has for long been a close association between museums and anthropology.

if the attempts at the analysis of art as communication prove successful, anthropology by that means will have an effect upon psychology and linguistic theory.[107]

7. Music

We have seen that in the study of visual art anthropology is in the process of consolidating its achievements by imposing its characteristic styles of research. The case with music is for the moment different. The study of music of non-literate societies and, more widely, of non-European societies was during the first half of the twentieth century nurtured by some university departments of anthropology in the U.S.A. and Europe and largely ignored by the more conventional musicologists. For the latter, music was an art belonging almost exclusively to the European tradition. The exotic element in musicology was represented for the most part by the popular traditions collected and analysed within the folklore studies of continental Europe. Since about 1950 that general trend has been reversed, and as the musicians and musicologists have begun to espouse ethnomusicology, the anthropologists, in the narrow sense of that term, have appeared largely to disengage themselves from its study. It is the one càse in which the prefix 'ethno-' signals an advance in scholarship and an anthropological withdrawal; we need to be alert to its significance and consequences. While ethnomusicology 'peut être définie comme la musicologie des civilisations dont l'étude constitue le domaine traditionnel de l'ethnologie',[108] the anthropologists are the junior partners in the enterprise. (There are of course a few – too few – anthropologists who are musicologically qualified.)

Perhaps the crux of the difficulty, apart from the lack of musical competence on the part of the run-of-the-mill ethnographer, is the distinctive character of music as an art: as a musicologist one may know its structure, but as an anthropologist one is hard put to it to relate that structure, when one knows it, to the culture within which the music is produced.[109] That strain, all else aside, marks a cleavage between musicology and anthropology, and at the same time offers the challenge to bring them together. We may agree that music communicates. But what and how?[110]

107. For general work on the study of art by anthropologists, see the many references in POIRIER (ed.), *Ethnologie générale* (1968), especially MERCIER, 'Anthropologie sociale . . .', pp. 988 sqq. And cf. JOPLING (ed.), *Art and Aesthetics in Primitive Societies. A Critical Anthology* (1971).

108. ROUGET, 'L'ethnomusicologie' (1968), p. 1339. The reader may be referred to that survey for *inter alia* its bibliographical data (supplemented by the items mentioned in this sub-section) and its information on recordings. And cf. MERRIAM, 'Ethnomusicology' (1968), p. 562.

109. Cf. MERRIAM, *The Anthropology of Music* (1964), p. 3: 'Ethnomusicology carries within itself the seeds of its own division . . .'. The book is reviewed extensively and by scholars from all over the world in *Current Anthropology* 7 (2), 1966.

110. Cf. LÉVI-STRAUSS, *Mythologiques**. *Le cru et le cuit* (1964), pp. 22-38, especially p. 26 (English translation, *The Raw and the Cooked. Introduction to*

While in much of continental Europe the folklore tradition of musicology has pursued its course,[111] ethnomusicology has during the last few years exhibited a number of newer trends. In the first place, there has been a tendency partly to disengage the study of non-European music from the framework established within Western musicology, the non-Western musical cultures being examined in their own terms. One stimulus for this develop- ment has been the emergence of a body of scholars within the 'new' nations who, in studying their own music by the basic methods devised within the Western tradition, yet bring to their work a view from the inside. A related movement, although one which embraces the foreign investigators, might be called the field worker's 'internalization' of non-European music by his study of practical performance and composition, an effort apparent chiefly in those cultures where the systematic teaching of music is an indigenous tradi- tion, for example in the civilizations of Asia.

During the first half of the century ethnomusicology was in search of the 'authentic', that is to say, musical systems uninfluenced by the West, in much the same manner as many ethnographers sought in more conventional branches of anthropological investigation, and in the same period, to abstract or ignore the Western forces impinging upon institutions and ideas. But in recent work musical change and acculturation are elevated to the rank of a chief problem; and the adoption of an historical approach for its treatment forms a link with the historians of Western music.

The newer view of non-European music has carried over to the study of the musical culture of minority groups, above all in the United States. We have witnessed a revived interest in the study of Afro-American music in the Americas as a whole, in that of the American Indians as a minority culture (rather than as an isolated group of remnant cultures), and in the music of bilingual communities. An extension of this interest has led to the study of the musical culture of certain definable groups (for example, adolescents) within general populations, and to an emphasis being put upon the music of urban life. Ethnomusicology now becomes relevant to a very wide range of social interests, and its practitioners, by a sort of applied anthropology, play a rôle in establishing the cultural identity of societies and groups within societies.[112]

Ethnomusicology in the traditional fields has, increasingly since about 1960, become specialized and (in the social scientist's jargon) problem- oriented. The older style of research was aimed at characterizing the total musical culture of a unit (society or tribe); the newer style seeks typically to investigate a particular technique or problem. A recent issue of the journal

---

a Science of Mythology: I (1969), pp. 14-30, especially p. 18).

111. And very sturdily in the Socialist countries. Note, e.g., the *Corpus Mu- sicae Popularis Hungaricae*, begun in 1951, in, to date, six great volumes.

112. See, e.g., WEMAN, *African Music and the Church in Africa* (1960); PAWLOWSKA, *Merrily We Sing. 105 Polish Folksongs* (1961). Various series of ethnomusicological recordings in the U.S.A. are used largely by listeners belong- ing to the cultures whose music is represented; e.g., *Songs of the Redman*, Sound- chief Enterprises and Indian House Records, Taos, New Mexico.

Ethnomusicology,[113] for example, includes a survey of oboes in India, an investigation from various points of view of a single Hausa song, and a study of music and the structure of town life in northern Afghanistan.

New techniques of analysis have appeared. Computers, although not greatly used (yet experiments have been going on for the last twenty years or so), have made an impact on ethnomusicology.[114] A particularly important development in the use of machines has been the attempt objectively to reduce musical sound to visual form; the machines, usually called 'melographs', have been developed in, among other places, the University of California at Los Angeles, the Hebrew University, Jerusalem, and the University of Oslo. Efforts have been made to devise descriptive and analytical procedures and techniques for coping with aspects of music not traditionally studied, such as the manner of the use of the human voice, tone colour in singing and instrumental music, and the relationships between singers and performers in ensembles. Further along this line of development, exercises have been mounted to correlate types of performance with types and configurations of culture. From the study by Lomax and his colleagues, for example, there have emerged hypotheses on, among other matters, the relation between work groups and complex choruses, and that between the elite supervision of work and solo singing. In this study it was found that 'a culture's favorite song style reinforces the kind of behavior essential to its main subsistence effort and to its central and controlling social institutions'.[115]

In earlier ethnomusicological research the musicians of non-Western cultures tended to be treated anonymously, and it was implied that all members of a culture were more or less equal in their musical competence and participation. There is now much more readiness to treat musicians as individuals and to accord them something of the treatment given to their counterparts in the West. The studies of individual musicians, of their biographies and their contributions to musical culture, parallel the trend in other fields of anthropology by which individual creativity ceases to be concealed behind the overgeneralized formulas of cultural style and social homogeneity.[116]

It will be seen, therefore, that ethnomusicology shows some marked trends of development, but it is clearly hampered in moving towards a true anthropology of music by the preponderance within it of narrower musicological concerns. Most ethnomusicological research is still centered upon the de-

113. 14 (3), 1970.

114. The Society for Ethnomusicology (U.S.A.) is forming a study group on the use of computers. And see SUCHOFF, 'Computer applications to Bartok's Serbo-Croatian material' (1967) and 'Computerized folk song research and the problem of variants' (1968). Cf. *Studia Musicologica Academiae Scientiarum Hungaricae* (1965) for several papers on experiments with computers in research on folk music, read at the Budapest Conference of the International Folk Music Council.

115. LOMAX *et al., Folk Song Style and Culture* (1968), p. 133. A similar movement towards connecting musical (and dance) forms with social structure is to be noted in East European studies.

116. See, e.g., NETTL, 'Biography of a Blackfoot Indian singer' (1968); TRACEY, 'The Mbira music of Jeje Tapero' (1961); and (in a quite different vein) *Who's Who of Indian Musicians* (1968).

scription and comparison of music. It cannot reach into music as culture until, as in the case, *mutatis mutandis,* of visual art, literature, and technology, music ceases to be treated only as a special subject and becomes a part of more rounded attempts to treat thought, feeling, and behaviour.[117] And much the same can be said about an even more neglected branch of study, that of dance.[118] Of course, there are difficult technical problems in the way of achieving a satisfactory anthropology of music and dance; but that there are such problems follows from the specialized skills of the cultures from which most anthropologists come; they limit the ethnographer's vision and lead him to be insensitive to or uncomprehending of major aspects of the cultural life of the peoples he undertakes to observe. The 'total' suffers from the musicologist's specialization and from the anthropologist's lack of technical competence.[119]

8. *Literature*

The pioneers of anthropology, often men-of-letters themselves, moved easily between ethnology, folklore, and the studies of Eastern or Western classical literature in which they had received their earlier training.[120] Travellers and missionaries [121] who supplied them with observations and texts were also for the most part grounded in a literary education, and though they may have concerned themselves more with ethnology and language than with intrinsically literary studies (oral art and tradition being then particularly the province of ethnology and folklore) [122] they showed some feeling for verbal skill

117. Linguistic theory may prove important; cf. BRIGHT, 'Language and music. Areas for cooperation' (1963).

118. For references see ROUGET, 'L'ethnomusicologie' (1968), pp. 1383 sq. And see *VIIe Congrès International des Sciences anthropologiques et ethnologiques,* Vol. 6 (1970), pp. 7-145.

119. In addition to the works already cited, see: KUNST, *Ethnomusicology* (3rd edn., 1959); NETTL, *Theory and Method in Ethnomusicology* (1964); MERRIAM, *Ethnomusicology of the Flathead Indians* (1964) and 'Ethnomusicology revisited' (1969); STOCKMANN, D., 'Das Problem der Transkription in der musikethnologischen Forschung' (1966); HOOD, 'Music, the unknown' (1963); KOLINSKI, 'Recent trends in ethnomusicology' (1967); LAADE, *Die Situation von Musikleben und Muskiforschung in den Ländern Afrikas und Asiens und die neuen Aufgaben der Musikethnologie* (1969); KATZ, 'Mannerism and cultural change. An ethnomusicological example' (1970); *VIIe Congrès International des Sciences anthropologiques et ethnologiques,* Vol. 7 (1970), pp. 221-347. Soviet work in this field may be exemplified by the following: contributions by EVALD, AKSENOV, VINOGRADOV, and KVITKA in STOCKMANN, E., STROBACH, CHISTOV (= ČISTOV), & HIPPIUS (eds.), *Sowjetische Volkslied- und Volksmusikforschung. Ausgewählte Studien* (1967); VINOGRADOV, *Musika Gvinei* (= Music of Guinea) (1969).

120. For example, Sir James Frazer and Jane Harrison, Marcel Mauss and Max Müller, and Renan and Robertson Smith, in relation to Western, Eastern, and Semitic classical literature respectively.

121. In Africa alone there were Krapf, Callaway, Hahn, Koelle, Christaller, Bleek, Chatelain, Guttmann, Junod, and many others.

122. As late as 1962 in the preface to his *Primitive Song,* C. M. (Sir Maurice)

and artistry. Hence they are still consulted by students of anthropology who work on language and literature.

The vigorous growth of a specifically *social* anthropology between the two World Wars tended (but more in Britain than in the rest of Europe or America) to weaken anthropological links with literary scholarship. Poets and novelists [123] increasingly explored the literary interest of anthropological writings, and literary history and criticism took on a more sociological character. But as W. H. Whiteley has observed: [124]

... anthropologists who collected texts did so for their anthropological value, and as Doke has pointed out '... the mere recording of ethnographic, historical and technological texts need not *ipso facto* contribute much to the literature of a people'. Even in very recent times ... anthropological interest in historical texts has been directed solely at the historical value ... Following on the period of initial activity at the turn of the century, the collection of traditional material lapsed: social anthropologists concentrating on institutional, synchronic studies of individual societies; linguists on structural or grammatical studies; and missionaries on pastoral work.

In attempting to establish the scientific credentials of their subject, anthropologists during the inter-war period thus neglected the wider literary interest of the textual material they had at their disposal. Even today field workers whose tape-recorders enable them to collect as much in a few days as their predecessors could in many weeks, do not always sufficiently differentiate between texts of primarily linguistic or anthropological value, and those in which the literary resources of a language are much more fully, and often consciously, deployed.

But the scientific principles of the anthropology of that time have now been either assimilated or modified, and scholars who then made great advances in the subject by adhering to them have since brought their knowledge and discrimination to bear on the literatures they then left to one side. Certainly for students of literature in anthropology today the most rewarding earlier studies are by those for whom 'science', 'literature', and 'history' had not appeared to be quite distinct vocations.[125]

Among these H. M. and N. K. Chadwick[126] in their substantial *The Growth of Literature* promoted the study of non-European oral compositions

---

BOWRA wrote of attempting 'to break into a field which has not, as far as I know, been explored in any history of literature'. Many teachers of literature have indeed allowed their interests to be limited by established university curricula.

123. English readers will think of D. H. Lawrence, T. S. Eliot, and Ezra Pound, to mention only the most obvious. Arthur Waley may be cited also as a literary figure who did much (in his translations from the Chinese) to accustom cultivated readers to literary interests and principles very different from their own.

124. *A Selection of African Prose: I. Traditional Oral Texts* (1964), p. 10.

125. Neither of the two outstanding anthropologists, Sir Edward Evans-Pritchard and Claude Lévi-Strauss, has neglected the profounder intellectual and imaginative questions raised for an anthropologist in this respect. And see Clyde KLUCKHOHN, *Anthropology and the Classics* (1961).

126. CHADWICK & CHADWICK, *The Growth of Literature* (3 vols., 1932-40). Vol. 3 is of particular relevance to this subject.

with the authority of scholars eminent in more conventionally academic studies. The complementarity of scientific and literary understanding was also assumed by (for example) M. Griaule and his associates, whose influence is still felt in the progress of modern French work,[127] and such Americans as F. H. Cushing, Ruth Benedict, Paul Radin, and M. J. and Frances Herskovits.[128] In Britain, Malinowski, advocate of an anthropological science though he was, kept open channels of communication with literary critics and philosophers, as his appendix to I. A. Richards and C. K. Ogden's *The Meaning of Meaning* (1923) testifies. His extensive published texts with commentaries, intended as a contribution to anthropology, also show awareness of some literary problems.

Folklorists too have continued to connect anthropological and literary investigation. Folklore has always been a part of literary scholarship, both through philology and by pursuing the interests and values of the unlettered majority of the population underlying established literary works.

This 'common culture' of historical periods has been widely explored by literary historians and critics,[129] and is of central importance to anthropologists studying literature and to creative writers, since it represents the communal tradition against which the individuality of particular authors may be assessed.

If folklore was partially eclipsed for a time by the rise of other social studies, it was because it seemed to represent a merely curious enthusiasm for details of popular speech and custom on the part of more educated members of the community whose social class was higher than that of their informants. Intellectuals from the 'folk' themselves, and others suspicious of academic condescension to them, have thus often held that the anthropological study of oral literature reduced it to 'folklore'.[130] Chinua Achebe, for example, has said: [131]

The prose tradition of non-literate peoples is often presumed to consist of folktales, legends, proverbs and riddles ... I would go so far as to say that they represent the least important part. If one takes the Igbo society which I know best, it seems quite clear that the finest examples of prose occur not in those forms but in oratory or even in the art of good conversation. Riddles and proverbs ... are cast in a rigid mould and cannot be varied at will. Legend ... and folk-tale ... are more flexible but only within a certain framework ... Serious conversation

127. For example, that sponsored by the Institut d'Ethnologie de l'Université de Paris under the auspices of Mm. Michel Leiris and André Martinet.

128. Much is owed to the example of Franz Boas.

129. Hoggart's *The Uses of Literacy. Aspects of Working Class Life with Special Reference to Publications and Entertainments* (1957) is one example among many.

130. Among the French-speakers the situation has probably been rather different. The connexion for example between Lucien Lévy-Bruhl and L. S. Senghor, with its important implications for the literary discussion and achievement associated with *Présence africaine,* seems to have no parallel in the English-speaking world, where such genuine literary and artistic dialogue comes later. The work of Ulli Beier in West Africa and now in Papua is noteworthy here.

131. Foreword to Whiteley, *A Selection of African Prose, I* ... (1964), p. vii.

and oratory, on the other hand, call for an original and individual talent and at their best belong to a higher order.

In the last twenty years these objections have had less and less force. Such a compilation as *The Study of Folklore* by Alan Dundes [132] shows how students of oral and written language and literature, of anthropology, of folklore and psychology, once more have begun to see their subjects as aspects of a common enquiry into the nature and history of the imagination, and at a more sophisticated level than before. Thus modern anthropological theory itself owes much to discussions of symbolism and metaphor in European literary criticism, to psychoanalysis and so forth.[133]

Many anthropologists also share with literary critics, folklorists, linguists, and philosophers the structuralist universe of discourse, as characteristic of the present time as 'the comparative method' was of the past. For literary studies, structuralism is significant in seeking a framework of discussion which would include in principle all serious expressions of human imagination and thought.[134] And though anthropologists discussing literature necessarily dwell in detail upon the differences of style and function in oral and written compositions, they recognize also that at a deeper level they raise common problems.

The overlap between anthropology on the one hand and folklore and literary studies on the other brings the Soviet contributions to the forefront, for they stand out by the thoroughness of their compilation and by their advancement of the techniques of analysis, including the structuralist.[135] The ten-volume work on world literature being prepared by the Gorky Institute of World Literature of the Soviet Academy of Sciences, surely the most ambi-

---

132. DUNDES (ed.), *The Study of Folklore* (1965). TAYLOR's 'Folklore and the study of literature' and BASCOM's 'Folklore and anthropology', included there, have a particular bearing on the subjects discussed in this comment. Bascom also indicates the close collaboration between the Modern Language Association and the American Anthropological Association. And see DUNDES, 'Oral literature' (1968); and CHISTOV (= ČISTOV) & TUTILOV (eds.), *Fol'klor i ètnografija* (= Folklore and Ethnography) (1970).

133. Two examples from India may be cited: VATUK, 'Protest songs of East Indians in British Guiana' (1964), and 'Let's dig up some dirt. The idea of humour in children's folklore in India' (1969).

134. See, e.g., the commentary on Baudelaire's poem 'Les chats' by JAKOBSON & LÉVI-STRAUSS, in *L'homme* (1962) and LÉVI-STRAUSS's reflections on Rimbaud's *Sonnet des voyelles* in relation to the experience of South American Indians: *Tristes Tropiques* (1955), p. 121 (English translation, *World on the Wane* (1961), p. 126).

135. See, for Soviet contributions to literary and folklore studies, the bibliography to SOKOLOVA, 'Sovetskaja fol'kloristika k 50-letiju Oktjabrja' (= Soviet folklore studies to the 50th anniversary of the October Revolution) (1967); and ČISTOV, *K voprosu o principah klassifikacii žanrov ustnoj narodnoj prozy* (= On the Classificatory Principles of Oral Popular Prose) (1964). There are many collections of regional and ethnic folklore as well as of the folklore of the working class. For this last see BASANOV (ed.), *Ustnaja Poèzija rabočih Rossii* (= Oral Poetry of the Workers of Russia) (1965); and ALEKSEEVA, *Ustnaja poèzija russkih rabočih, Do-revoljucionnyj period* (= Oral Poetry of Russian Workers, Pre-Revolutionary Period) (1971).

tious project of the kind to be found, rests on important methodological antecedents, among them the so-called comparative-typological science of literature.[136] The structuralist element is to be particularly noted in Soviet research
on the epic and on fairy tales.[137]

The more mundane questions of literary history and sociology, of translation, textual authenticity, and critical evaluation, remain. The portable tape-
recorder has transformed and is transforming the study of literature and
music so rapidly that we should not forget that there were certain advantages
in the older method of recording by hand with the help of thorough local
exegesis. In the latter the student absorbed through direct personal contact
not only the complex local allusions found in much oral literature, but also
criteria of style and relevance, moral and aesthetic judgment, and details of
custom and tradition not likely to emerge in the speed of a mechanical recording. Hence for literature as for anthropology there is no substitute for an
informed mind able to seek the interpretation of a text on the spot. It becomes more and more apparent how much of an original text, especially in
poetry, defies translation into a European vocabulary coming from a very
different experience of living. Indigenous critical standards and artistic categories are among the topics urgently needing more investigation, a task in
which anthropologists have much to learn from studies in comparative
literature.[138]

As has been implied, the study of literature in anthropology has been and
still is in practice more involved with oral than with written work.[139] But
their direct experience of the transition many peoples are now making from
oral to written habits of communication may enable anthropologists more
than others to assess the aesthetic, social, historical, and psychological effects
of that change. They have indeed a remarkable opportunity to record in local
detail the social implications of literacy, and hence examine in concrete human terms what happens when authors can write and publish for a mass of

136. The 'comparative-typological' scheme was worked out by ŽIRMUNSKIJ. See
his *Vergleichende Epenforschung*, Vol. 1 (1961) and CHADWICK, N. K. & ZHIR-
MUNSKY, *Oral Epics of Central Asia* (1969).
137. See MELETINSKIJ, *Proishoždenie geroičeskogo eposa. Rannie formy i
arhaičeskie pamjatniki* (= The Origin of Heroic Epic ...) (1963) (English summary, 'The primitive heritage in archaic epics', 1970); *Edda i rannie formy eposa*
(= The *Edda* and Archaic Forms of Epic) (1968); and, with NEKLJUDOV, NOVIK, &
SEGAL, 'Problemy strukturnogo opisanija volšebnoj skazki' (= The problems of
the structural description of fairy tales) (1969) and 'Eščë raz o probleme strukturnogo opisanija volšebnoj skazki' (= Further thoughts on the problem ...) (1971).
Of course, modern research owes something to the pioneering work of PROPP,
Morfologija skazki (= Morphology of the Folk Tale) (1928), a second edition of
which appeared in 1969, with a postface by MELETINSKIJ. For a translation of that
second edition see *Morphologie du conte* (1970).
138. E.g., LORD, *The Singer of Tales* (1960). The series 'Classiques africains',
Paris, and 'The Oxford Library of African Literature' concern themselves with
such standards. A volume in the latter series, FINNEGAN, *Oral Literature in Africa*
(1970), is likely to prove influential. Another series published in Paris is 'Langues
et littératures de l'Afrique'.
139. Cf. JASON, 'A multidimensional approach to oral literature' (1969).

individual readers rather than sing and recite to a community present before them.[140] But the anthropologist's study of literature need not be confined to the oral literature of peoples culturally remote from his own. His interest in literature, like his interest in society, is in the total social context of experience, and (given the requisite literary and linguistic scholarship) there is no reason why he should not be as able to recreate this for historic written literatures as for those of small non-literate societies. And there is every hope that he will be so able.

9. *Technology*

There is a wider 'technology' and a narrower, for when the net is cast very wide, the study of technology encompasses what many anthropologists would classify under other heads. The distinction being made can most clearly be seen by a glance at the French tradition established by Mauss. In that tradition of *technologie culturelle* we are so far from being confined to the study of implements and techniques for the extraction of sustenance that we are obliged also to examine the human uses of the human body (gait, posture, decoration, and so on) and standardized modes of behaviour in relation to all material things (for example, cooking, eating, and locomotion). Moreover, the techniques of acquiring techniques — learning and apprenticeship — become relevant.[141]

For scholars who take a more restricted view of technology (they are the majority outside the French tradition), their subject is concerned above all with two things: the manufacture of useful objects and the physical apparatus involved in making a living. The techniques of the body (to use Mauss's expression) and the total structure of agriculture, fishing, cattle-herding, and so on, belong to the anthropological study of cultural forms and economic life. Yet even on this narrower interpretation, a hard-and-fast line cannot be laid down between technology on the one hand and anthropology on the other. As in the case of the study of the visual arts, there is an academic

140. For a recent example of work in this field see GooDY (ed.), *Literacy in Traditional Societies* (1968). BURRIDGE, *Tangu Traditions* (1969) is a most thorough and sensitive study of this and other fundamental changes in the imaginative experience of a single people.

141. See HAUDRICOURT, 'La technologie culturelle. Essai de méthodologie' (1968) and MICHÉA, 'La technologie culturelle. Essai de systématique' (1968). LEROI-GOURHAN's influence upon French studies also needs to be noted. See his *Evolution et techniques – L'homme et la matière* (1943; 2nd edn., 1971); *Evolution et techniques – Milieu et techniques* (1945); *Le geste et la parole – Technique et langage* (1964); *Le geste et la parole – La mémoire et les rythmes* (1965). For a German view, see HIRSCHBERG & JANATA, *Technologie und Ergologie in der Völkerkunde* (1966); and for examples of Soviet work, see SEMENOV, S. A., 'Izučenie pervobitnoj tehniki metodom eksperimenta' (= A study of primitive technology by experimental method) (1963) and *Razvitie tehniki v kamennom veke* (= The Development of Technology in the Stone Age) (1968); and, for a work by this author in English translation, *Prehistoric Technology* (1964).

infra-structure, so to say, that tends to enforce a greater distance between disciplines than is justified by their nature. When technology is based in the museum and anthropology in the field, the dialogue is difficult to sustain. Looking at the matter from the point of view of the technologist, we may say that his studies are divided into two broad categories: those which are above all concerned with technological processes in themselves, and those which try to place those processes within some sort of wide context and trace their interrelations with social life, the environment of the users, with other technologies, and so on. It is a fact that anthropologists show only a very limited interest in the former category of studies, and in doing so have handicapped their development.

Technological processes are directly observable, are generally capable of being measured, can be repeated under controlled conditions, and can be experimentally modified. The objects or goods produced frequently persist through time and are portable through space. The end- and by-products of many technological processes make them a potential area of co-operation between the overlapping disciplines of economics, archaeology, history, folklore,[142] and anthropology, but the practitioners of the last-named subject fail, from the technologist's point of view, to pull their weight. In their field studies they usually neglect to provide even the most simple and limited information on the technologies of the peoples they describe, a delinquency most marked among those brought up within the British tradition of social anthropology. Although a number of ethnographers still publish descriptions of technological processes based on their field research, their data are often grossly defective and the same is true of some archaeologists and museum specialists. To the ethnographer such data seem to be peripheral and are generally limited to the more noticeable aspects of a people's technology, that is to say, to the processes which are completed in a relatively short time and all of whose stages are easily understood by an observer of small technological knowledge. It is for that reason that ethnographers usually furnish accounts of iron-smelting, pot-making, and weaving. On their side, the museum-based students of material culture fail to pay attention to its social and cultural significance in any but the most general terms.

Full and accurate reporting of technological processes is of the essence. It has been pointed out, for example,[143] that domestic fuel supplies are crucial to the lives of all human societies, yet many ethnographers give no information of the type, quantity, or methods of the collection of fuel. The defects in the record may sometimes result from the fact that the events described are a reconstruction after indigenous processes have largely died out. The short time-span of observation is, as we have said, a further cause of the incompleteness of the data. Limited observation cannot furnish data about the differential skills of operators, variations in their patterns of procedure, the

142. On the direct relevance of the research done in continental European folklore, see, e.g., FÉL & HOFER, 'Über monographisches Sammeln volkskundlicher Objekte' (1965).

143. HEIZER, 'Domestic fuel in primitive society' (1963).

alternative strategies they follow to achieve the same products with materials of varying qualities, and so on. It has often been implicitly assumed that primitive technologies are inflexible and their sequences immutable; a single operation comes to be taken as the norm. As Scheans [144] and others have pointed out, even within a comparatively small area and an apparently unified technological tradition there may be major differences of socially important method and sequence. Again, Merrill has recently stressed [145] that technologies need to be viewed dynamically and that consideration must be given to the various strategies they offer in relation to the capital, skills, and ideals of the society using them; yet much ethnographic reporting is basically synchronic and static in approach. There is an almost complete failure to report quantities, temperatures, man-hours expended, and so forth. Perhaps most distressing of all, especially in relation to what anthropologists profess, field observers neglect to elicit native categories, taxonomies, theories, etc., where these concern technological processes. But in this respect, there is hope in the development among American scholars of the linguistically inspired techniques for the study of 'ethnoscience' and 'folk classification'. In the more conventional forms of anthropological analysis mention is often made of the crucial significance of objects as the points around which ideas, sentiments, and actions cluster, but the technological dimension is little explored. Light may be thrown on a great range of social relationships by focussing on a single material substance and its associated technology.[146]

Despite their relative incompetence in describing technological processes, anthropologists frequently show great interest in their relationships with the beliefs and ritual practices of the people they study. This interest has partly manifested itself in the discussion of the general nature and status of technological associations of particular processes. The analysis of a particular interstanding the universe,[147] and partly in the exploration of the ritual and mythological associations of particular processes. The analysis of a particular interpenetration of rites and techniques is exemplified in Tambiah's reworking of Malinowski's Trobriands ethnography.[148] There is an increasing flow of information about the symbolism and meaning of various artefacts and patterns produced by local technologies.[149] Lévi-Strauss has drawn attention to the possible conceptual significance of basic technological operations such as different ways of preparing food or making noise,[150] while the discussions on

144. SCHEANS, 'A new view of Philippines pottery manufacture' (1966).

145. MERRILL, 'The study of technology' (1968).

146. See, e.g., GARINE, 'Usages alimentaires dans la région de Khombole (Sénégal)' (1962).

147. See, e.g., *Technology and Culture* 6 (4), 1965, issue on *The Historical Relations of Science and Technology*; and *ibid.*, 7 (3), 1966, issue on *Towards a Philosophy of Technology*.

148. TAMBIAH, 'The magical power of words' (1969).

149. E.g., NEUMANN, *Wirtschaft und materielle Kultur der Buschneger Surinams* (1967). But cf. PRICE, 'Saramaka woodcarving. The development of an Afroamerican art' (1970).

150. *Mythologiques* *. *Le cru et le cuit* (1964), especially pp. 291-347 (*The Raw*

literacy involve analysis of the cultural and social consequences of the invention of writing.[151] The style of analysis associated with Sturtevant's work [152] treats artefacts as parts of ordered systems.

On the other hand, the major trend in the study of technology in relation to society is diachronic and largely North American. American studies of technology take in a wide range of phenomena and involve co-operative research and discussion by archaeologists, scientists, philosophers, anthropologists, and others.[153] The diachronic studies may be divided into three interconnected kinds: those principally concerned with tracing the diffusion of individual technologies and artefact types through space and time; those which aim at clarifying the interrelations of material culture, environment, and society in particular places over a limited period; and those which attempt to place such limited area studies in an overall developmental or evolutionary sequence or set of sequences.

'Simple' diffusion studies are still carried out, but are based increasingly on original field research and on better data. Area studies using a variety of approaches in order to cover as many factors as possible are becoming more common.[154] Models of the diffusion process have recently been made, variations have been simulated on computers, and the results tested against data from the observed diffusion of material goods and techniques.[155] Several solutions to 'Galton's problem' have been offered,[156] and older concepts such as 'cultural drift' have been scrutinized and reworked.[157]

and the Cooked (1969), pp. 285-342). On noise see also NEEDHAM, 'Percussion and transition' (1967).

151. See GOODY (ed.), *Literacy in Traditional Societies* (1968).

152. See C. 6 above, pp. 55-56.

153. See, e.g., the journal *Technology and Culture, op. cit.* Soviet studies of technology range widely, being in part descriptive, in part historical, and in part typological (as in the extensive work done in connexion with the production of ethnographic atlases). As examples of recent publications see: TOLSTOV (ed.), *Russkie. Istoriko-ètnografičeskij atlas* (= The Russians. Historical-ethnographic Atlas) (1967); LEVIN, M. G. & POTAPOV (eds.), *Istoriko-ètnografičeskij atlas Sibiri* (= Historical-ethnographic Atlas of Siberia) (1961); TOKAREV, 'K metodike ètnografičeskogo izučenija material'noj kul'tury' (= On methods of the ethnographic investigation of material culture) (1970); LIPINSKAJA, 'Nekotorye čerti sovremennoj material'noj kul'tury russkogo naselenija Altajskogo kraja' (=Some features of the present-day material culture of the Russian population in the Altai region) (1968); MKRTUMJAN, 'Formy skotovodstva i byt naselenija v armjanskoj derevne vtoroj poloviny XIX v.' (= Cattle-raising and daily life of Armenian villagers in the second half of the 19th century) (1968); DAVYDOV, 'Tradicionnoe žilišče Tadžikov Verhnego Zeravšana' (= Traditional dwelling houses of the Tadzhiks of Upper Zeravshan) (1969).

154. E.g., BOSER-SARIVAXEVANIS, *Aperçus sur la teinture à l'indigo en Afrique occidentale* (1968).

155. See HÄGERSTRAND, *Innovation Diffusion as a Spatial Process* (1968).

156. E.g., NAROLL & D'ANDRADE, 'Two further solutions to Galton's problem' (1963). 'Galton's problem' is that of deciding the effect of diffusion upon the correlations made in cross-cultural studies. And see NAROLL, 'Galton's problem' (1970) and DRIVER & CHANEY, 'Cross-cultural sampling and Galton's problem' (1970).

157. EGGAN, 'Cultural drift and social change' (1963).

Numerous area studies now try to trace the development of society over time by a combination of archaeological, linguistic, botanical, documentary, genetic, and ethnographic data.[158] In these studies technology and its material remains are crucial. At one level the debate is on the limitations or capacities of the technologies involved.[159] More complex attempts are being made to interrelate technology, environment, and society and to explain their alterations over time.[160]

Nearly all such studies can be brought into relationship with broad developmental and evolutionary theories, which, their roots deep in nineteenth-century thought, owe their present character in the U.S. mainly to the influence of Leslie White and Julian Steward. Evolutionary and functionalist anthropologies are brought closer together, the latter being persuaded away from their earlier preoccupation with a synchrony that puts all description upon one plane of time. In the second place, the attempt has now been abandoned to understand the relations between technology and society in terms of a simple interaction unrelated to their total environment. Terminologies have been refined [161] and exercises mounted to cross-check hypotheses by the use of the Human Relations Area Files.[162] There is a growing awareness of the importance of broad technological factors in the discussion of social forms,[163] while one of the most significant effects of the influence of White and Steward has been a heightened attention to the rôle of energy, and attempts have been made accurately to measure its production and consumption as a contribution to the understanding of the forms taken by society.[164]

On the one hand, then, anthropology appears to be passing through a period of rapprochement with archaeology (in the countries where until recently they had drifted apart). In part this movement is due to the general stimulus of evolutionary theories, in part to a shift within archaeology itself, particularly in North America, from a preoccupation with change in time

158. See the discussion of iron-working and Bantu expansion in WRIGLEY, 'Speculations on the economic prehistory of Africa' (1960); OLIVER, 'The problem of Bantu expansion' (1966); POSNANSKY, 'Bantu genesis' (1961). See also YEN & WHEELER, 'Introduction of Taro' (1968); WATSON, J. B., 'Pueraria: names and traditions of a lesser crop in the Central Highlands, New Guinea' (1968).

159. See, e.g., SHARP, *Ancient Voyagers in the Pacific* (1957); HEYERDAHL, *Sea Routes to Polynesia* (1968).

160. See, e.g., TIPPET, 'Fijian material culture' (1968); LAWRENCE, *Aboriginal Habitat and Economy* (1968); and BATHGATE, 'Maori river and ocean-going craft in Southern New Zealand' (1959).

161. E.g., BEALS, 'Food is to eat' (1964); GREENFIELD, 'More on the study of subsistence agriculture' (1965); and CONKLIN, 'The study of shifting agriculture' (1961).

162. See, e.g., UDY, *Organization of Work* (1959). On the Human Relations Area Files, see n. 262 below.

163. See, e.g., the discussion, in GOODY, 'Economy and feudalism in Africa' (1969), on the significance of the fact that wheeled transport and non-human power were absent from most of pre-colonial Africa.

164. See LEE & DEVORE (eds.), *Man the Hunter* (1968); PARRACK, 'An approach to the bio-energetics of rural West Bengal' (1969); and LEE, '!Kung Bushman subsistence. An input-output analysis' (1969).

and space to an interest in the reconstruction of social structure and ecological relations,[165] in which sort of enterprise anthropology becomes of the
first importance. Technology is seen to be an important link between the two
disciplines. On the other hand, a great number of field ethnographers still
seem uninterested in the details of technological processes. 'Museum' and
'field' stand for two different styles – that is a crucial fact that we shall need
to come back to in a more general context.[166]

D. FAMILIES OF STYLES AND PROBLEMS

Although what has already been said may furnish many indications of how
anthropology defines the limits of its endeavours and the kinds of problem
it chooses to tackle, the nature of the enterprise in general still remains to be
explored. Of course, the exploration is never-ending, for each self-interrogation comes to a temporary halt which leaves other paths to be followed. There
is no finitude in either facts or theory. The rôle of this section of the chapter
is to regroup, in some cases to elaborate, many of the points already made,
and to add new points, under a number of rubrics that will between them
cover the main styles of research as they are at the moment. We begin with
three characteristic 'total' styles before moving on to matters at a lower level
of generality.

1. *Functionalism*

Functionalism is more accurately called by the barbarous term 'structural-
functionalism'. Both elements in the latter name are traceable to the biological analogies that inspired the first generation of British social anthropology, but which are now, happily, no more than etymological residues.
Beyond the confines of anthropology we are clearly within a more general
sociological tradition that survives in the kind of scholarship represented by
Talcott Parsons. And although the hybrid term has little currency outside the
English language, the style for which it stands is widely known and practised.
Indeed, it is so deeply entrenched as a mode of analysis that some of the
people who are affected by the newer style of structuralism both proclaim
their continuing adherence to it and abide by its canons, even sometimes
forgetting that what they do under the name of the more novel style might
just as well have been classified under that of the older.[167] Nobody can fore-

165. See, e.g., BINFORD & BINFORD (eds.), *New Perspectives in Archeology*
(1968); DEETZ, *Invitation to Archeology* (1967); TRIGGER, *Beyond History. The
Methods of Prehistory* (1968); and LONGACRE, *Archeology as Anthropology. A
Case Study* (1970). And cf. in this volume the chapter on archaeology and prehistory by Sigfried J. De Laet, pp. 201-202.
166. See G, pp. 136-137 below.
167. A case in point is LEACH's 'The legitimacy of Solomon' (1966) which, offered as an exercise in structural analysis, and as a development from Lévi-Strauss's

see what future merging of the two main current styles will bring.

And in that connexion it is important to take account of the field work tradition that lies at the heart of the (structural-)functional mode. One may indeed deny to it the right to call itself a theory, in the sense that it says little more than that all parts of a social or cultural systems are interdependent; it is (one might possibly argue) no more than a set of instructions for the conduct of good field research, in that it guides the investigator to a detailed study of all the circumstances attending whatever it may be that he has placed at the focus of his attention. Malinowski did not invent field work but he imposed a modern pattern upon it, and those who, all over the world, emulate his style are required by it painstakingly to tease out the multiple connexions among persons, events, rules, institutions, ideas, practices and rites in the living material they have under their gaze. Lévi-Straussian structuralism knows no field method of its own, and in the work of its leader one can find very little upon which to model a style of field research to match that of the older tradition. It follows that as the canons of structuralism become more widely accepted among men for whom intensive field work is important, so the shape of structuralism is likely to alter. Eclecticism is by no means always to be recommended, for it may lead to vague and insipid work, but the marriage of the field methods of functionalism with the theoretical outlook of structuralism may be fertile of robust and determined offspring. There is perhaps the risk that, with the structuralists wedded to 'theorizing' and the functionalists doggedly attached to the 'field', we may live to see the day when, as in Frazer's time, theoreticians and field workers will be distinct and unequal partners. But it is unlikely.

As for its theory, some of the difficulties inherent in the functional mode have been alluded to. It grew up to sever the apron-strings by which it was first tied to its evolutionary mother. Concentrating on the study of primitive societies for which the historical evidence appeared (in the absence of any appetite for it) to be lacking or grossly deficient, practitioners of the mode created, often quite consciously, the fiction that they were dealing with timeless entities which upon analysis would be demonstrated to consist of an intricate mechanism of interacting parts. (It will be remarked that a mechanistic analogy overlaid the biological.) And if the societies under study were in a vacuum of time, then they tended also to be in a vacuum of space, for it was also a convention that the entities were circumscribed by clear limits – as they had to be if they were to be treated as exhaustively self-causing.

But such restrictive conventions were never intrinsic to the mode, and as time has gone on its potential flexibility has come to be realized in practice. The firmly bounded societies have become fields of social relationships which overlap with other such fields. Time re-enters. The total and unifying structures are reduced to configurations of perhaps only loosely aggregated parts, the mechanism allowing for much free play between them. Yet struc-

---

work, can be linked up easily enough with the author's pre-Lévi-Straussian treatment of Kachin myth.

tural-functionalism still has its methodological problems; they arise from its preoccupation with totality, however vaguely it be defined. They were touched on in earlier contexts and must now be restated.

If a method aims at seizing the total it will be either impatient with generalization or, at the other extreme, over-generalized, so to say, in its generalization. On the one hand, it rejects the ripping of institutions or practices out of their total context; on the other, it presents a particular totality as a case for general consideration. For example, matriliny among the Trobrianders cannot be understood outside the context of Trobriand society; that society is the type of a primitive society. The comparative method continues to wrestle with the problem of what and how to isolate for comparison. Some structuralists appear to think that they have avoided the problem by rejecting the method; that they have not succeeded is shown by their inevitable use of the basic categories of the discipline: kinship, politics, marriage, witchcraft, and the like. It is all the more striking that they sometimes burden themselves with such categories as 'feudalism' and 'caste', to chain themselves more firmly to the method they abjure.

A totalizing field method, based upon the powers of observation of the lone investigator, is essentially self-limiting. By it a small and isolated society may be grasped. But what is to happen when the anthropologist wants to turn to societies of wider scale? Radcliffe-Brown's answer (and not his alone) was to encourage the study of communities; it is not a completely satisfactory solution, for the arbitrary nature of the small unit then becomes transparent. No amount of village studies in a complex society is going to rise above local particularism to reach to the character of the society that englobes its villages, unless the villages are understood in relation to that society. And it follows that the efforts made by anthropologists in the functional tradition to tackle the study of complex societies entail a radical departure from the field method it enshrines. To say that one cannot directly observe the whole of such a society is a truism; to say that one cannot study: it at all is nonsense. And the solution to the problem lies along two paths. One of them is the investigation of limited sectors (family, legal system, religion, and so on); the other is the recourse to alternative methods of study documentary evidence, statistically based surveys, team-work, and the like. The first course sacrifices totality, the second directness of observation. But there is no escape. Functionalism, like every other kind of anthropology, has to learn to live with the consequences of its growing ambitions and to pay the price of its increasing sophistication.

Much of the viability of the mode is rooted in its ambiguity, for it can encompass people of different persuasions and with different aims. 'Function', as has been pointed out *ad nauseam*, has many meanings. Functionalism can embrace both those who seek 'understanding' from the relation of parts to whole and those whose ambition it is to arrive at 'explanation' by the attribution of causal effect to one or more of the things in relationship. The mode can then be seen to span the dividing line between the scientific and anti-scientific wings of the discipline, when cause is taken to be the characteristic goal of the one and intuitive comprehension of the other. If we now switch from the observer to the observed, then again we see the ambiguity: 'thougts' may function in the minds of the members of a society to make sense of their world and to realize the values after which they strive; or they may exist outside the range of their consciousness to make them act in a manner whose consistency it is the triumph of analysis to show. It is a fact of life that men are motivated by their norms and ideals; it is also a fact of life that they are driven on unawares by their unconscious thought and their conditions. Functionalism allows for the analysis of both and permits different scholars to throw the emphasis in different directions. It is not an accident that structural-functionalists appeal at various times to the work of Marx, Max Weber, Durkheim, and Parsons. It is not surprising that they may be open to the viewpoints of structuralism, 'cognitive anthropology', social psychology, and the like.[168]

There is a moral and political side of the matter to be mentioned. Both structuralism and evolutionism have their ready answers to the problem of human difference and worth. The former places all men, at all times, on the same plane, for they are alike in the principles which govern their behaviour and thought, and any unevenness in development among groups averages itself out – one group is economically more advanced but religiously 'underdeveloped', another shows the opposite, and so on. Evolution demonstrates that different groups are at different stages or levels of development, but, strung out along the line of advance, they are all equal in their potentiality for forward movement. Now, the functionalists also base themselves upon the principle of human unity, but they are apt to give the impression that their attachment to the idiosyncrasy of cultures rests on a conviction that the human universe is made up of a myriad of entities of fixed difference – whence in part the common attack on them for their 'reactionary' and 'conservative' views. A sad irony lies in the fate of the scholar who, carrying the principle of cultural relativity so far as to make it the basis of a philosophy of moral relativity, thinks of himself as the very model of tolerance and is reproached for the arrogance of his suggestion that the members of other societies are not like him. In a similar fashion, because an earlier generation of scholars pressed the case for a gentle treatment of indigenous systems within the framework of colonial conditions, their successors are sometimes accused of wanting selectively to stop the clock of development. The fact of the matter is that the functionalists are no more committed to a 'conservative' viewpoint than the adherents of any other style of anthropology. If they sometimes seem to be, then they are suffering for their delicate sense of cultural autonomy and of the dignity of cultural difference.[169]

168. On functionalism cf. MARTINDALE (ed.), *Functionalism in the Social Sciences* (1965) and LAZARSFELD, 'Sociology', in *Main Trends . . ., Part I: Social Sciences* (1970), pp. 103-111.

169. NADEL, *The Foundations of Social Anthropology* (1951) remains an admirable guide to many of the questions discussed in this sub-section. Examples of recent writing on them will be found in Part IV/A of MANNERS & KAPLAN (eds.), *Theory in Anthropology. A Sourcebook* (1968).

2. Evolutionism

The rôle of Lewis H. Morgan as an ancestor of functionalism has already been referred to. In that context it was pointed out that Fortes dedicated his recent book on kinship to the American forerunner. A similar dedication is to be found in Lévi-Strauss's *Les structures élémentaires de la parenté,* and we see at once that we are dealing with a fertile progenitor, an impression much increased by the knowledge that, unmediated in the one case and through the influence of Marx and Engels in the other, both American scholarship and that of the Communist world draw support for their evolutionary theories of culture and society from a common source. It is a remarkable backward convergence.

Of course, 'evolutionism' is not the name by which scholars in the Socialist countries would describe what they do; for, basing themselves on Marxism, they dissociate themselves from the other philosophical and theoretical elements that may cluster around the idea of evolution in the 'West'. Yet, in the large-scale view which we must take here of anthropological thinking, we may recognize the 'Eastern' approach to human development as belonging in the general class that embraces evolutionist tendencies elsewhere.

The Soviet anthropologists look upon historical materialism as the main feature of their school. It has by no means prevented the emergence of a powerful trend since the Second World War to make the study of contemporary life the chief aim of their science, but it stamps their work with an historical character and maintains among them a continuing concern with problems of both the general and particular patterns of the development of human society and culture. One important consequence of this style is that there is in the Soviet Union less differentiation than there is generally in the 'West' between social/cultural anthropology on the one hand and archaeology, historical linguistics, and certain aspects of physical anthropology on the other. For Soviet ethnography devotes itself to, among other problems, the genesis of the specifically human, the genesis of ethnic entities, and the migrations of peoples, as well as to present-day ethnic processes.[170] A second and related consequence is that the whole of prehistory and history can be

---

170. Some of the relevant references have been cited. See in addition: BROMLEJ & ŠKARATAN, 'O sootnošenii istorii, ètnografii i sociologii' (= The interrelations of history, ethnography, and sociology) (1969); TOKAREV, 'Die Grenzen der ethnologischen Erforschung der Völker industrieller Länder' (1967); ARTANOVSKIJ, *Istoričeskoe edinstvo čelovečestva i vzaimnoe vlijanie kul'tur* (= The Historical Unity of Mankind and the Mutual Influences of Cultures) (1967); KOZLOV, 'O ponjatii ètničeskoj obščnosti' (= The concept of the ethnic unit) (1967); ČEBOKSAROV, 'Problemy tipologii ètničeskih obščnostej v trudah sovetskih učenyh' (= Problems of the typology of ethnic units in the works of the Soviet ethnographers) (1967); EREMEEV, 'Jazyk kak ètnogenetičeskij istočnik' (= Language as a source for ethnogenesis) (1967); KUBBEL', 'Voprosy razvitija sovremennoj kul'tury stran Afriki v svete leninskogo učenija o kul'turnoj preemstvennosti' (= Questions of cultural development in African countries today in the light of the Leninist teaching on cultural continuity) (1970).

brought within one framework, to reject the view that anthropology is above all concerned with the primitive.

Yet obviously primitive society occupies an important place in Soviet studies, and to the history of that society much attention is given. Soviet scholars begin by postulating a specifically primitive social system as the first socio-economic formation in the past of all peoples. They give particular attention to the clan as the cell of the structure of primitive society, and they are no less concerned with the community and its place in history. All their investigations follow the materialist conception of the historical process established by the founders of Communism, according to which private property, the monogamous family, classes, and the state are historically conditioned and historically transient social institutions. As we have already seen in part in C.1 above, modern Soviet scholarship has made a number of modifications to Morgan's general periodization of primitive history and of the development of marriage and kinship relationships.[171]

The situation in the United States is different. There the evolutionists are one among a number of competing groups, while the Morganian heritage has been reworked after a period during which the dominance of Boas and his immediate followers broke the line of succession by dismissing evolutionism in favour of ethnographic particularism.[172] American evolutionism revived stands primarily in the names of two scholars, Leslie White and Julian Steward, who have been responsible for inspiring a group of younger men now devoted to the promotion of a number of theses in the evolutionist tradition. White's intellectual position is particularly revealing in that the basis from which he starts, being in his own language 'culturological', is at once Tylorian and Durkheimian. Evolutionary and functionalist themes are welded to produce a view of human society and culture moving through a 'temporal sequence of forms'. From this kind of analysis the historical mode is, as White sees it, sharply distinguished, for his concern is with classes of events and with generalization. Technological, sociological, ideological, and sentimental components make up cultural systems, but they are not of equal causal weight, for the first factor is held to be basic and determinative of the form and content of the others. Perhaps most distinctively of all, White proposes a law of cultural development in terms of the amount of energy harnessed per capita.[173]

That is one kind of evolutionary theory; it belongs in the same intellectual tradition as that of Morgan. Steward's case is different, for what is now of interest is adaptation to environmental and social situations, a cultural ecolo-

---

171. In addition to the works already cited, see: KNYŠENKO, *Istorija pervobytnogo obščestva i osnovy ètnografii* (= History of Primitive Society and the Bases of Ethnography) (1965); PERŠIC, A. I., MONGAJT & ALEKSEEV, *Istorija pervobytnogo obščestva* (= A History of Primitive Society) (1968).

172. For a summary of Boas's reaction to the evolutionary arguments of his day, see MEAD, M., *Continuities in Cultural Evolution* (1964), pp. 6 sq.

173. See especially WHITE, *The Evolution of Culture. The Development of Civilization to the Fall of Rome* (1959).

gy within whose framework may be studied, when the evidence is to hand, examples of micro-evolution at work. Unilinear evolution gives way here to multilinear, the latter being 'concerned with cause-and-effect relationships of limited cross-cultural occurrence rather than with processes common to all cultural development'.[174]

In the work of younger men the two styles are brought into relation with each other by being made complementary halves of a more general formulation. There is general evolution (on the Whitean model) and specific (on the Stewardian), 'any given change in a form of life or culture' being 'viewed *either* in the perspective of adaptation *or* from the point of view of overall progress'.[175] It becomes clear that each of the two styles connects up readily enough with other styles: specific evolution with the historical study of social and cultural change, both specific and general evolution with the structural-functional analysis of the interaction between parts of total systems. The second connexion is shown in an interesting and sober fashion in Elma R. Service's *Primitive Social Organization. An Evolutionary Perspective*,[176] in which the problems of evolutionists and those of the functionalists are confronted and merged. There is, of course, nothing surprising in this development, for we have already seen how a careful handling of the theme of development is in no way incompatible with a moderate functionalism. Culture and Society have obviously changed over the course of history; the problem is to investigate changes in particular cultures and societies with the hypothesis in mind that some regularities in the mutations may be detected.

The analogy with, or derivation from, Marxist theory is apparent in certain aspects of the general evolutionary 'school' in the United States.[177] The affinity is perhaps clearest in Marvin Harris's *The Rise of Anthropological Theory* (1968), to which reference was made in another context. The strategy there summarized and commended 'states that the explanation for cultural differences and similarities is to be found in the techno-economic processes responsible for the production of the material requirements of biosocial survival. It states that the techno-economic parameters of sociocultural systems exert selective pressures in favor of certain types of organizational structures and upon the survival and spread of definite types of ideological complexes

---

174. STEWARD, 'Introduction' to STEWARD *et al., Irrigation Civilizations. A Comparative Study, A Symposium on Method and Result in Cross-Cultural Regularities* (1955), p. 1.

175. SAHLINS & SERVICE (eds.), *Evolution and Culture* (1960), p. 13.

176. 1962. See also STEWARD, *Theory of Culture Change* (1955); GOLDSCHMIDT, *Man's Way* (1959).

177. But the views of members of the 'school' do not wholly commend themselves to Soviet scholars. See, e.g., ARTANOVSKIJ, 'The Marxist doctrine of social progress and the "cultural evolution" of Leslie White', in *Soviet Anthropology and Archeology* (1964-65), where White, praised for his adherence to Morgan's basic ideas, is rebuked for also being a Tylorian and for lacking an understanding of the significance of Marxist-Leninist dialectics. See also AVERKIEVA, 'L. G. Morgan i ètnografija S.Š.A. v XX veke' (= L. H. Morgan and ethnography in the U.S.A. in the twentieth century) (1968).

... it does not commit itself to the explanation of any specific sociocultural type or any specific set of institutions'.[178]

There is a majesty in the evolutionary outlook. It scans the whole of the human horizon in its quest for regularity in development, and for that reason throws out bridges to archaeology on the one hand and to the history of civilizations on the other. For this sort of anthropology, the category 'primitive' is in principle only incidental, and if the surveys of human development often stop short of the civilizations, then it is because the evidence becomes too complex to handle. The humanism of the structuralists (if they will allow the term) is the search for a basic humanity; that of the evolutionists lies in their vision of a vast panorama of human development. But both structuralists and evolutionists (at least those in the 'West') show their anthropological limitations in the no more than tentative ventures they make outside the field of the 'primitive'. In theory, all mankind is ours; in practice, we are trained into more modest styles of work.

Moreover, the grandness of the evolutionist vision is diminished when scholars apply themselves to the detailed study of the particulars of history and of social and cultural change. In the long view, there is a beautiful order; in the short, a recalcitrant variety. From this angle, the large contingent of functionalists may be seen to occupy and work in humdrum fashion the middle ground between the ecstatic extremes of structuralism and evolutionism. Each of the three styles may oppose the other two either individually or in allied pairs; they seem to be parts of a triangular system of knowledge.

3. *Structuralism*

Structuralism is both a method of analysis and a collection of theories. As the former it reaches across a broad spectrum of systematic knowledge, within which anthropology is one small area. For obvious reasons, the theories relevant to anthropology extend less widely, yet even in their case it would be unwise to ignore their potential generality. For structuralism in our discipline springs up from within a broad philosophical movement which, while it may sometimes be castigated as a fad of French intellectual exuberance or dismissed as a mere incident in a parochial Parisian war against existentialism or some other school of totalizing thought,[179] is nonetheless of great intellectual vigour and of international interest.[180]

But even if we ignore its generality in order to concentrate on what it has contributed or can contribute to anthropology, we are still obliged to look

178. *Op. cit.*, p. 241.

179. See, e.g., Aron, *Marxismes imaginaires. D'une sainte famille à l'autre* (1970), especially pp. 322 sqq.

180. Two recent studies argue this case: Piaget, *Le structuralisme* (1970) (English translation, *Structuralism*, 1971); and Lane (ed.), *Structuralism. A Reader* (1970). For slightly earlier works see Wahl (ed.), *Qu'est-ce que le structuralisme?* (1968) and Boudon, *A quoi sert la notion de structure?* (1968) (English translation, *The Uses of Structuralism*, 1971).

beyond our own borders. For example, it is frequently stated that the linguistic movements associated with Saussure, Trubetzkoy, and Jakobson, and the literary analysis pioneered by Propp, are fundamental to structuralism in anthropology.[181] Such influences pointing towards an exogenous origin need, however, to be balanced against movements native to the discipline. The notion of structure was implanted in it by the sociologizing science shaped by Radcliffe-Brown in the English-speaking world.[182] The formal procedures were sketched in by the work of a group of Dutch scholars associated with Leiden University; indeed, their studies of both kinship and ritual are in a direct line of ancestry to the latest structuralist exercises.[183] Moreover, Lévi-Strauss himself places his French origins in Mauss. And if the sources are international, so are the consequences. Lévi-Strauss is not the whole of French social anthropology (not by far), nor are his followers all French.

If structuralism were merely formal analysis we should not be able to confine the discussion to the style associated with Lévi-Strauss, for we should then have to take into account some of the parallel work done, for example, by the practitioners of 'ethnoscience', 'formal ethnography', and so on in the United States.[184] Something more is at stake. It is the determination to marry the concept of structure to the notion of transformation, such that the analyst's task is to delineate structures, to transform them by manipulating their internal relations and to establish a set of realized transformations within the body of existing ethnographic knowledge. By such means infinite contingency may be brought down to a limited base of necessary principles. It is not *a* society or *a* culture which is now in question, but the restricted foundation of possibilities from which all societies and all cultures arise and on the basis of which they generate their apparently endless variety. And this kind of exercise diverges radically from what might be termed American structuralism by putting the emphasis on the deduction of structures from observable reality and by locating them below the level of consciousness of the men among whom they work. It is not how men see their reality ('cultural' or 'natural') that is so important; it is how what they see and how they act can be accounted for by deeper layers of a reality they can scarcely know.

The Lévi-Straussian programme first began to be realized on a grand scale in *Les structures élémentaires de la parenté* (1949). It has moved on, via the study of totemism, to that of myth, in four volumes of *Mythologiques*.[185] The

181. As far as Lévi-Strauss is concerned, the linguistic influence is apparently mainly that of phonology, whence the emphasis on distinctive features and binary opposition. 'Transformation' in his work seems also to have a derivation from biology.

182. On Radcliffe-Brown in relation to Lévi-Strauss, see the sustained comparison in MARIN, 'Présentation', pp. 15-64, in RADCLIFFE-BROWN, *Structure et fonction dans la société primitive* (1970). Of course, Radcliffe-Brown's notion of structure places it at an empirical level, but it was important in the development of anthropological ideas that the notion of structure be implanted.

183. See, e.g., DE HEUSCH, 'Les points de vue structuralistes en anthropologie et leurs principaux champs d'application' (1968).

184. Cf. SCHEFFLER, 'Structuralism in anthropology' (1966), pp. 75 sqq.

185. *Le cru et le cuit* (1964); *Du miel aux cendres* (1966); *L'origine des manières*

kinship study rests (to put the matter as briefly as possible) on communication as the driving force in the formation of incest prohibitions and the exchange of women in marriage, on the possibilities of systems of such exchange, and on the examination of some of these possibilities. The transition from the study of modes of action and modes of thought together to that of modes of thought by themselves is marked in a passage in the first volume of *Mythologiques*.[186] This structuralism is a method of analysis (by means of transformations and a binary code), and in that regard it enriches bodies of ethnographic data that might otherwise have for long lain inert and opaque. It is a theory; it traces all possibilities of cultural reality (but rejects the charge of reducing them) to the basic mechanism of human thought; it is therefore in the last analysis about the architecture of the mind (*esprit*). We start from cultural and social variety and finish with mental unity. Along the way, one version of a system (a structure) is shown to be the ordered reworking of another. (Compare the audacious treatment of the transition from 'totemism' to caste.[187]) Men invent and elaborate social orders, myths, ideas, and so on, but the reality of their freedom to innovate and embroider is the constraint of the deeply underlying principles embedded in their nature.

The difficulties in stating the Lévi-Straussian position arise in part (it must be said) from the abundance of words and their vibrant ambiguity, and in part from the obfuscation in the critical literature that has grown up in the last five years or so. The difficulties in accepting what appears to be said are of several kinds. The first is the apparent arbitrariness of the structures deduced,[188] and the absence of a criterion for choosing the best among the alternative structures postulated by different analysts. (It is perhaps rather like the situation we might imagine in which, in a detective novel, rival sleuths produce equally plausible hypotheses to account for the known facts of a crime without the possibility of any further fact coming forward to decide which, if any, is right.) The second difficulty takes us back to a matter already touched on in section B: the problem of time. If transformations can transform across time and space without regard for temporal or cultural continuity (Freud's myth of the Oedipus myth being part of the corpus of Oedipus myths, Australian 'totemism' and Hindu caste part of one system),

---

de table (1968); and *L'homme nu* (1971). For expositions (and in the second case considerable criticism) see Simonis, *Claude Lévi-Strauss ou la 'Passion de l'inceste'*. *Introduction au structuralisme* (1968) and Leach, *Lévi-Strauss* (1970). See also Sperber, 'Le structuralisme en anthropologie' (1968) for admiring criticism. (This last essay has some interesting remarks on the difficulty structuralists have in dealing with the subject of politics: pp. 169, 219.) And cf. for an 'Eastern' view, Meletinskij, 'Klod Levi-Stross. Tol'ko ètnologija?' (= Claude Lévi-Strauss. Is it only ethnology?) (1971).

186. P. 18: 'Derrière la contingence ... il doit l'être partout.' (*The Raw and the Cooked* (1969), p. 10: 'In *Les Structures* behind what seemed to be the superficial contingency ... it must also be determined in all its spheres of activity'.)

187. In Chapter 4 of *La pensée sauvage* (1962) (*The Savage Mind*, 1966).

188. A criticism that can be countered, however, by asserting that such structures are no more arbitrary than those devised by the functionalists. Cf. Ardener, 'The new anthropology' (1971), pp. 458-459.

then not only is cause abandoned as a category (and deliberately so) but time has no significance.

A third difficulty relates to the second: men, on this view, do not advance. What they were at the beginning they are now, for they differ only in the contingent and, in a sense, the superfluous. And while this may be a heartening doctrine when read against the background of the arrogant formulations of racism and Western superiority, it cancels hope for the progress of rationality in the ordinary meaning of that term. There is a passage in an older work which highlights the problem. In *Race and History* we are told that the Australian aborigines, albeit backward in economic life, 'are so far ahead of the rest of mankind that, to understand the careful and deliberate systems of rules [of kinship] they have elaborated, we have to use all the refinements of modern mathematics'. So far so good. But: 'The Australians, with an admirable grasp of the facts, have converted this machinery into terms of theory ... They have gone further than empirical observation to discover the mathematical laws governing the system, so that it is no [sic] exaggeration to say that they are not merely the founders of general sociology as a whole, but are the real innovators of measurement in the social sciences.' [189] There are, in fact, two intertwined difficulties here. The first is the apparent immobility in level of thought. The second is its locus. If man is the subject of history in humanism, then in structuralism the subject is structure. It is not the Australian aborigines who, in common language, may be said to have thought out the mathematics of kinship, but some other entity which non-structuralists would not anthropomorphize so. The psychological problem raised is put by an otherwise admiring exponent in a passage culminating in the following words:

So, then, the history of intelligence is not simply an 'inventory of elements'; it is a bundle of transformations, not to be confused with the transformations of culture or those of symbolic activity, but antedating and giving rise to both of these. Granting that reason does not evolve without reason, that it develops by virtue of internal necessities which impose themselves in the course of its interactions with the external environment, nevertheless reason has evolved, from the level of the animal or the infant to the structural anthropology of Lévi-Strauss himself.[190]

It would be an impertinence to both Lévi-Strauss and his host of eloquent commentators to pretend that structuralism can be so shortly treated. But it has to be characterized in order that it may take its place here as one of the major traditions now at work. Whatever one's doubts and criticisms, one

189. LÉVI-STRAUSS, *Race and History* (1952), p. 28 (original French text republished as *Race et histoire* (1967); see pp. 48-49).
190. PIAGET, *Structuralism* (1971), p. 114. (*Le Structuralisme* (1910), p. 100: 'L'histoire de l'intelligence n'est pas un simple "inventaire d'éléments": elle est un faisceau de transformations qui ne se confondent pas avec celles de la culture ni même de la fonction symbolique, mais qui ont débuté bien avant elles deux et les ont engendrées; si la raison n'évolue pas sans raison, mais en vertu de nécessités internes qui s'imposent au fur et à mesure de ses interactions avec le milieu extérieur, elle a tout de même évolué, de l'animal ou du nourrisson humain à l'ethnologie structurale de Lévi-Strauss.')

cannot resist the impression that one is dealing with the most fascinating of current formulations, which, if it does not convince, then has this advantage, that it marvellously concentrates and stirs the mind.[191]

It is a matter of general knowledge that 'French' structuralism owes much to intellectual developments in Eastern Europe, for in addition to the older scholarship represented by the names of Trubetzkoy and Propp, an important element in present-day work in the 'West' is formed by scholars of Eastern European origin – Jakobson, Greimas, Kristeva, Todorov, etc. spring to mind. And at first sight it may seem paradoxical that structuralism plays so small a rôle in one of its 'homelands'. Yet, by once more adjusting our vision of anthropology in Eastern Europe and the U.S.S.R. to make it include folklore and literary studies, we are able to see that structuralism is a by no means negligible element in the Socialist countries. It has as yet made little impact on anthropology in a narrow sense, in, for example, social organization and material culture, but it has established a base from which further developments may be made.

After a period of decline, structuralism was rehabilitated in the Soviet Union in the early 1960's, at least as far as linguistics and folklore studies were concerned. In the other Socialist countries the movement seems to have been carried furthest in Romania, mainly as a result of the work done by Mihai Pop and his pupils.[192] Structuralist research has been conducted in Hungary since 1962, and at the present time it can be said that, within the field of folklore studies, greater advances are being made in some centres of the Socialist world (Moscow, Tartu, Bucharest, Budapest, and Brno) than in the 'West'.[193]

191. The reader may be referred to the following sources in addition to those already cited: POIRIER, 'Histoire de la pensée ethnologique' (1968), pp. 58 sqq.; MANNERS & KAPLAN (eds.), *Theory in Anthropology. A Sourcebook* (1968), Pt. VIII: 'Structuralism and formal analysis' (which has papers on both the American and Lévi-Straussian versions of structuralism); HAYES & HAYES (eds.), *Claude Lévi-Strauss: The Anthropologist as Hero* (1970) (particularly useful for its display of Anglo-Saxon attitudes); POUILLON, 'L'œuvre de Claude Lévi-Strauss' (1967); PINGAUD et al., *Claude Lévi-Strauss* (1965); POUILLON et al., *Problèmes du structuralisme* (1966); CUISENIER et al., '*La pensée sauvage* et le structuralisme' (1967); MOULOUD et al., *Structuralisme et marxisme* (1967). For an example of American support see ROSMAN, 'Structuralism as a conceptual framework' (1970), which has the additional advantage of suggesting the application of structuralist ideas to African data. For a German reaction see HAUCK, 'Die "strukturale Anthropologie" von C. Lévi-Strauss' (1968). The range of Lévi-Strauss's influence may be judged from the contributions to POUILLON & MARANDA (eds.), *Echanges et communications. Mélanges offerts à Claude Lévi-Strauss* (2 vols., 1970).
192. This work was summed up in several papers given at the Fifth Congress of the International Society for Folk Tale Research held in Bucharest in 1969. Especial attention was given to Pop's paper, 'La poétique du conte populaire'.
193. See VOIGT, 'Az epikus néphagyomány strukturális-tipológikus elemzésének lehetőségei' (= Possibilities for structural-typological analysis of epic folk traditions) (1964). See also the material grouped in 'Modellálás a folklorisztikában' (= Modelling in folklore studies) (1969); HOPPÁL & VOIGT, 'Models in the research of forms of social mind' (1969); VOIGT, 'Structural definition of oral (folk) literature' (1969); VOIGT, 'Towards balancing of folklore structuralism' (1969); MELE-

4. *Ethnohistory*

Ethnohistory (in the view of many) cannot exist. Yet there are ethnohisto-
rians. The second assertion is easily proved – witness the existence of a journal called *Ethnohistory* in the United States, a *Journal of African History* in
England, and a body of scholars who write in *Cahiers d'études africaines* in
France; and these are only specimens. The first proposition is a matter of
interesting debate, for while it may in the end be quite inconclusive (for who
is to legislate against some writers calling what they do by a special name?),
it raises the important issues which spring from a recent confluence of
streams. To begin with politics: as one writer has put it, the right to history
has become a matter of claim by nations and peoples about whom no history
has yet been written. As for scholarship, two lines of development intersect,
if not converge: historians grow more sociological and at the same time
widen the range of their interests to include parts of the world in respect of
which the documentary evidence is slight; anthropologists, on their side, increasingly gaze back into the dimmer time to which, in the case of many,
they had been previously blinded by the dazzling brilliance of the present.
That is to say, there have of late been major shifts in scholarly perception.

The contention that ethnohistory cannot exist rests on the very proper view
that there is good history and bad history, but no systematic account and
analysis of the past that exists apart from history.[194] On that view, ethnohistory runs the risk of being another name for the kind of shoddy history
created by the inexpert use of the total range of possible evidence. And it
becomes clear that what is being registered in the debate is an awareness of
the danger inherent in the novel situation where historians, trained to handle
the written record with scrupulous care and systematic scepticism, may be
beguiled by the unwritten documents to which they now have recourse, and
where the anthropologists, traditionally the producers of primary sources,
may lay clumsy hands upon the secondary.

But there is more to it than that, for the anthropologist as well as the historian has to learn how to amass, sort, and interpret the novel sorts of primary
unwritten document. Now, of course, it is true that historians are not all of
them novices in treating such things as archaeological and linguistic evidence, nor all the anthropologists unused to handling material, oral, and

---

TINSKIJ, 'Structural typological study of folklore' (1971).

The influence of contemporary French structuralism on some Soviet scholars
is marked, although they are firm in their rejection of the atemporal element in it.

Our survey of general styles stops at this point to give way to a treatment of
styles of lesser range. In a fuller survey of present-day anthropology, the discussion
of functionalism, evolutionism, and structuralism would probably be followed by
an account of diffusionism, the varieties of Marxism, and psychoanalytical anthropology. That account cannot, alas, be given here.

194. Cf. the spirited article, BRUNSCHWIG, 'Un faux problème: l'Ethno-histoire'
(1965). To avoid misinterpretation, it must be pointed out that 'ethnohistory', as it
is used in 'Western' scholarship, is *not* synonymous with the history of ethnic
groups.

literary data about the past; but it is certainly true that ethnohistorical exercises are becoming so common that by no means all the writers who engage in them are adequately alert to the problems of method they raise. We may concentrate on oral tradition,[195] which for a number of reasons has a special place in anthropological study.

In functional studies, which were reacting against an earlier tradition of the misuse of oral evidence, a persuasive doctrine was developed according to which all statements made by informants which purported to be about the past were to be taken as statements about the present, in the sense that they were justificatory of present social arrangements (group membership, social alignments, privileges, status, and so on). And in fact, by concentrating on the data from some kinds of pre-literate society it was not difficult to show that genealogies and myths, above all, were finely adjusted to particular structural 'needs' of the social systems within which they were collected. We are, of course, dealing with Malinowskian charters, and no inferences for history could be drawn from them. It is now, at a later stage of scholarship, clear that the scepticism was too widely applied. The situation confronting the ethnographer is in reality one where he must make a judgment, in the light of the social system he is studying, about which statements on the past are nothing more than charters and which may have evidential value. For example, the oral histories recited by professionals associated with a royal court are politically shaped; but it does not follow that in all respects they insert only that which is politically expedient. They may have an historical potential which, taken together with other evidence, builds up into a corpus of data about the past. Two things above all are essential: that the ethnographer or the historian know in great detail the society whose past he wishes to investigate, and that he discriminate finely among classes of oral documents — the word 'myth' may be too easily extended to cover them all. The historian must in addition have some anthropological insight into the kind of society he is dealing with; for one threat to ethnohistory from history is that the historians may too easily transfer to exotic societies the assumptions they make about their own. It is worth stressing the significance of the fact that there is emerging within American, French, and British scholarship a trend to train people thoroughly in both the disciplines of anthropology and history.

Evidence may be added from artefacts, language, and of course written documents. (These last show a tendency to increase as they are sought. A generation less curious was more easily convinced that they did not exist.) In studies involving long time-spans, data from botany, zoology, and human genetics may be relevant. To put them together calls for remarkable deftness. But we must move on from methods to purpose and achievement.

Ethnohistorical studies may be roughly grouped into three kinds. In the first, the anthropologist seeks to provide some historical run-up to an other-

195. A key work is Vansina, *De la tradition orale. Essai de méthode historique* (1961) (English translation, *Oral Tradition. A Study in Historical Methodology*, 1965).

wise synchronic account; the history is incidental. In the second, the time dimension is prominent, and an attempt is made to trace a course of development. In the third, we revert to synchrony, but now it is a synchrony set back in time; the anthropologist is concerned to treat a body of evidence about a past state of affairs as he would a present one if he were in the field. The first kind of study differentiates the anthropologist from the historian; the second and third kinds do not – the last serves to remind us that not all historical writing (*pace* some theorists) is diachronic and concerned with change. The first kind of ethnohistoriography may be little more than a literary flourish or polite nod in the direction of the growing fashion for historicizing, and the genre as a whole might so degenerate. But even if the historical preface serves no rôle in explanation, then at least it has the great virtue of reminding the reader of the study that what is being described in the body of it has a firm location in a real time.

The second genre is an instrument for the study of change and takes its place among both the evolutionary and other varieties of it. Indeed, whether an attempt is made to trace the movement through time of a whole social or cultural system or alternatively of some delimited sector of it (agriculture, kinship, technology, chieftainship, and so on), the writing of this sort of ethnohistory is intrinsic to all kinds of anthropology,[196] with the notable exception of structuralism (and even there the possibility is not, in the view of some, totally excluded). In the third genre, the analyst must have at his disposal a dense texture of data, for, diachrony being eschewed, there is no time dimension along which sparse evidence can be strung. And the writer is necessarily preoccupied with written documents. They may be secondary sources (for there is room for an anthropological interpretation of what historians and others have already written) or primary, when the ethnohistorical vocation calls for a total devotion to established historical technique.[197]

A variation of the last genre needs to be noted, because of the growing tendency for the same society to be restudied, either by the same ethnographer or different ones, at successive periods of time. The primary sources are the notebooks of the field worker(s); the secondary what is published on the basis of them. There can be no doubt that this is the best kind of historical material for anthropology, for the prospect is opened up of a cumulation of diachronic studies, spanning, say, fifty years, all of them incorporating data collected within the framework of a related set of theoretical assumptions and by professional observers.[198]

196. Obviously, this variety of historiography is particularly important in Soviet scholarship, which concerns itself with the history of groups whether the evidence is easy or difficult to come by.

197. It must not go unremarked that, particularly in the ethnohistory done in North America, much of the research is carried out by scholars who identify themselves as archaeologists.

198. The discussion has been about ethnohistory as a branch of anthropology. In a wider context we should have needed to touch on those sorts of ethnohistorical writing that, by feeding upon local, ethnic, and national interests, would

The question is inevitably raised whether the flowering of ethnohistorio-graphy may not prove to produce weeds in the garden of anthropology. If the profession were still small and any diversion from the classical field method of enquiry therefore a marked injury to it, then of course there would be cause for worry. But that is far from being the case, at least in the populous centres of the discipline, and some degree of specialization is not only likely but welcome, partly because of the opportunity it affords to converse with historians. On the other hand, a preoccupation with the past would have this disadvantage, that it would diminish the capacity of anthropology to engage in a dialogue with its subject matter. The past cannot talk back; it is exotic and dumb. The present is exotic and, potentially at least, voluble in its re-plies. We do not need to follow Lévi-Strauss in his polemically inspired pessi-mism about the objectivity of historiography that appears towards the end of *La pensée sauvage*, where we are assured that history 'n'est donc jamais l'histoire, mais l'histoire-pour'.[199] But it is true that whatever the objectivity history may attain, it is arguable that it cannot match that form of it which arises from the possibility that the analyst's facts and models may be balanced and modified by the replies of the people who know the facts and their aggregation from inside.[200]

5. *Approaches from linguistics*

There appears to be only one national anthropology, the American, of which it may be said that a large part of linguistics is fully and formally within its ranks – and for that reason the most interesting and important developments

---

merit study as examples of history as charter and history as prejudice. There are, of course, examples to be drawn from all over the world, east and west, north and south.

199. *Op. cit.*, p. 341 (*The Savage Mind*, p. 257).

200. In addition to the works already cited, see: EVANS-PRITCHARD, *Anthro-pology and History* (1961); THOMAS, 'History and anthropology' (1963); STURTE-VANT, 'Anthropology, history and ethnohistory' (1966); DESCHAMPS, 'L'ethno-histoire' (1968); POIRIER, 'Ethnologie diachronique et histoire culturelle' (1968); LEWIS (ed.), *History and Social Anthropology* (1968); COHN, 'Ethnohistory' (1968); GREENBERG, 'Culture history' (1968); COHN, 'History and political science' (1970); VANSINA, 'Cultures through time' (1970). The Russian literature is very large, but may perhaps be exemplified by: TOLSTOV, 'Nekotorye problemy vsemirnoj istorii v svete dannyh istoričeskoj ètnografii' (= Some problems of world history in the light of ethnohistorical data) (1961); KOZLOV, 'Nekotorye problemy teorii nacii' (= Some problems of the theory of the nation) (1967); and TOKAREV, 'K posta-novke problem ètnogeneza' (= On the problem of ethnogenesis) (1949). In Latin America, especially in Peru and Mexico, historiography has always bulked large in anthropology, the archaeological past being linked to the colonial past, and that in turn to the present. See, e.g., VILLONES, *Introducción al proceso de aculturación religiosa-indígena* (1967); AGUIRRE BELTRÁN, *Medicina y magia: el proceso de aculturación en la estructura colonial* (1963). To take an example from another part of the world, most Australian ethnohistory has been done in close collabora-tion with prehistorians and been based upon archaeological, documentary, and ethnographic evidence. See, e.g., HIATT, B., 'The food quest and economy of the

spring from anthropological linguistics in the United States, typified in recent time by the research of Lounsbury and Hymes. Elsewhere the institutional arrangements of the two disciplines allow for dialogue and mutual influence but not integration, while in some countries (for which Britain was until recently a good example) even the interchange is at a low level of intensity. It is clear that a 'main trend' lies in this very quarter; language moves closer to the centre of anthropological attention. The transition from philology to linguistics has directed the study of language into the social sciences.

The componential and transformational analyses already touched upon have made their fullest impact upon world anthropology by their approaches to the study of kinship, but in fact they have ranged much more widely. Any coherent set of terms (a terminology) in any field of social or cultural life can be brought to their notional laboratory; folk taxonomies of various sorts (botanical, zoological, medical) have been dissected as well as, although to a lesser extent, the lexical sets ordering aspects of social institutions (for example, law and religion).[201] The point was made in C.1 and must be repeated here, that these modes of analysis are not intended to be competitive with other and older approaches to the study of institutions; they do only so much, by laying out the order or alternative orders within verbal systems and, perhaps (there is doubt), providing maps of the cognitive perceptions of the speakers who use the systems. Criticism that they fail to account for variation in usage is beside the point, as is the less understandable attack which accuses them of putting back the anthropological clock to a time when a superficial view of society made its study rest upon the features of its vocabularies. The limitations within which most such analyses are consciously conducted are a) that they are merely contributory to a wider study; b) that they ignore significant variation in usage; and c) that they can by definition be applied only to those features of life for which terminologies exist – not every important aspect of social or cultural life is summed up or expressed in a vocabulary, the relation between language and culture (to use the old formulation of a problem) being of immense complexity.[202] As for this last matter, we may say that a language is at once a partial index of a culture to the outsider and a selective meta-language in which a community can express some but not all of its social and cultural life. What we are seeing in the formal modes of analysis is the coming to fruition within anthropology of the

---

Tasmanian aborigines' (1967). The following studies in German may be mentioned: HIRSCHBERG, 'Kulturhistorie und Ethnohistorie. Eine Gegenüberstellung' (1966); and SCHLESIER, 'Sippen-Diagramme und lokale Ethnohistorie' (1966).

201. See, e.g., TYLER (ed.), *Cognitive Anthropology* (1969); GLADWIN & STURTEVANT (eds.), *Anthropology and Human Behavior* (1962); HAMMEL (ed.), *Formal Semantic Analysis* (1965); ROMNEY & D'ANDRADE (eds.), *Transcultural Studies in Cognition* (1964); HYMES (ed.), *Language in Culture and Society* (1964). See also KAY, 'Some theoretical implications of ethnographic semantics' (1970). And cf. pp. 114-117 below in E. 4).

202. Doubtless, both critics and some proponents of componential analysis will not be content with this formulation; there are differences in aims among the champions. But it may serve as an approximation.

twentieth-century exercise of establishing the presence of structure in language. We now know that structures are detectable in the kinds of language in which anthropology is especially interested; the new problem for some is to establish and analyse the diversity and complexity of the *functioning* of structures in language, and to try to develop concepts and methods for showing the functional organization of languages in the social and cultural lives where they are used. For others the impact of modern linguistics is to be found above all in the inspiration it offers to anthropologists in their efforts to delineate structures of social behaviour and relationships: linguistic methods are to be employed analogically in the analysis of such social phenomena as kinship relations, rites, and eating habits, a variety of work which is best exemplified in the writings of Lévi-Strauss.[203]

The formal analyses of language are typically synchronic, but a new line in the direction of diachrony has been developed in a recent study of colour terminology [204] in which the authors argue that there is a scale among colour vocabularies such that when they are ordered from those with the fewest terms to those with the most, the appearance of additional terms is not random but almost wholly predictable. There is no question here of reverting to older and naiver ideas about the evolution of 'primitive' to 'advanced' languages; a case is being made for abandoning the assumption that there are not stable regularities of a developmental kind among languages.

Ethnographers, however casually, have always been conscious of the flexibility of a linguistic code in its everyday use, at least when they have had enough command of the language of the people they were studying to note the difference, say, between the formulations of commands (politely indirect or bluntly forthright) or between verbal forms in a gradation from affection to hostility. They are matters of common observation in any society. Yet the drive for an ethnography of speaking comes from the side of the linguists – true, a minority of them – who find themselves drawn on by their interest in the relations among units beyond the sentence to consider the status of sentences as acts, the relations among speakers in speech events, and the strategies employed by the speakers. The trend is represented in the work of William Labov,[205] which has demonstrated that to explain linguistic change one must have data in their ethnographic context. It is central to the approach that one abandons the simplifying abstraction 'homogeneous speech communities' in favour of methods to deal with the fact that in each community there is a stratification of socially marked linguistic features (pronunciation and style).

This kind of linguistic consideration has a bearing on a traditional interest within anthropology: the classification of languages for the purpose of historical reconstruction. It is said in the usual run of argument that classification is possible by features retained from a common ancestor, by features shared through borrowing within a common area, and by features shared by

203. For a recent statement see LEACH, 'Language and anthropology' (1971).
204. BERLIN & KAY, *Basic Color Terms* (1969).
205. *The Social Stratification of English in New York City* (1966).

members of a common linguistic type. It is increasingly recognized that there must also be classification according to function: status as vernacular, lingua franca, literary language, ritual language, and the like. The historical questions posed about pidgins and creoles, for example, are less productive than are functional ones, which may show that retained, borrowed, and typologically induced features all converge, giving rise to parallels among, say, pidgins between which there is no historical connexion.

An approach now emerging rests on the injunction to think, not of 'a language' in a community, but of the total repertory of ways of speaking available to members of the community. The ways of speaking have distributions and are contrastive in meaning. What in effect is being done by this approach is to bring back into study the variation in usage that structural and formal linguistics would not tackle. Variation may be examined in terms of social status (or rôle) and situation or from the point of view of the plurality of functions in the use of language.[206] And it is at once obvious both that anthropologists have long been aware of these points and that they now have the opportunity, by means of their ethnographic work, to contribute to a growing branch of linguistic enquiry. For example, there is the problem of norms of interpretation and strategies pursued in the choice of linguistic means. The status of an utterance as a command, insult, endearment, and so on, rests in part on how the hearer interprets it – as a request, joke, affront, etc. What latitude is permissible? A linguistic approach or response may be made in any one of a number of different ways, and it is the job of ethnography to register the range of choice and establish the motivations of the various options. For some linguistically inclined anthropologists, questions of this sort are likely to be more informative in the answers they bring than the structural analysis of *a priori* categories such as 'language' and 'myth', for the hinge between language and society is then seen in the organization of behaviour, that is to say, in speaking itself.

One way of giving a focus to such newer forms of systematic enquiry would be to undertake comparative studies of modes of verbal persuasion and of rhetoric. The categories 'speaking truthfully', 'commanding', 'threatening', 'speaking unguardedly', and so on, might then be specifiable in a manner which does not rely on the categories embedded in the language of the analyst. Anthropology has come a long way from the day when such terms as 'uncle' and 'aunt' were thought to be applicable in all systems of kinship; there remains a mass of equally clumsy categories to be subdued by their being reduced and subtilized.[207]

206. See, for example, FINNEGAN, 'How to do things with words: performative utterances among the Limba of Sierra Leone' (1969).
207. In addition to the works already referred to, see: HAUDRICOURT, 'Linguistique et ethnologie' (1968); ARDENER (ed.), *Social Anthropology and Language* (1971); GUMPERZ & HYMES (eds.), *Directions in Sociolinguistics* (1970); HYMES (ed.), *Pidgenization and Creolization of Languages* (1970); LEFEBVRE, *Le langage et la société* (1966); TAMBIAH, 'The magical power of words' (1969); GREENBERG, *Anthropological Linguistics* (1968); GUMPERZ & HYMES (eds.), *The Ethnography of Communication* (1964); MILLER, 'Language' (1970). In Eastern Europe and the

6. *Approaches from psychology*

Any statement about the relation between anthropology and psychology that begins from the position that they differ by the one dealing with culture and society and the other treating the individual, runs up against a formidable theoretical difficulty – or rather, it runs away from it. It is of course obvious that individuals exist in a sense in which societies and cultures do not; but the obviousness of that statement is deceptive, for the word 'individual' here means a physical presence. And as soon as we conceive of the individual as being human in his behaviour (including his use of his own body) we are in the same world of inference and abstraction as contains 'society and culture'. Only new-born babies and feral men are nothing but individuals in the first sense; all others are known as individuals by virtue of their being in society. We are individuals, and can be studied as such, only because we are formed in the company of other individuals. Anthropology and psychology deal with one reality, and even when the attempt is made to get behind culture to the underlying mechanisms of mind and brain which it presupposes, the psychologists still cannot shake off the anthropologists, who, whether of the ethological or structuralist variety, are determined to follow them into the depths. It is true that there once existed a flourishing school concerned with the study of 'culture and personality' (now much declined); it could justify itself only by defining some things out of culture which were then allocated to individuals, and if the Tylorian view of culture was maintained ('that complex whole' which includes any 'capabilities and habits acquired by man as a member of society') the exercise was impossible.

Within the field of human behaviour which is common to them, anthropology and psychology for the most part choose different problems, and when they tackle the same problems they employ characteristically different methods. The first discipline is wedded to contextual analysis and wide-scale comparison and is preoccupied with norms and regularities; the second prefers experiment and is fascinated by variation and deviation. But a scholar might be trained in both disciplines (some have been) and so bring to bear upon a problem common to the two traditions the methods and techniques drawn from both. We shall be concerned here with precisely that attempt to use psychological styles within anthropology, for to try to deal with the con-

Soviet Union the most interesting linguistic development relevant to anthropology appears to be in the field of communication; see HOPPÁL & VOIGT, 'Kultura és komunikáció' (= Culture and communication) (1969); HOPPÁL, *Egy falu kommunikációs rendszere* (= The System of Communication in a Hungarian Village) (1970); and in other styles see IVANOV, V. V., & TOPOROV, *Slavjanskie jazykovye modelirujuščie sistemy* (= Slavic Language Model Systems) (1965); IVANOV, V. V.. 'Dvoičnaja simboličeskaja klassifikacija v afrikanskih i aziatskih tradicijah' (= Dualist symbolic classification in African and Asian traditions) (1969). The reader may also be referred to the remarks in JAKOBSON, 'Linguistics', in *Main Trends . . .*, *Part I: Social Sciences* (1970), especially pp. 428 sqq.

verse, and so cover the whole of the overlap between the two disciplines, would be to exceed our brief.[208]

The vast range of ethnographic observation lends itself to the tackling of psychological problems on a wide comparative basis, either by recourse to the literature (in which case the data stored and sorted in the Human Relations Area Files are of help) or by the mounting of correlated field studies. John W. M. Whiting's study of 'Socialization process and personality'[209] and Roy G. D'Andrade's of 'Sex differences and cultural institutions'[210] are examples of the first method, which is open to the same criticism (but no more so) as that which greets all studies resting in a statistical manner upon information culled from varied sources. The second method, much closer to the central field work tradition, is exemplified in a group of six field studies in various parts of the world on child rearing.[211] This method clearly needs to be more extensively used, not simply for psychologically phrased problems but for a great number of others, for it introduces into a classically idiosyncratic method of enquiry a measure of standardization such that the data collected are more homogeneous than those gathered in a series of independently conducted studies.

In taking over a set of instruments along with a group of problems, the ethnographer as psychologist often finds that he has to adapt the former to the exotic circumstances in which he works. In the heyday of the American school of 'culture and personality' the equipment was Rorschach and Thematic Apperception Tests, but they have by and large dropped out of fashion, doubtless in part because of the scepticism that always attends the use in strange settings of psychological instruments devised within the special conditions of Europe and North America. Again, there was a time when some anthropologists were eager to contribute to the debate on the measurement of intelligence within different cultures, and that interest too has greatly diminished. It is as though anthropology taken as a whole is interested in speculating about the mental foundations of social and cultural life, but wary of the traps laid for those who set out to study them. In effect, the important tasks of what we may call psychological anthropology are left increasingly to the psychologists, who, taking to the field and putting themselves to school among the anthropologists, are developing a new comparative psychology of their own.[212] On the other hand, ethnographers still show themselves willing

208. It would include, for example, the use by psychologists in exotic societies of 'participant observation' in the attempt to establish a general context within which to conduct tests and experiments, and their scanning of the ethnographic record for evidence of correlations between practices and cognitive or emotional style.

209. In Hsu (ed.), *Psychological Anthropology. Approaches to Culture and Personality* (1961). See also another collective work of the same period: Kaplan (ed.), *Studying Personality Cross-Culturally* (1961).

210. In Maccoby (ed.), *The Development of Sex Differences* (1967).

211. Whiting, B. (ed.), *Six Cultures. Studies of Child Rearing* (1963). See also Minturn & Lambert, *Mothers of Six Cultures. Antecedents of Child Rearing* (1964).

212. See, for example, the *International Journal of Psychology* (Paris), founded in 1966, which is almost entirely devoted to cross-cultural experimental psychol-

to apply new techniques of investigation devised by their psychological colleagues [213] and to participate in joint enquiries. An example of the latter is to
be found in *The Influence of Culture on Visual Perception*,[214] which brings
up to date the treatment of a problem deeply rooted in the history of both
disciplines. It is perhaps worth noting that one reason for the overshadowing
of anthropological work in comparative psychology by that done by the psychologists is the emergence of a greater corps of psychologists than of anthropologists in some of the countries where the social sciences have been more
recently established.

Up to this point we have taken 'psychology' to represent an academic
discipline which, although heterogeneous in its intellectual origins, has internationally a common style. Especially when 'culture and personality' studies
flourished, our discipline was particularly under the influence of psychoanalytic theory; that influence remains,[215] but it is much reduced in its effect
upon style of research, even while it is widely spread as a single element in
the total intellectual equipment of the anthropologists of many countries: it
is, after all, part of the cultural heritage of North America and a large part
of Europe, and its academic presence is often reinforced by the psychoanalytic treatment to which many anthropologists have submitted themselves.
(The treatment has in turn sometimes produced ethnographers converted to
psychoanalysts and operating as both.) [216]

While the decline of psychoanalytic anthropology has been matched by a
rise in attention to genetic and experimental psychology, some aspects of
which we have glanced at, there remains a third psychological extension of
anthropology to be noticed: into psychiatry. Here again the psychoanalytic
element is strong in places and some psychiatrists have been anthropologically trained or at least influenced by anthropology. Yet because psychiatry
is a branch of medicine, and therefore an applied science, equipped with a
highly specialized apparatus of knowledge and technique, the rôle of the
anthropologist in it must be limited. He may collaborate in studies with psychiatrists and broach subjects of immediate interest to them, but he cannot,
unless he is one himself, bring psychiatry fully within the fold of his discipline.[217]

---

ogy; the *Journal of Cross-Cultural Psychology* (West Washington State College,
Washington); and PRICE-WILLIAMS (ed.), *Cross-Cultural Studies* (1969).

213. Such as the 'semantic differential technique'. See OSGOOD, 'Semantic differential technique in the comparative study of cultures' (1964) and the same
author's 'On the strategy of cross-national research into subjective culture' (1968).

214. SEGALL, CAMPBELL, & HERSKOVITS (1966). And see FRENCH, 'The relationship of anthropology to studies in perception and cognition' (1963).

215. See, e.g., MUENSTERBERGER (ed.), *Man and His Culture. Psychoanalytic
Anthropology after 'Totem and Taboo'* (1969); DEVEREUX, *Essais d'ethnopsychiatrie générale* (1970). For a survey of the interaction between anthropology and
psychoanalysis, see NACHT, 'Psychanalyse et ethnologie' (1968).

216. One might suppose it absolutely necessary in psychoanalytic research to
have a knowledge in depth of the language of one's informants; and that must
presumably put a brake upon psychoanalytic study of the exotic.

217. For a survey see BASTIDE, 'Psychiatrie sociale et ethnologie' (1968). See

Although some anthropologists – particularly those who hold the view that was disputed at the beginning of this sub-section – profess a lack of interest in psychological questions, the fact remains that all of them, be they naive soever, are concerned with the underlying problem of 'human nature'.[218] If they are conscious of attempting to apply themselves to its study their approaches are various: through structuralism, functionalism, evolutionism, linguistics, psychology, or ethology. In the last analysis, the contemplation of social and cultural variability leads to reflection upon how it is generated from a common human base – and while ideas about racial differences may still in some quarters have a residual effect, anthropology has long since passed the stage where any gross biological differences among groups of men is held to be explanatory of cultural variation. The base may be sought in psycho-physical properties, in a heritage from primate ancestry, in universal mental structures, in common human needs. In that sense, psychology is central to anthropology, and the pursuit of the questions it raises is obviously endless. It is one of the longest-range 'main trends'.[219]

7. *Approaches from ethology*

The anthropological interest in that common human nature to which we have just referred and which transcends both outmoded racialism and the drive to comprehend cultural diversity, has of late been given impetus by developments within ethology, the modern study of animal behaviour. But that 'ethology' should be only one letter short of 'ethnology' is both a typographical and a scientific hazard. As for the latter, we can see by looking at some popular writings which stress the innately aggressive character of *homo sapiens* and its built-in sense of territoriality that too ready a zoomorphization of human behaviour can lead to conclusions which succeed in combining the trivial with the fantastic. The relevance of ethology to anthropology has to be sought in more restrained speculations.[220]

---

also OPLER, M. K. (ed.), *Culture and Mental Health. Cross-Cultural Studies* (1959); PAUL & MILLER (eds.), *Health, Culture and Community* (1955); LINTON, *Culture and Mental Disorders*, ed. by DEVEREUX (1956); DEVEREUX, *Essais . . .* (1970) and *Mohave Ethnopsychiatry and Suicide: The Psychiatric Knowledge and the Psychic Disturbances of an Indian Tribe* (1961).

218. For an interesting meditation on this theme see OPLER, M. E., 'The human being in culture theory' (1964).

219. In addition to the works already cited, see: BASTIDE, 'Psychologie et ethnologie' (1968); FISCHER, J. L., 'Psychology and anthropology' (1965); BARNOUW, *Culture and Personality* (1963); WALLACE, *Culture and Personality* (1961); PELTO, 'Psychological anthropology' (1967); HUNT (ed.), *Personalities and Cultures* (1967); MAYER (ed.), *Socialization* (1970); SPIRO, 'Culture and personality' (1968); PRICE-WILLIAMS, 'Ethnopsychology I: Comparative psychological processes' and 'Ethnopsychology II: Comparative personality processes' (1968); MÜHLMANN, 'Ethnologie und Völkerpsychologie' (1961).

220. It needs to be emphasized that this sub-section is not about ethology as

In a framework wider than that of ethology on its own we may note how in recent years there has been a change in the anthropological vision of the relation between human and non-human animal life; and that change has involved a major shift in the view of the rôle of culture itself. It now no longer seems plausible, as once it did, to conceive in human history of a sudden transition from non-human/no culture to human/culture. Instead, culture can be seen (or at least hypothesized) to have played a part in the very process by which man evolved from proto-man; the basic features marking human distinctiveness (language, tool-making, and the prohibition of incest) are themselves to be viewed as gradually evolving phenomena.[221] In this perspective it becomes necessary to raise all over again the problem of the evolution of human social and mental forms from their non-human antecedents, the development of basic social units and ties, the relations between the sexes, and social hierarchy standing high on the list of questions.[222] It is nineteenth-century Anthropology in a refreshingly new guise, and a promise of profitable co-operation between social and cultural anthropologists on the one side and the biologists (including of course the physical anthropologists) on the other.[223]

But the impetus to a renewed evolutionary view of human life is only part of the importance of the ethological inspiration. Its other, and perhaps more important, part lies in its encouragement to anthropology to consider the value of studying man within a zoological framework and through that study to concentrate on both the unity of human life and the limits within which it can be lived. Those limits presuppose a biological determinism which is then

---

such (a vast subject in itself) but about some aspects of the significance of ethology for anthropology. For some parallel remarks in regard to psychology, see PIAGET, 'Psychology', in *Main Trends . . . Part I: Social Sciences* (1970), pp. 258 sqq. where ethology is referred to as animal psychology. On primate behaviour in general, see DeVore, 'Primate behavior' (1968). And cf. *Understanding Aggression* (1971), especially TIGER, 'Introduction', and BIGELOW, 'Relevance of ethology to human aggressiveness'.

221. For a succinct statement see GEERTZ, 'The transition to humanity' (1964). And cf. Fox, 'The cultural animal' (1971). Some of the field studies of primate behaviour have contributed to the debate on 'the transition to humanity'.

222. See, e.g., Fox, 'In the beginning: aspects of hominid behavioural evolution' (1967); and TIGER, *Men in Groups* (1969). From the zoological side see CHANCE & JOLLY, *Social Groups of Monkeys, Apes and Men* (1970).

223. There has been a trend among some social and cultural anthropologists in recent years to rid themselves of the belief, generated in the reaction to nineteenth-century racialism and by the then liberating doctrine of Durkheimian sociology, that biology and the study of culture must be kept apart. We are perhaps now at the beginning of a period in which physical anthropology and social/cultural anthropology will be brought closer together once more by the relevance to both of genetic and cultural change. For an example of the significance of the findings in genetics, see NEEL, 'Lessons from a "primitive" people' (1970); LIVINGSTONE, 'Physical anthropology and cultural evolution' (1968); and for a slightly earlier work see BENOIST, 'Du social au biologique. Etude de quelques interactions' (1966). Cf. JOHNSTON *et al.*, 'Culture and genetics' (1970). Unfortunately the topic is too complex to be handled here.

at once modified by the further assumption that they are the basis upon which transformations (to use a fashionable term) are generated. In opposition to the evolutionary view, this one sets time and development to one side in order to produce a kind of structuralism. Without (its proponents hope) falling into biological reductionism, this sort of ethological approach seeks a way of viewing cultural variations (the transformations) against a background conception of man as an animal of a particular kind endowed with a particular range of social responses and potentialities.[224] The collaboration called for between anthropology and ethology is made the easier of attainment by the adoption within the latter of concepts and points of view generated within the social sciences. Ethology looks upon animal behaviour not merely as the product of individual potentialities and drives but as the product of social systems, and it is significant that in a recent work the 'structure and function' which were once transferred from the biological to the social sciences are now seen biologically through their social science refractions. That work refers to Durkheim, Radcliffe-Brown, Malinowski, and Lévi-Strauss.[225]

Within ethology we find a human ethology. The specialism has mushroomed in the United Kingdom (for example, in Birmingham, Cambridge, London, and Edinburgh) and, in continental Europe, in Munich; and it has close links with groups of scholars, albeit non-ethological, working along similar lines in a number of places in the United States.[226] Human ethology involves the prolonged and intensive observation of human behaviour (gesture, posture, facial expression, and so on) in various kinds of social situation in the attempt to identify 'behaviour elements' from which may be built up the basic repertory of the face-to-face social behaviour of the species.[227] On one view, human ethology should be able to reveal the behavioural heritage on which, in some sense, social systems are constructed. But in precisely what sense are they so constructed? The significance of human (and doubtless non-human primate) social behaviour rests upon the social context in which it is generated and performed; and behaviour and society cannot be so simply separated and analysed apart. Behaviour does not, of course, just well up from individual motivations but is a response to prescriptions and expectations relevant at all levels of society, lower and higher. But while human ethology may be limiting itself unduly by concentrating on face-to-face encounters it may also lead to our reaching a more sensitive and comprehensive view of social interaction precisely because it so concentrates. Building in particular upon the pioneering studies by Goffman,[228] it might be

224. See, e.g., the treatment of the structural relations between the sexes in TIGER, *Men in Groups* (1969) and CALLAN, *Ethology and Society. Towards an Anthropological View* (1970), Chap. 8. This book contains a wide-ranging discussion and a useful bibliography, to which the reader may be referred.

225. CHANCE & JOLLY, *Social Groups* ... (1970), pp. 16 sq.

226. E.g., P. Ekman's group in San Francisco; A. H. Esser's in New York; R. L. Birdwhistell's in Philadelphia; and S. S. Tomkins's in New Brunswick.

227. Cf. GRANT, 'Human facial expression' (1969).

228. See, e.g., GOFFMAN, *Behavior in Public Places* (1963). Other work bearing

able to account for the articulation of social life through 'ritual' [229] at the level of face-to-face encounters, and relate the patterns that emerge to both the universal (species-specific) and the variable aspects of human society on the largest scale. If it succeeds it will feed both appetites of anthropology: for the general and the universal (human nature/Culture) and for the particular and local (cultures). Ethology will then be seen to be not an aberration (as it is in the view of some) but an important element in the total range of styles to which this section of the chapter has been devoted.[230]

8. *Social and cultural change; applied anthropology*

Anthropologists sometimes give the name 'Social/cultural change' to courses of instruction in the universities; that name is also the label of a would-be specialism among some professionals. But we shall take the view here that it is a pseudo-subject produced by a false assumption that change and stability can be clearly segregated in the practice and teaching of the discipline. Like other important pseudo-subjects, of which 'race relations' is an example, it has its pragmatic and pedagogical uses, but it ought never to be marked out as a separate and distinct thing. Indeed, enough has already been said in this chapter to show that change over longer or shorter spans of time is a constant theme in anthropological work; for even the functionalist studies of a generation ago, which seemed to be wedded to timelessness, paradoxically brought time and change to the forefront when they treated the impact of modern forces upon 'traditional' societies.

But it is precisely this concern with modern transformations that justifies some special comment. There are, in fact, several reasons for the great interest now being taken in 'social and cultural change'. One of them is the dramatic alteration in the political map of the world, many new states taking the place of colonies. Another is the passion for economic development (except in a very few countries where it appears to have succeeded in making life uncomfortable). And the very technology which facilitates or urges on social change magnifies that change by spreading the news of its consequences around the globe.

---

on this topic is to be found in HALL, 'Proxemics' (1968); BIRDWHISTELL, 'Kinesics' (1968) and 'The kinesic level in the investigation of the emotions' (1963); and SCHEFLEN, 'The significance of posture in communication systems' (1964). See also WATSON, O. M., *Proxemic Behavior. A Cross-Cultural Study* (1970).

229. But there is a serious problem both in deciding how to use the term 'ritual' in human behaviour and another in bridging the gap between the anthropologist's uses of the term and the ethologist's. On the latter, see HUXLEY (ed.), *Ritualization of Behaviour in Animals and Man* (1966).

230. For another recent appraisal of the topic see SARLES, 'Communication and ethology' (1970). And see EIBL-EIBESFELDT, *Ethologie: die Biologie des Verhaltens* (1966) (English translation, *Ethology: The Biology of Behavior*, 1970); and CROOK, 'Social organization and the environment. Aspects of contemporary social ethology' (1970).

The hunger for social improvement and economic development makes our generation eager to plan, and many of the most interesting social and cultural changes of the day arise from political acts of will. To these changes anthropologists are attracted either as detached observers or as allies of the promoters. In the latter rôle they are applying their knowledge; we shall come later on to 'applied anthropology', but we need to realize that many of the anthropologists working in their own countries and morally committed to their development or improvement find themselves half-way between the study of social change and applied anthropology. They are scholars convinced of the needs of their societies for anthropological knowledge and aware of the consequences of their findings for political action. It is clear that such an anthropologist is often in a delicate position in that, while conducting research that responds to the demands of his country, he must satisfy himself and the world community of anthropologists that what he is doing is technically valid and intellectually important. Apart from anything else, 'developing' countries in their haste may require of their few anthropologists that they discover and make available knowledge which cannot be produced at speed. On the other hand, that kind of pressure is seen by some anthropologists in the Third World to have brought its advantages, for it has led them to perceive anthropological problems in modern phenomena (urbanization, industrial organization, health programmes, land reform, local government, and so on) and to experiment with ways of carrying out their enquiries quickly and efficiently. Moreover, since the anthropologist is the field social scientist par excellence and is often prepared to carry out on the ground the economic and political investigations neglected by his colleagues in economics and political science, he soon acquires a general competence that leaves him both technically and morally strengthened.

The study of social change in modern conditions has the further characteristic that it forces upon anthropologists the realization that they are working within a complex entity, a state, in which all social phenomena are likely to be affected by decisions taken and plans formulated at the centre. The more conventional units of study (tribe, village, district, and so on) may not be so relevant as they once were, while new forms of cultural, political, and religious leadership, new 'classes', and new kinds of social organization ('tribal' associations, 'caste' associations, trade unions) come to the centre of attention. These too call for innovations in field technique. And we are able to see why anthropologists in the Third World often look upon their obligations as citizens as an opportunity for the advancement of their discipline. Of course, the direction in which they may move − away from one-man ethnography towards multidisciplinary research, away from intensive field work during one or two years to investigation spread over decades − may come increasingly to differentiate the anthropologists of (some parts of) the Third World from their colleagues elsewhere. And we may need to learn to tolerate the difference without deploring it.

It is often said, and with some justice, that anthropologists working in colonial societies in the old days were blind to the total political and social environment within which they conducted their studies of small communities or of tribes. In independent states they are not likely to make the same kind of mistake, and they have there the chance of studying the way in which all groups and elements respond to the post-colonial situation. The old bias in anthropology towards the study of the rural and the powerless is now being corrected, and work is undertaken on elites and politicians as well as on those whom they lead.

Some present-day trends, which cry out for closer study, seem to be detectable. In the first place, there is a tussle between the urge to claim a distinctive cultural heritage (on a national up to a continental scale) and the desire to enter into a more international cultural community. Second, in the process of nation-building two striking phenomena emerge: the growth of micro-nationalisms which may struggle against the nation, and the construction of legitimating pasts – the making of national histories.

If we now turn quickly to the anthropology of development we see that it must by its nature be comprehensive; only some of its priorities can be touched on here. It is obvious that it must begin from a position in which it seeks to understand the multiple connexions among material conditions, techno-economic resources, social organization, religious beliefs, and values. From that general base it may move to study the obstacles to and modes of the transmission of technical messages, their differential reception by distinguishable groups and groupings, and the sociology of knowledge which underlies the perceptions and acts of those responsible for creating and implementing plans. When development is in train it becomes important to analyse its consequences for, among other things, changes in the nature and quality of social relationships and gross structural changes in key forms of groups (family, village, local political community, and so on). As examples of more specific matters for study, we may suggest as topics of great interest the development of new legal forms and the attempts (sometimes by codification) to impose entirely novel jural norms; and the shifts in inter-ethnic relationships attendant upon new economic and social arrangements.

It is, of course, a matter of prime interest to anthropology to examine the difficulties in the way of its reinforcing its presence in the 'new' countries, for the discipline can only complete itself, for reasons discussed earlier, if the Third World enters fully into the intellectual exchange. The more reflective and less practical social sciences obviously have lower attractive power than the subjects which lead direct to political and administrative office, and anthropology may as a result have difficulty in recruiting new members. And there are other problems which arise from the anthropologist's status as an intellectual.

On a pessimistic view (which even if it is exaggerated, at least has the advantage of alerting us to the dangers) the pace of progressive change in many of the 'new' countries may in the next decade be hampered by certain defects. In the first place, the scholastic rivalries of the wider intellectual world may be imprudently imported. It does not matter very much, after all, in terms of its impact on the lives of ordinary people, whether the anthropology of a 'developed' country is psycho-analytical, structuralist, evolutionist, or functionalist. It may matter a great deal if these intellectual schemes are to be applied in studies from which practical consequences are to flow. There is a case for stressing the importance of a balanced and well-proportioned discipline of investigation and analysis. Above all, there is a danger in those reduced and impoverished schemes of research which, for example, operate with simple notions of social class and class exploitation or, as in some forms of neo-Marxism, with equally rudimentary concepts of power and dominance. That class and power may be crucial is not in question; it is the illegitimate (and incidentally un-Marxist) generalization and reductionism which are to be guarded against, for they amount in themselves to an anti-anthropology which in its self-defeat defeats the profitable study of social change.

There is a threat from another quarter. There is always the possibility that anthropology may be dispensed with in 'new' countries either because it is seen to be an expensive and useless luxury (against which charge it does its best to defend itself by a sober and determined effort to study and analyse social change) or because it appears along with sociology to contain a built-in capacity to generate social and political criticism of a radical kind. In favour of this latter charge there is some evidence from Europe and North America which already has had its effect on the attitude towards the sociological disciplines in the universities of some 'new' countries.[231]

It will be seen that reflection on the study of social and cultural change in the Third World leads on to a discussion of a kind of meta-anthropology: the anthropology of the rôle and position of anthropology. Some (by no means all) of its conclusions may be discouraging.[232]

231. Whatever the reason, anthropology seems to have been generally on the retreat in the universities of French-speaking Africa since 1968.

232. For a recent example of anthropological self-appraisal see WARMAN, NOLASCO ARMAS, BONFIL, OLIVERA DE VÁZQUEZ, and VALENCIA, *De eso que llaman antropología mexicana* (1970).

The themes outlined in these paragraphs cover only a small part of the field of social and cultural change, and some important topics (e.g., innovation, assimilation, race and inter-ethnic relations) have been neglected for lack of space. The following items in the vast literature may be mentioned: MAIR, *Anthropology and Social Change* (1969); MERCIER, 'Anthropologie sociale . . .' (1968), pp. 1004 sqq.; POIRIER, 'Dépendance et aliénation: de la situation coloniale à la situation condominiale' (1966); MURPHY, 'Cultural change' (1967); STEWARD (ed.), *Contemporary Change in Traditional Societies* (3 vols., 1967); VOGT, 'Culture change' (1968); EGGAN, *The American Indian. Perspectives for the Study of Social Change* (1966); SRINIVAS, *Social Change in Modern India* (1966); RUDOLPH, ' "Akkulturation" und Akkulturationsforschung' (1964); SIXEL, 'Inkonsistenzen in Transkulturationsprozessen' (1969); EPSTEIN, A. L., 'Urbanization and social change in Africa' (1967); LITTLE, *West African Urbanization* (1965); LLOYD, *The New Elites of Tropical Africa* (1966) and *Africa in Social Change* (1967); BALANDIER, *Sens et puissance. Les dynamiques sociales* (1971). Naturally, a great deal of Soviet ethnography is taken up with the theme of change. And although little field research has been conducted in the Third World by anthropologists from the U.S.S.R. and the other Socialist countries, their writings show much interest in contemporary change in Asia and Africa. See, e.g., ČEBOKSAROV, 'Ėtničeskie processy v stranah Južnoj i

We may turn to applied anthropology. Except where the view is taken that scholarship and action in the real world are inextricably intertwined, anthropologists may seek either to apply their knowledge, so to say, from the outside, or, taking on the rôle of the organizer of change, make their professional knowledge a part of their action. The distinction is perhaps best illustrated by the contrast between the anthropologist answering the call to advise a government or international agency on a problem (health education, nutrition, land reform, local government, and so on), and his colleague who becomes a national or international bureaucrat charged with the promotion of change in the same fields. There is, therefore, an academic applied anthropology and an extra-academic one. And the former is more closely connected with the study of social and cultural change.

The argument must begin from this point because quite different opinions are held on the extent to which anthropology can in reality be applied. On the one side, scholars say that, presented with a practical problem, they can study the context in which it arises and suggest the consequences of alternative solutions (including that of no action); on the other, that their skill in social relations and their special knowledge enable them to take over responsibility for formulating a programme of change and carrying it through. The first sort accuse the second of failing to understand that as soon as they take to organizing they cease to operate as anthropologists; the second may charge the first with the crime of heartless academicism. There is little dialogue between them and much talking past each other. It is, for example, quite wrong of the second kind of applied anthropologist to accuse the first of a spurious ethical neutrality, for by agreeing in the first place to offer advice of any sort a scholar has chosen to site himself within a congenial set of values: he does not set up shop to sell his services to all comers and would not (to take a simple example) advise the government of the Republic of South Africa on its policy of *apartheid* if he was out of sympathy with its aims. Nor, symmetrically, is it likely to be true in all circumstances that the anthropologist who commits himself to the rôle of organizer and promoter is lost to his science; his analysis of his own experience as a doer in a complex field of forces can become part of the record for the study of social and cultural change. But there is one point upon which nearly all anthropologists are agreed: applied anthropology is more like politics than engineering. It does not rest upon a secure and precise theory, but takes any strength it has

---

Jugo-Vostočnoj Azii' (= Ethnic processes in the countries of South and South-East Asia) (1966); ARUTJUNOV, *Sovremennyj byt japoncev* (= Present-day Japanese Way of Life) (1969); EREMEEV, 'Osobennosti obrazovanija tureckoj nacii' (= The specificity of Turkish national formation) (1969); GAVRILOVA, 'Svoeobrazie processov urbanizacii v Nigerii' (= Specificity of the processes of urbanization in Nigeria) (1969); BERNOVA, 'Sovremmenye ètničeskie processy na Malyh Zondskih ostrovah' (= Present-day ethnic trends in the Malay Archipelago) (1969). And there is of course a vast literature on social change within the U.S.S.R. itself. As an example see SERGEEV, *Nekapitalističeskij put' razvitija malyh narodov severa* (= The Non-Capitalist Development of the Small Peoples of the North) (1955).

LINCOLN CHRISTIAN COLLEGE AND SEMINARY

from general principles, wide experience, and skill in assessing the realizability of interests.

All anthropology changes with the world in which it is practised, but the response of applied anthropology in particular is more noticeable. Indeed, much of the recent literature on it may in some ways soon be out of date. It charts the shift from applications in the colonial field to international technical co-operation, from problems of economic, administrative, and medical improvement to those of community development and educational expansion. But in a few years it may need to incorporate more grandiose schemes for remedying the world's ills and internationalizing its peoples.[233] That is to say, there is just perceptible the beginning of a trend to try to make of anthropology a healer of the large-scale ills that particularly strike the sensibilities of the young: war, racialism, environmental pollution, poverty, sexual inequality . . .[234] One may predict that, the smaller-scale problems having proved difficult enough to handle, the larger ones will remain elusive. But it does not follow that their intractability will discourage the mood in which they are approached, for idealism is not always daunted by experience.

Of course, there is no doubt that whatever the obstacles in its way, some internationalizing of applied anthropology is highly desirable. In the first place, the level of suspicion between countries is in many cases now so great that it can be overcome, to allow any sort of anthropological research in foreign parts to proceed, only by means of international sponsorship. That would place a special burden upon Unesco and the other U.N. specialized agencies or on some non-governmental international body; they might, quite understandably, not care to take it up. In the second place, all programmes of applied anthropology carried out in one country by people from another are an unreciprocated gift that damages the status of the recipients; there is inequality to begin with between donor and receiver; it is reinforced by the

233. In April 1971 the Center for the Study of Man, Smithsonian Institution, Washington (D.C.), called a meeting for May, in Chicago, to start off a programme 'to encourage and to coordinate worldwide interdisciplinary research on anthropological problems suggested by the most pressing problems facing mankind . . .'. In the view of some anthropologists, their subject must justify itself by its practitioners taking part extensively in tackling practical problems; and they can do so best by working with narrower specialists (economists, engineers, and the like) in order that these colleagues may benefit from anthropological wisdom.

234. The anthropological members of the Barbados Symposium, January 1971, say *inter alia* that the 'anthropology now required in Latin America is not that which relates to Indians as objects of study, but rather that which perceives the colonial situation and commits itself to the struggle for liberation. In this context we see anthropology providing on the one hand, the colonised peoples those data and interpretations both about themselves and their colonisers useful for their own fight for freedom, and on the other hand, a redefinition of the distorted image of Indian communities extant in the national society, thereby unmasking its colonial nature with its supportive ideology. In order to realize the above objectives, anthropologists have an obligation to take advantage of all junctures within the present order to take action on behalf of the Indian communities.' – 'Declaration of Barbados', World Council of Churches, Programme to Combat Racism, PCR 1/71 (E), mimeographed, p. 5.

act of giving. A denationalized agency would be more welcome. But to make these points is not to show a simple way out of the difficulty; one is merely speculating about what the near future may hold.

It may also hold a new standing for applied anthropology within the profession. The second-best status conventionally accorded it is often remarked upon in some countries; theory is for the high-fliers, application for the drudges. There is another side to the matter: anthropologists do not reckon to teach their subject to would-be research workers in anything less than a full-scale professional education, yet they often instruct administrators, health workers, and the like in the elements of applied anthropology in such a way as to lead to the conclusion that applied anthropology is something that can be done by common sense and a minimum of technical knowledge. It is not surprising that applied anthropology comes to be viewed in places as a poor man's anthropology. If the omens are being correctly read and the drive for a 'committed' anthropology grows strong, then applied anthropology will shift its position, moving to the top rank. From that vantage point it may certainly assuage the hunger for 'relevance' (not necessarily by action), but its effects upon the discipline as a body of knowledge and theory may be less benign.

What above all distinguishes the new voice is its note of urgency. The older applied anthropology, suffused as it might be by an intensely moral view of what needed to be done, was more patient – as indeed it needed to be according to the canon that social life is complex and not easily to be directed into new paths. A more revolutionary conception of change, a cataclysmic view of human progress, especially if wedded to romantic notions of scholarship upon the barricades, is likely to exert its influence upon the way in which applied anthropology is to be reshaped. Not all the voices speaking in an urgent tone belong to the young. The Editor of *Current Anthropology* (Sol Tax) in his 'Letter to Associates' No 49 (in the October 1969 issue) reported on differences of opinions within world anthropology on the priorities of research. He went on to say:

I conceive three tasks for world anthropology to be equally urgent: (1) the human problem of the forced acculturation or physical destruction of peoples who appear to stand in the way of the interests of stronger peoples; (2) the scientific problem of the rapidity of change of traditional forms, whether due to force or the consequences of wanted changes, which forever destroys the data for the understanding of the historical variety of human forms that may help us to guide our future; (3) the problem of educating people, including other scientists and engineers, in the anthropological points of view needed both to make programs of modernization more effective and to ameliorate their negative human consequences.

The second point need not concern us for the moment. The first falls within the definition of applied anthropology in that it implies some kind of political intervention to protect weak groups. It is clearly a very delicate matter, for the old colonialist powers can no longer be blamed, and there are always different views of what constitutes forced acculturation. The principle is fine, but there is little chance within a world community of getting agreement on a defined group of cases. The third point raises to a high level a kind of self-assurance that anthropologists usually confine to their private conversations. But even if we grant that by their special knowledge and understanding anthropologists are in a position to play a much larger rôle in educating their colleagues in other disciplines in order to ease the course of modernization, how precisely are they to do so? Can we be sure that the propaganda and the brief courses of instruction will produce the required effect? One might at least hope that both will be tested against their results before the profession begins to divert to the operation such scarce resources as might better be spent on anthropological research. The popularization of the subject is not unquestionably a good thing for anybody involved. But that cautionary note is likely to be drowned out by the voices crying for more anthropology in the schools, training colleges, and universities, whatever the strain on a small profession and whatever the damage to its standards of scholarship. The trend is certainly towards a wider diffusion of the subject.

Perhaps the special duty that anthropology owes to the world at large might best be discharged by its organizing a critical survey of the applied anthropology of the last twenty-five 'years and by its developing, preferably under international auspices, programmes of training and research to ensure the presence in every country of a group of scholars able to give counsel and guidance on (to follow Tax's scheme of urgent tasks) the protection of weaker groups, the recording of disappearing forms, and the smoothing of the path of modernization.[235]

235. Changes in the conception and range of applied anthropology can be followed in the journal *Human Organization*, founded as *Applied Anthropology* in 1941. For developments in the fifties and sixties see also: various contributions in 'Problems of application', in KROEBER (ed.), *Anthropology Today. An Encyclopedic Inventory* (1953); NADEL, 'Applied anthropology' (1963, but written in the early fifties); GOODENOUGH, *Cooperation in Change. An Anthropological Approach to Community Development* (1963); TAX, 'The uses of anthropology' (1964); LEBEUF, 'Ethnologie et coopération technique' (1968); MAIR, *Anthropology and Social Change* (1969); FOSTER, *Applied Anthropology* (1969); MAIR, 'Applied anthropology' (1968); BENEDICT, B., 'The significance of applied anthropology for anthropological theory' (1967); 'Anthropology and the problems of society', in SMITH & FISCHER (eds.), *Anthropology* (1970); BROKENSHA & PEARSALL, *The Anthropology of Development in Sub-Saharan Africa* (1969); RUDOLPH, 'Entwicklungshilfe und Sozialwissenschaften' (1961). And for a very recent work see BASTIDE, *Anthropologie appliquée* (1971). Soviet 'ethnography' has quite clearly played a part ever since the Revolution in forming and implementing cultural policy for the national minorities (e.g., through the Northern Institute in Leningrad): see, e.g., GAGEN-TORN, 'Leningradskaja ètnografičeskaja škola v dvadcatye gody' (= The Leningrad ethnographic school of the twenties) (1971) . . . An idea of the sharpness of the current debate on the anthropologist's responsibilities towards the people he studies can be got from the group of papers under the title 'Anthropologie et impérialisme' in *Les Temps modernes* (1970-71). As an excellent example of the anthropological endeavour to help practical people understand what is involved in promoting development in foreign countries, see JOSSELIN DE JONG, *Contact der continenten* (1969).

E. METHODS AND TECHNIQUES OF RESEARCH

In the preliminary discussions in sections A and B it was shown that, as a distinctive method of research by anthropologists, field work appeared on occasion to be in danger of dominating both their thought and their subject matter. Section E has, therefore, two chief tasks: to round out the account of modern field work, and to provide a summary of the other important methods of research against which field work has to be measured. All social scientists are familiar with Poincaré's quip to the effect that sociology is the science with the most methods and the least results. The contrary view, that anthropology and sociology are not occupied enough with problems of method, has at times tended to be voiced inside those professions.[236] In present-day anthropology there is certainly no lack of talk about method; the self-interrogation to which anthropology submits itself is clearly visible in the questions it poses about the manner in which it goes about its work.

1. *The practice of field work*

'... l'expérience ethnologique est à l'origine monographique et comparative.' [237] Field work is above all monographic, but from time to time an effort is made to make it conform to the comparativism which is intrinsic to anthropological method. Indeed, the story of field work, when it comes to be written, may turn out to be a history of the indecisive struggle to convert a personal experience into a 'scientific' one, the personal constantly prevailing over each new attempt to 'scientize' it. For, at bottom, nearly every ethnographer covets the experience of a prolonged and intimate relationship with the exotic unknown which he seeks to convert (let us be honest and confess that the process is mysterious) into the experience of himself. It is no surprise to teachers of anthropology to discover that those students who carry out other forms of research feel themselves not only deprived of moral and intellectual excitement but also inferior as professionals to their fellows who have ventured abroad.[238]

It is not for us to trace here the development of field method into its modern form of 'participant observation'.[239] We may merely state that in

236. Cf. NADEL, *The Foundations of Social Anthropology* (1951), p. v.

237. LEROI-GOURHAN, 'L'expérience ethnographique' (1968), p. 1819.

238. On the personal experience, some works have been cited above, p. 20, n. 24; see also LÉVI-STRAUSS, *Tristes Tropiques* (1955) (English translation, *World on the Wane*, 1961); Georges BALANDIER, *Afrique ambiguë* (1957) (English translation, *Ambiguous Africa*, 1966); CONDOMINAS, *L'exotique est quotidien: Sar Luk, Vietnam* (1965). The degree to which, given the nature of the field experience, 'objective' data can be said to be established is not often and well enough discussed. A psychoanalytical anthropologist, DEVEREUX, has tackled the problem in *From Anxiety to Method in the Behavioral Sciences* (1967).

239. See, e.g., RICHARDS, 'The development of field work methods in social anthropology' (1939); POIRIER, 'Histoire de la pensée ethnologique' (1968), pp. 41 sqq.

most of the traditions now making up social and cultural anthropology the ideal technique in the field consists in prolonged observation and the penetration of informants' categories by the use of the vernacular.[240] Professionals always rightly deny the validity of a claim that an ethnographer has completely merged himself into the exotic community he has studied; but they all secretly pride themselves, when they have been lucky or skilful enough, on having made the leap from being a total stranger to an intimately received quasi-citizen. When the community is in effect a society, then field work of that sort offers the chance of recording the data for a 'total' account of what is studied. Wholeness is all.

But anthropology is torn away from this ideal method. Its beautiful amateurism is eroded by the need to adopt stricter techniques of observation and measurement – photography, tape-recording, census-taking, administration of questionnaires, random sampling, and so on. Some of the more modern methods of field work are made necessary precisely because the entity under study is no longer a small and closed community. And when the ethnographer comes to think of himself as above all a specialist (economic anthropologist, linguist, kinship expert . . .) and concentrates upon one institutional complex, then he is condemned (if that is the right way of putting it) to a segmented view of social and cultural life, and to the increasing use of more and more refined techniques for the collection of his data. All these developments are reflected in two books which demonstrate the present condition of the art of field work [241] – potentially specialized, highly technical, and ambitious to do more than study merely the 'primitive'.

But the fact that most field work remains a one-man job, despite the sophistication of the newer techniques, suggests that the old monographic tradition dies hard.[242] The logic of specialization is the necessity of teamwork. There have been a few attempts to form field teams comprising anthropologists and other social scientists (of which the Ashanti study in the Gold

240. Of course, despite the emphasis placed nowadays on the use of the informant's language, a great deal of ethnography has always been done through interpreters or by means of a lingua franca, and much of it has been good. However, the confidence one reposes in ethnographic reporting must depend to a large extent on the degree to which the field worker could handle the language of the people whom he describes, while the efficiency of field work is greatly affected by the interposition of interpreters. Cf., e.g., BERREMAN, *Behind Many Masks* (1962).

241. JONGMANS & GUTKIND (eds.), *Anthropologists in the Field* (1967) and EPSTEIN, A. L. (ed.), *The Craft of Social Anthropology* (1967). It may be surmised that the middle sixties saw the realization of the full meaning of the changes in field work method that had been building up. See also GRIAULE, *Méthode de l'ethnographie* (1957) and LEBEUF, 'L'enquête orale en ethnographie' (1968); PELTO, *Anthropological Research. The Structure of Inquiry* (1970), pp. 213-271; and NAROLL & COHEN (eds.), *A Handbook of Method* . . . (1970), Pt. III, 'The field work process'.

242. Husband-and-wife teams have already been referred to (p. 14, n. 13); they have been quite common, especially among American field workers. The advantages of the arrangement are obvious, but doubtless they sometimes have the disadvantage of creating a separate domestic unit where what is preferable is a closer association of the ethnographer with his informants.

Coast, as it was then, during the Second World War and the Chicago study of Chiapas in Mexico are good examples); [243] there have been more attempts at correlated field studies by teams of ethnographers, either scattered in different places (as in the case of the Six Cultures Project referred to in D.7) or concentrated upon one or a group of communities. The Harvard study in east-central Java in the 1950's and the studies organized by Griaule on the Dogon are illustrations of the latter. And between the extremes of lone ethnography and tightly co-ordinated team-work lie many more loosely conceived plans of joint research, characteristically arising from a situation in which a senior scholar directs his pupils to some aspect of 'his' society or area that he himself has left untouched or under-examined. One might wish that it were possible to state that a 'main trend' has been established to carry forward this kind of co-ordinated field study on an increasing scale, but there is little hard evidence of it, for lone ethnography, the highly individualistic pursuit of the control by one man of one great body of ethnographic data, persists at the ideological heart of the discipline.[244] The humanistic experience dominates the scientific impulse. Many do not regret it, and they are confirmed in their judgments by the success achieved by the lone ethnographers who, with the experience of the exotic behind them, turn their professional eyes to gaze upon their own societies.

How to establish rapport, use informants, observe events, follow up cases, count the countable, compile genealogies, avoid over-commitment, dodge if not solve moral problems, and a thousand other things are part of the professional small-talk of anthropologists even when they are not organized into themes for formal instruction in field technique. Methods of recording are also much discussed, but one problem seems rarely to be confronted: the storage and retrieval of field notes. Of course, the matter arises from that personal character of the field experience we have noted. A set of field notes is doubly confidential: it contains private information about the people studied and about the ethnographer. No wonder then that anthropologists are reluctant to make them publicly usable; and it will be guessed that all attempts to form 'data banks' of ethnographic raw notes are likely to meet with stubborn resistance.[245] It is right that it should be so; yet some way must be found for making available for general use some half-processed forms of raw notes if a large part of the thousands of field investigations are not irretrievably to be lost.[246] Of how many ethnographers could it safely be said

243. In some cases the need for a team of mixed skills has been avoided by a single ethnographer being equipped to work in an additional discipline (history, economics, law, demography, psychology).
244. Although lone ethnography is practised in Eastern Europe and the U.S.S.R., the accent is there placed upon collective research.
245. It is of course possible that anthropologists would make use of archives in which their notes could be stored for a fixed period of years before being made available. A 'fifty-year rule' might answer.
246. Of course, some kinds of ethnographic data, lacking a confidential character, are often systematically stored and classified for general use. Cf. PROPP (ed.), *Metodičeskaja zapiska po arhivnomu hraneniju i sistemetizacii fol'klornyh mate-*

that they had used all their data in their published work? The future success of comparative study, regional ethnography, and ethnohistory (not by any means an exhaustive list) depends directly upon some solution to the problem of making field material more generally usable. But there are grounds for hope, not optimism. What a sadly perverse profession anthropology must appear to the historians, for they, avid for the remnants of the past, must watch with astonishment a body of scholars who systematically destroy their evidence.

Field work is an art and can be taught only up to a point. The talent for it does not always go with great intellectual qualities, and there is the risk that description and theorizing may be segregated in a manner more characteristic of earlier periods of the history of the discipline. But it is not likely to happen, for the reason implied in all that has been said on the subject of field work: it is too central to the image that anthropology creates of itself for itself, and all the chairborne activities, such as historiography and computer work, that keep the professional out of the field are counterbalanced by the quest for personal experience that raises anthropology from knowledge of the external world to insight into men-in-social-relationships.[247]

2. *Statistical methods in field work*

The increasing recourse to statistical methods in the gathering of field data is due, more obviously, to the need to draw samples from large entities (e.g., in urban studies), and, less obviously but more interestingly, to the desire to introduce exact measures into the examination of things hitherto quantified too vaguely. Demographic and economic examples may be taken.

There are clearly great difficulties in the way of demographic work in societies where, for example, age is not expressed in years or fertility cannot be established. Yet anthropologists have probably been more cautious than was necessary with the restricted demographic data they have been able to collect; and too few anthropologists have chosen to compute replacement rates in order to assess whether populations are increasing, declining, or remaining stable.[248] The most important advances in anthropological demogra-

rialov (= A Handbook of Methods for the Archiving and Cataloguing of Folklore Materials) (1964).

247. In addition to the works already cited, see: PANOFF & PANOFF, *L'ethnologue et son ombre* (1968); CASAGRANDE (ed.), *In the Company of Man: Twenty Portraits by Anthropologists* (1960); GOLDE (ed.), *Women in the Field: Anthropological Experiences* (1970); SPINDLER (ed.), *Being an Anthropologist. Fieldwork in Eleven Cultures* (1970); the various items in the series (SPINDLER & SPINDLER, eds.), 'Studies in anthropological method'; FREILICH (ed.), *Marginal Natives: Anthropologists at Work* (1970); CONKLIN, 'Ethnography' (1968); POWDERMAKER, 'Fieldwork' (1968); BERREMAN, 'Ethnography: Method and product' (1968; *Fältarbetet. Synpunkter på etno-folkloristik fältforskning* (= Field Work..Aspects of Ethno-Folkloristic Field Research) (1968); PENTIKÄINEN, 'Depth research' (in press – 1972).

248. Attempts to compute these rates are to be found in, for example, ARDENER,

phy seem to have come in the study of the domestic cycle [249] and in that of divorce. The latter provides an excellent example of the advance within anthropology from vague propositions to statistically complex formulae. The older ethnographers are not criticized for recording that divorce was 'rare' or 'frequent'; their successors are expected to make use of the different measures introduced by present-day anthropologists, and they may one day need to increase their statistical skills to the extent of being able to put to use Barnes's latest technique for analysing marriage durations by a life-table method.[250]

In the collection of economic data, techniques have been constantly refined. It was obvious that attempts would be made to estimate value and cost in the absence of media of exchange; anthropologists have resorted to measuring either time [251] or energy [252] expended in the pursuit of various economic activities. T. S. Epstein [253] has quite recently reviewed many of the procedures to be applied in the collection of economic data. Very briefly, they involve, for example, the careful definition of consumption units with the use of weights to allow for the differences in age and sex composition of households; the collection of income and expenditure budgets, ideally on a day-to-day basis; the collection of time budgets, the calculation of critical densities and the carrying capacities of land; and the measurement of field sizes and their yields. Sampling procedures have had to be devised for the recording and measurement of daily economic activities. Salisbury (*op. cit.*) chose a sample of twelve Siane men (New Guinea) and followed each for three different weeks in the year, measuring the time spent on each of their daily activities. A different kind of measurement is to be found in a study of the Tsembaga of New Guinea by Rappoport (*op. cit.*); concerned with the study of the interdependence of human and pig populations within one ecological system, he measured food intake and estimated the amounts of energy expended on various tasks.

It is nowadays by no means unusual for anthropologists to gather quantitative data in the field, but the sample survey, which in a sense typifies the application of statistics to the study of society, is resorted to in nearly all

---

Divorce and Fertility. An African Study (1962); BROWN & WINEFIELD, 'Some demographic measures applied to Chimbu census and field data' (1965); BOWERS, 'Permanent bachelorhood in the upper Kaugel Valley of Highland New Guinea' (1965); and HENIN, 'Marriage patterns and trends in the nomadic and settled populations of the Sudan' (1969).

249. See FORTES, 'Time and social structure. An Ashanti case study' (1970, first published 1949).

250. BARNES, 'The frequency of divorce' (1967). The question of demographic research in anthropology is surveyed by IZARD & IZARD, 'L'enquête ethno-démographique' (1968), although the references are now somewhat out-of-date.

251. SALISBURY, *From Stone to Steel: Economic Consequences of a Technological Change in New Guinea* (1962), p. 106. On time sampling see BROOKOVER & BLACK, 'Time sampling as a field technique' (1966).

252. RAPPOPORT, *Pigs for the Ancestors* (1967), p. 256.

253. EPSTEIN, T. S., 'The data of economics in anthropological analysis' (1967).

cases only by those anthropologists working in urban areas.[254] In general, such surveys have been limited to the gathering of basic demographic data and been used to furnish background for the intensive studies of sectors or facets of urban life pursued by more or less traditional methods of anthropological enquiry. But a few anthropological statistical surveys have been aimed at producing information for the study of particular problems. To limit the examples once more to those from Africa: Maclean surveyed attitudes towards modern and traditional modes of treating illness in Ibadan, Nigeria; [255] Dubb administered a questionnaire to about 1,000 members of an African separatist church in East London, South Africa, in order to test the reality of the division between 'Red' (i.e., traditional) and 'School' Xhosa; [256] and Hammond-Tooke collected cases of misfortune and death among the Xhosa to enable a statistical test to be made of hypothesized differences between rural and urban people in the interpretation of misfortune and its sources.[257]

But there remains among many anthropologists – especially from within the *social* anthropological tradition – an uneasiness about the use of survey techniques, and in particular an hostility towards attempts to measure attitudes or opinions; surveys are held to be all right in their place (subordinate) but treacherous once promoted. On the other hand, the American *cultural* anthropological style appears more receptive, its practitioners often administering schedules and questionnaires.[258] A particularly interesting case is to be found in Elder's work,[259] which shows how an attitude survey of a stratified* random sample of 200 people in a village in Uttar Pradesh (India) served to correct conclusions earlier reached from participant observation, and how, later, a nation-wide survey was mounted in India to investigate changes in 'traditional' attitudes.

Of course, it cannot be debated here how far statistical methods of enquiry in the field can or ought to be taken, but it may be worth pointing out two different reasons for supposing that from this point in time on there may be a slowing down in the progress of the use of those methods. The first is that they require for their successful application a thorough statistical

254. For some African examples see READER, *The Black Man's Portion. History, Demography, and Living Conditions in the Native Locations of East London, Cape Province* (1961); STENNING, *Documentary Survey of Crime in Kampala, Uganda* (1962); PAUW, *The Second Generation. A Study of the Family among Urbanized Bantu in East London* (1963); KAPFERER, *The Population of a Zambian Municipal Township* (1966); COHEN, A., *Custom and Politics in Urban Africa. A Study of Hausa Migrants in Yoruba Towns* (1969).

255. MACLEAN, 'Hospitals or healers? An attitude survey in Ibadan' (1966).

256. DUBB, 'Red and School. A quantitative approach' (1966).

257. HAMMOND-TOOKE, 'Urbanization and the interpretation of misfortune. A quantitative analysis' (1970).

258. See, e.g., MCGINN, HARBURG, & GINSBURG, 'Responses to interpersonal conflict by middle-class males in Guadalajara and Michigan' (1965); CHANCE, 'Acculturation, self-identification, and personality adjustment' (1965); GRAVES & ARSDALE, 'Values, expectations and relocation: the Navaho migrant to Denver' (1966); and RODGERS, 'Household atomism and change in the Out Island Bahamas' (1967).

259. ELDER, 'Caste and world view. The application of survey methods' (1968).

training on the part of the anthropologist; he seldom has it and rarely en-
sures it for his pupils. The second reason is that the very nature of anthropological enquiry, which seeks to contextualize that upon which it concentrates,
may act as a brake upon the use of a method that isolates and atomizes, although in carefully worked out studies of heterogeneous communities, a
statistical approach may itself be part of the process of contextualizing. That
statistical methods are important to the field anthropologist is not in ques-
ion; but they are unlikely to command his allegiance to the extent illustrated
by many of his colleagues in sociology and psychology.[260]

3. *Large-scale comparison*

Systematic comparison is part of almost every anthropologist's work at some
stage of his intellectual career. Most, however, confine themselves either to
the literature on the regions of the ethnographic world they know intensively
or to exercises in which they bring together what they know well with what
they cull from a wide selection of the published work. But to the compara-
tivist of a sterner sort these undertakings are not in fact systematic, and if he
casts about for a rigorous method he will soon find that it was invented long
ago in the history of the subject. From Tylor through Steinmetz, Nieboer,
and Hobhouse, Wheeler, and Ginsberg to the recent developments associated
with Murdock and those whom he has influenced there flows a tradition of
the statistical correlation of facts drawn from better or worse samples of
society and culture.[261] In our own day the tradition is embodied in the
Human Relations Area Files in New Haven, Conn.,[262] and the journal
Ethnology.[263]

260. See, e.g., MITCHELL, 'On quantification in social anthropology' (1967);
and SPECKMAN, 'Social surveys in non-western areas' (1967). Cf. the discussion in
GUILLAUMIN, 'Des modèles statistiques pour l'ethnologue' (1968); and see HONIG-
MANN, 'Sampling in ethnographic field work' (1970); BENNETT & THEISS, 'Survey
research in anthropological field work' (1970). For the application of statistical
methods in anthropological work on European life, see, e.g., SARMELA, *Perinneaineiston kvantitatiivisesta tutkimuksesta* (= On Quantitative Methods in Folk
Tradition Research) (1970). For some Russian references, see ANDREEV & GAVRILEC
(eds.), *Modelirovanie social'nyh processov* (= Modelling of Social Processes)
(1970) and references in that work.

261. An extremely useful compilation of leading contributions in the tradition
is to be found in MOORE, F. W. (ed.), *Readings in Cross-Cultural Methodology*
(1961). But not all the pieces in the book are in the tradition. See also FORD (ed.),
Cross-Cultural Approaches. Readings in Comparative Research (1967).

262. Where ethnographic data are sorted and classified on a massive scale.
Sets of the files (either full-size or on microfilm) are kept in 99 institutions, all of
them in the United States, except for 11 in Canada, 5 in Japan, 3 in Germany, and
one each in France, Netherlands, Denmark, Sweden, India, Korea, Nigeria, Australia, and New Zealand. See MOORE, F. W., 'The Human Relations Area Files'
(1970). For countries with poor libraries the Files provide a valuable source of
data.

263. *Ethnology* is edited by G. P. Murdock. See MURDOCK, *Social Structure*
(1949) and *Culture and Society* (1965), Pt. VI.

Because much may be (and has been) said in criticism of the method, it will be wise to begin by distinguishing between intrinsic and extrinsic difficulties. In the latter class falls above all the eminently practical problem of covering the relevant sources of the facts to be considered and of evaluating their relative quality as evidence. In principle, such difficulties are surmountable, even though one may tremble at the prospect of being responsible for the massive work of retrieval, translation, and evaluation.[264] (Computers might conceivably do the first, possibly the second, certainly not the third.) The methodological problems are of another order altogether, and in the view of many insurmountable, for, as they see the matter, the exercise can lead to no trustworthy conclusions. What is to be compared? How can one apply probability statistics to non-random samples? How can one leap from statistical to scientific inference? And even if in a simple exercise of correlation some statistically significant relationship is found between two things, how is one to push the analysis to a more satisfactory stage at which factors other than those considered so far can be brought into the analysis, for a great many things may intervene between the two variables? If one is in any sense a functionalist, one suspects that the number of variables involved in almost any problem is so enormous that the method must be abandoned, to give way to a more modest study in which the societies taken into account resemble one another very closely, their few differences then perhaps emerging as significantly interconnected.

Not all the criticism levelled against the tradition is despairing.[265] Some take the view that there are problems which, given the necessary sophistication of method, are susceptible of solution. Others see in the tradition only a dead-end, or at least one so beset by statistical difficulties that little is likely to emerge from it.[266] But it would be surprising if a method of comparative study so highly institutionalized were suddenly to collapse, and it is a fair guess that it will continue in the seventies to command a scholarly attention increasingly sharpened by statistical wisdom.[267] What most anthropologists

264. These tasks have, of course, been carried out by the Human Relations Area Files for many years.

265. See, for example, the essay (first published in 1952) by KÖBBEN, 'New ways of presenting an old idea: the statistical method in social anthropology' (1961). And see Ginsberg's reflections, fifty years later, in the reprint of HOBHOUSE, WHEELER, & GINSBERG, *The Material Culture and Social Institutions of the Simpler Peoples* (1965). Cf. KÖBBEN's later paper, 'Why exceptions? The logic of cross-cultural analysis' (1967) and NAROLL, 'What have we learned from cross-cultural surveys?' (1970).

266. A current critique on statistical grounds is to be found in DRIVER, 'Statistical refutation of comparative functional causal models' (1970). See also LEACH, 'The comparative method in anthropology' (1968); COHEN, Y. A., 'Macroethnology: large-scale comparative studies' (1968).

267. Cf. PELTO, *Anthropological Research* ... (1970), especially pp. 281-302; ROKKAN, 'Cross-cultural, cross-societal and cross-national research', in *Main Trends ...*, Part I: *Social Sciences* (1970), especially pp. 655 sqq., 667; and NAROLL & COHEN (eds.), *A Handbook of Method* ... (1970), Pts. V ('Comparative approaches', pp. 581-685), VI ('Problems of concept definition for comparative studies', pp. 689-886), and VII ('Special problems of comparative method', pp. 889-1007).

would probably join in condemning is not the philosophy behind the method but the exaggerated claims made for its power – especially when what it has achieved is held up as evidence of the scientific status of the discipline; that way lies scientism.

Comparativists in the Tylor-Murdock tradition may easily turn the tables on their critics by asserting that the latter are committed to doing in a haphazard fashion what they themselves are striving to put on a basis of formality and rigour. And that is a telling reply, for try as they will anthropologists can never evade the problems of establishing universal categories of facts and of bringing them into relationship with one another. They may imagine that they can dissolve misleading categories, such as 'ancestor worship' and 'chieftainship', or even the more basic ones of 'kinship' and 'property'; but they are then either forced back upon an alternative set of categories (which in turn are subject to the kind of criticism they themselves have used) or, having rejected all observers' categories in favour of those embedded in the cultures studied, they are marooned in a wilderness of incomparables. It is one thing to say that our conventional anthropological categories are too crude; it is another to abandon the notion of externally imposed categories. It is one thing to be alert to the need to see institutions and acts through the categories of the people who live in and through those institutions and acts; it is another to retreat into a barren cultural relativity. Some structuralists appear to believe that they can escape the evils of what they deem to be old-fashioned comparativism by plunging into the categories of the people they study to re-emerge into a purified world of transformable structures. But while they may succeed in destroying our faith in outworn typologies and fruitless induction, which is all to the good, they are still with their colleagues in handling the common coinage of the discipline.

Leach's attack on comparison and 'butterfly-collecting' in the first Malinowski Memorial Lecture (1959) and his advocacy of a sort of mathematical reasoning for the production of a different sort of functional analysis, assumes (how could it do otherwise?) that there is a common language of discourse in anthropology that makes the terms 'brothers', 'brothers-in-law', and 'social relations' intelligible to his audience: 'If you feel you must start with assumptions then let them be logical (that is mathematical) assumptions – such as that the social relation between brothers must of necessity be in some sense the opposite of the social relations between brothers-in-law'.[268] If a meta-Leach were now to argue with the same eloquence that 'social relations' was a silly prejudice in the minds of anthropologists he would be a Prince of Darkness not of Light. In fact, the strenuous sophistication of the structuralists is sometimes cruder than that of the more conventional comparativists, for we find in the writings of the former such under-analysed categories as 'feudalism' and 'myth'. Comparison involves a constant and determined effort to transcend its own limitations, but we can no more evade the basic logic of categorization than we can jump out of our own skins.

268. *Rethinking Anthropology* (1961), p. 27.

4. *Mathematics, computers, and formal analysis*

It might be imagined that the subject of mathematics would inevitably take us out of the 'field' into the study (if not into the computer laboratory) and lead us only from the particular to the general. That is not the case, and for a reason that an argument of this chapter may have already suggested: the whole enterprise to which anthropologists devote themselves forces them to switch back and forth between the abstractions of generalized models of human society or culture and the concrete particulars of real societies or cultures. On the one hand, anthropologists dominate the real world with their categories; on the other, they try to infiltrate the categories of a myriad divergent societies. When mathematics enters the scene it cannot do other than serve both anthropological passions.

The bibliography of work in the last five years or so on what may be termed mathematical anthropology is vast and cannot be printed here,[269] which is perhaps just as well, since by being listed in the absence of a long and thorough discussion, the work might seem more mathematical, more coherent, and more advanced than it really is.[270] To date the promise is more important than the achievement, however brilliant and enlightening individual contributions may have been. Indeed, one might go so far as to assert that a chief virtue of the present mathematical work is that it makes us look back upon our disciplinary past to realize that we have in some sense been doing mathematics all along: certain kinds of logical operation and attempts at quantification which now rush to the banner of mathematics have a long history in the subject.

It is difficult to think of a body of theory in anthropology that does not call for mathematical treatment, for any theory that conceives of society or culture as a system is committed to the notion of the interrelationship of parts, and all conceptions of cultural consensus and conformity on the one hand and of degrees of complexity on the other involve notions of measure and scalar arrangement. It is perhaps more obvious that anthropological work on exchange leads directly into mathematical realms, and everybody knows that marriage as exchange, for long hovering on the edge of explicit mathematization, took the plunge in 1949 – in André Weil's contribution, 'Sur l'étude algébrique de certains types de lois de mariage (Système Murn-

269. The full bibliography prepared for this sub-section is in Eugene A. HAMMEL, *Mathematics and Anthropology*, as yet unpublished. It needs to be noted that the bibliography and the discussion in this sub-section are concerned with mathematics in the broad sense of a style of thought and not in the narrow sense of a method composed of particular symbols and techniques. It follows that there is an overlap between this discussion and that of linguistics elsewhere in the chapter, pp. 87-90. For another recent survey of the subject see HOFFMANN, 'Mathematical anthropology' (1970), and for two collections which illustrate recent work see KAY (ed.), *Explorations in Mathematical Anthropology* (1971) and RICHARD & JAULIN (eds.), *Anthropologie et calcul* (1971).

270. Nonetheless, the bibliographical information given in this sub-section is fuller than elsewhere in the chapter, because readers probably need more guidance on this topic than on the others.

gin)', to Lévi-Strauss's *Les structures élémentaires de la parenté*. It is clear that some of the most inspiring theories of social behaviour rest upon notions of quantity, which need translation into the language of the mathematician – not so much by the mathematician, or by the anthropologist rethinking his data after they have been collected, as by the ethnographer mathematizing as he goes along in the field.

And in that connexion we ought to remember that by studying culture, anthropologists are usually supplied by the subjects of their study with the quantifiable and translatable entities they need for their mathematical operations. Informants *name* things and events, and so provide to the analyst the basic discrimination of items which will permit the use of the techniques of formal logic, the simpler operations of set theory, and the application of whatever aspects of Boolean algebra may go with them. And informants *classify* the objects of their universe, and so furnish the indispensable condition for the use of more complicated aspects of set theory, such as relations of inclusion and contrast. Ethnographic semantics (ethnoscience and its connected styles in American structuralism [271]) is based on these simple principles. In the third place, informants *evaluate* the objects in their universe, and in doing so they enable the analyst to move from the mathematics of nominally scaled to that of ordinally scaled items. He may then judge the consistency in and conditions of variation in evaluation by means of more powerful mathematical devices. Again, social behaviour takes place in time, and whether the anthropologist uses informants' concepts of time or imposes his own chronological measures, he can once more move on to powerful kinds of mathematical expression. Similarly with counting: particularly in systems of exchange, where things are exchanged in such a fashion as to permit statements of equivalence and allow the establishment of interval or even ratio scales, the mathematics appropriate to such scales can be readily employed.

Yet there are barriers to the diffusion of these mathematical techniques. There is an old and familiar assertion that the application to human data of rigorous techniques destroys their richness. In fact, it has to be recognized that while to describe events by using a mathematical system imposes a 'bias' upon them, the distortion does not differ in kind from that entailed in the use of other linguistic systems, for mathematics is only a special kind of language. Of course, we expect to be limited in the kinds of event to which we can apply mathematical methods, since mathematics is a form of discourse characterized by precision of definition, non-redundancy, rigorous syntax, and lack of entropy of information. A natural linguistic system, on the other hand, characterized by ambiguity, will minimize analytical precision and maximize the area to which it can be applied. All systems of classification, all lexicons, impose their bias. The important thing is to be aware of the different biases inherent in the different systems and not simply dismiss one of them out of hand.

Many of the larger issues of social and cultural theory are basically quanti-

271. See above, C.1 and D.5.

tative in nature but never reach mathematical expression for want of an anthropological sensitivity to mathematical relationships and of a capacity to devise operational procedures. We always face the problem of perceiving that a social relationship is quantitative and of choosing the kind of mathematics to apply in particular cases. Theoretically important problems are not solved by inappropriate mathematical techniques, nor are trivial problems made more important by the application to them of difficult mathematical techniques. In the use of new modes of analysis a sense of relevance and proportion is especially to be nursed. Certainly, one must adjust one's mathematics to one's theory and not expect a particular mode of mathematical analysis to answer for all aspects of one field of enquiry. For example, enough was said on the subject of kinship terminology in C.1 and D.5 above to make it plain that one kind of approach to its study is not going to suffice, and a rounded attack on the problem will need to include techniques that demonstrate the complementarity and essential unity of different analyses.[272]

Naturally, it may be objected to much work that it is narrow in range, but a start has to be made where a start may be made; and there is no point in dismissing humbler enterprises simply because they fail to tackle the grand problems of social or cultural theory. And one begins with the simplest appropriate mathematical techniques, for to lavish complicated methods upon simple enough problems or to use mathematics only in an exhortative but non-rigorous way, is not only a waste of effort but very bad propaganda.

Some of the resistance to mathematical methods springs from an exaggerated view that they cannot handle all ethnographic facts. Indeed they cannot, especially when they are used in respect of data which have not been collected for a mathematical purpose and by a means that takes mathematical considerations into account. Mathematization should start from the very beginning of an enterprise and not be brought in as a belated curer of the defects of unmathematically collected facts. The principle involved is the very same that, arising from the ethnographic methods established by, among others, Boas, Malinowski, and Mauss, insists on the purposeful gathering of data in the knowledge that their nature is shaped by the theoretical force that inspired their collection.

On the other hand, not all *post factum* applications of mathematical methods to inappropriately gathered data are unproductive. A mathematical model, informed by some persuasive and ultimately correct theory, may, by being applied to a body of data, produce results so far out of line with those data as to cast strong doubt on the ethnography – itself warped by the assumptions of the verbal model used in its collection. Moreover, a mathemati·

272. See HAMMEL, 'Further comments on componential analysis' (1964) and 'Anthropological explanations: style in discourse' (1968); NERLOVE & ROMNEY, 'Sibling terminology and cross-sex behavior' (1967); ROMNEY & D'ANDRADE, 'Cognitive aspects of English kin terms' (1964); BURLING, 'Cognition and componential analysis: God's truth or hocus-pocus?' (1964), 'Rejoinder' (1964), 'Burmese kinship terminology' (1965), and 'American kinship terms once more' (1970); D'ANDRADE, 'Procedures for predicting kinship terminologies from features of social organization' (1971); BOYD, 'Componential analysis and the substitution property' (1971).

cal model may produce results which are just not in the data at all. These results may be at a low factual level, as when a generative analysis of a kinship terminology predicts terms for types of kinsman omitted from the ethnography; and then the correctness of the analysis is checkable by further field work. Or at a higher level the results may point to the existence of structural features not hitherto detected.

From these preliminary remarks we may turn to what has been achieved. Several useful surveys and symposia have appeared in the last few years. The work on ethnographic semantics is reviewed in a number of publications.[273] Hymes's symposium volume [274] on the uses of the computer is still instructive, although in many ways it remains an unfulfilled prospectus. A number of works survey the various applications of mathematics;[275] so much have they been in the field of kinship that one book concentrating on it [276] leads us to almost all of them. In addition to some recent studies demonstrating the quantitative nature of social theory [277] and illustrating the dispute between 'science' and 'art',[278] there have been useful discussions of narrower compass on the rôle and character of formal and mathematical analysis in which the authors seem to agree at least that some degree of formality is appropriate.[279]

In the field of semantic structures a great deal of attention has of late been given to their formal properties in a way that often suggests useful devices

273. COLBY, 'Ethnographic semantics. A preliminary survey' (1966); HAMMEL (ed.), *Formal Semantic Analysis* (1965); STURTEVANT, 'Studies in ethnoscience' (1964).

274. HYMES (ed.), *The Use of Computers in Anthropology* (1965).

275. E.g., BUCHLER & SELBY, *Kinship and Social Organization* ... (1968); HOFFMANN, 'Mathematical anthropology' (1970); KAY (ed.), *Explorations in Mathematical Anthropology* (1971); *Calcul et formalisation dans les sciences de l'homme* (1968); and cf. REVZIN, *Modeli jazyka* (= Language Models) (1962); MOLOŠNAJA (ed.), *Strukturno-tipologičeskie issledovanija. Sbornik statej* (= Papers on Structural-Typological Investigations) (1962); DENISOV, *Principy modelirovanija jazyka* (= Principles of Language Modelling) (1965); APRESJAN, *Idei i metody sovremennoj strukturnoj lingvistiki* (= The Ideas and Methods of Contemporary Structural Linguistics) (1966); ŠTOFF, *Modelirovanie i filosofija* (= Models and Philosophy) (1966); GORSKIJ (ed.), *Gnoseologičeskie problemy formalizacii* (= Gnoseological Problems of Formalization) (1969); VOIGT, 'Modellálási kisérletek a folklorisztikában' (= Research on folklore models) (1969).

276. BUCHLER & SELBY, *Kinship* ... (1968).

277. See, e.g., LANE, 'Introduction' [to *Structuralism*] (1970).

278. BERREMAN, 'Anemic and emetic analysis in social anthropology' (1966); HAMMEL, 'Anthropological explanation ...' (1968); HAMMER, 'Some comments on formal analysis of grammatical and semantic systems' (1966); KAY, 'Some theoretical implications of ethnographic semantics' (1970).

279. BURLING, 'Cognition and componential analysis ...' (1964) and 'Rejoinder' (1964); HAMMEL, 'Further comments ...' (1964); HOFFMANN, 'Mathematical anthropology' (1970); HYMES, 'On Hammel on componential analysis' (1965) and 'Reply to Coult' (1966); COULT, 'On the justification of untested componential analyses' (1966); BARNES, 'Rethinking and rejoining: Leach, Fortes, and filiation' (1962); FRAKE, 'Further discussion of Burling' (1964); KORN & NEEDHAM, 'Permutation models and prescriptive systems. The Tarau case' (1970).

of quantification.[280] Particular note should be taken of the work [281] which touches on the problems of the modelling of semantic structures when they are only indirectly given in the testimony of informants. Of course, the greatest range of techniques has been lavished upon kinship terminology, the use of formal mathematical techniques being most apparent in the application of the theory of groups and matrices, from the early suggestions by Weil [282] to the most recent critique by Korn and Needham.[283]

The recent literature goes far beyond the narrow field of kinship. Mathematical techniques or styles of analysis have been used in the fields of economics,[284] law,[285] social ranking,[286] acculturation,[287] religion,[288] divination,[289] proxemics and interaction,[290] and sociolinguistics,[291] among others. Decision models and game theory have come to the fore,[292] although the appropriate formal mathematics has seldom been rigorously applied. The study of deci-

280. E.g., BERLIN, BREEDLOVE & RAVEN, 'Covert categories and folk taxonomies' (1968); CONKLIN, 'Ethnogenealogical method' (1964); KAY, 'Comment on Colby' (1966) and 'On the multiplicity of cross/parallel distinctions' (1967); TYLER, 'Parallel/cross. An evaluation of definitions' (1966).

281. BRIGHT & BRIGHT, 'Semantic structures in Northwestern California and the Sapir-Whorf hypothesis' (1965); BERLIN, BREEDLOVE & RAVEN, 'Covert categories . . .' (1968).

282. *Op. cit.* in LÉVI-STRAUSS, *Les structures élémentaires* . . . (1949). See also COURRÈGE, 'Un modèle mathématique des structures élémentaires de parenté' (1965), reprinted in RICHARD & JAULIN (eds.), *Anthropologie et calcul* (1971).

283. 'Permutation models and prescriptive systems . . .' (1970).

284. JOY, 'An economic homologue of Barth's presentation of economic spheres in Darfur' (1967); SALISBURY, 'Formal analysis in anthropological economics. The Rossel Island case' (1969); COOK, 'Price and output variability in a peasant-artisan stoneworking industry in Oaxaca, Mexico. An analytical essay in economic anthropology' (1970).

285. POSPISIL, 'A formal analysis of substantive law: Kapauku Papuan laws of land tenure' (1965).

286. FREED, 'An objective method for determining the collective caste hierarchy of an Indian village' (1963); HAMMEL, 'The ethnographer's dilemma: alternative models of occupational prestige in Belgrade' (1970).

287. GRAVES, 'Psychological acculturation in a tri-ethnic community' (1967).

288. DURBIN, 'The transformational model of linguistics and its implications for an ethnology of religion. A case study of Jainism' (1970).

289. JAULIN, *La géomancie. Analyse formelle* (1966; and, in a shorter version, as 'Analyse formelle de la géomancie', in RICHARD & JAULIN (eds.), *Anthropologie et calcul*, 1971).

290. CHAPPLE, 'Toward a mathematical model of interaction: some preliminary considerations' (1971); WATSON, O. M., & GRAVES, 'Quantitative research in proxemic behavior' (1966).

291. LABOV, 'Phonological correlations of social stratification' (1964); FISHMAN & HERASIMCHUK, 'The multiple prediction of phonological variables in a bilingual speech community' (1969).

292. E.g., BARTH, 'Segmentary opposition' (1959) and *Models of Social Organization* (1966); BUCHLER & NUTINI (eds.), *Game Theory in the Behavioral Sciences* (1969); KEESING, 'Statistical models and decision models of social structure. A Kwaio case' (1967); MAZUR, 'Game theory and Pathan segmentary opposition' (1967); MONBERG, 'Determinants of choice in adoption and fosterage on Bellona Island' (1970).

sions made by individuals has the advantage over other modes of social analysis that the observable units are numerous, and being so allow us the more easily to test against reality the predictions made from models.

Social process, which frequently consists of allocation and exchange, lends itself to mathematical treatment. Mathematical modelling is common in demography and genetics,[293] while especially instructive examples in other fields are those concerned with the problem of equilibrium or the continued working of social systems, as, for example, Fischer's work on the Natchez,[294] Hoffmann's on the use of Markov chains to analyse age-grade systems,[295] the work of Gilbert and Hammel, Leach, and Livingstone on prescriptive marriage systems [296] and Hammel's work on patterns of preferred ritual sponsorship.[297] The study of networks of relationships likewise cries out for mathematical treatment, but is less well developed. As in the case of the applications of game theory, those of graph theory are largely inspirational even when important, and at the present time much of the discussion is still about what aspects of graph theory can usefully be applied.[298]

Index formation and scaling have been popular in anthropology. Some recent attempts are exemplified in the measurement of simple rates such as those of divorce [299] and 'endogamy',[300] in the definition of the limits of social aggregates,[301] and in the comparison of scaled data.[302] As for the drawing of causal inferences, Blalock [303] has treated the matter of inferring causal con-

293. E.g., COALE, 'Appendix: Estimates of average size of household' (1959); FALLERS, 'The range of variation in actual family size. A critique of Marion Levy, Jr.'s argument' (1965); HAJNAL, 'Concepts of random mating and the frequency of consanguineous marriages' (1963).

294. FISCHER, 'Solutions for the Natchez paradox' (1964).

295. HOFFMANN, 'Formal versus informal estimates of cultural stability' (1965) and 'Markov chains in Ethiopia' (1971).

296. GILBERT & HAMMEL, 'Computer simulation and analysis of problems of kinship and social structure' (1966); LEACH, 'The structural implications of matrilateral cross-cousin marriage' (1961); LIVINGSTONE, 'The application of structural models to marriage systems in anthropology' (1969).

297. HAMMEL, *Alternative Social Structures and Ritual Relations in the Balkans* (1968), esp. pp. 56-65.

298. E.g., BARNES, 'Graph theory and social networks. A technical comment on connectedness and connectivity' (1969); BARNES, 'Networks and political process' (1969); HARRIES-JONES, ' "Home-boy" ties and political organization in a copper-belt township' (1969); KEMENY, SNELL & THOMPSON, *Introduction to Finite Mathematics* (2nd edn., 1966), Chap. 7; MAYER, 'The significance of quasi-groups in the study of complex societies' (1966); MITCHELL, 'The concept and use of social networks' (1969).

299. BARNES, 'The frequency of divorce' (1967).

300. ROMNEY, 'Measuring endogamy' (1971).

301. HACKENBERG, 'The parameters of an ethnic group: a method for studying the total tribe' (1967).

302. HAMMEL, *The Pink Yoyo. Occupational Mobility in Belgrade ca. 1915-1965* (1969); HAMMEL, 'The ethnographer's dilemma' (1970); KOZELKA & ROBERTS, 'A new approach to nonzero concordance' (1971); ROBERTS, STRAND & BURMEISTER, 'Preferential pattern analysis' (1971).

303. BLALOCK, 'Correlational analysis and causal inference' (1960) and *Causal Inferences in Nonexperimental Research* (1961).

nexions from correlational analyses, while connexions of an evolutionary kind are dealt with in several works.[304] Guttman scaling has also been used in the analysis of the propriety of social behaviour.[305]

But mathematics more popularly means computers, even though interest in them is not matched by the quantity of the work actually accomplished. There have been general discussions of their use,[306] and examples of the employment of the computer in processing data are to be found in the fields of genealogy,[307] social mobility,[308] museology,[309] networks of ritual relations,[310] cycles of household development,[311] cultural choices among alternative models,[312] and semantic analysis.[313] A particularly important experiment, in its implications for teaching as well as for research, is the current work by Elizabeth Colson and T. Scudder in online data retrieval. Using the information system REL (Rapidly Extensible Language System) and Tonga (Zambia) data, they have been able to recover data along various dimensions by putting questions to the system in a slightly standardized variety of *English*.[314]

Allowing the anthropologist to process volumes of data he could not possibly tackle by hand, the computer is at once a blessing and a curse. The analyst may easily underestimate the time and effort needed to prepare his data even for a standard program. More particularly, he should never underestimate the cost in time and money of making even the smallest changes to existing programs, let alone of developing new ones. And computers sometimes produce errors, either because of the wrong specification of inputs or because of the changes continually being made to most computer systems.

304. CARNEIRO, Ascertaining, testing and interpreting sequences of cultural development' (1968) and 'Scale analysis, evolutionary sequences, and the rating of cultures' (1970); GRAY, 'A measurement of creativity in Western civilization' (1966); NAROLL, 'A preliminary index of social development' (1956); BERLIN & KAY, *Basic Color Terms* (1969).
305. GOODENOUGH, 'Rethinking status and role: Toward a general model of cultural organization of social relationships' (1965); HAGE, 'A Guttman scale analysis of Tikopia speech taboos' (1969).
306. E.g., GARDIN, 'A typology of computer uses in anthropology' (1965); LAMB & ROMNEY, 'An anthropologist's introduction to the computer' (1965); CUISENIER, 'Le traitement des données ethnographiques'/'The processing of ethnographic data' (1971); MARANDA, 'L'ordinateur et l'analyse des mythes'/'The computer and the analysis of myth' (1971).
307. E.g., COULT & RANDOLPH, 'Computer methods for analyzing genealogical space' (1965); GILBERT, 'Computer methods in kinship studies' (1971).
308. HAMMEL, *The Pink Yoyo* ... (1969).
309. E.g., GUNDLACH, 'Zur maschinellen Erschliessung historischer Museumbestände' (1968).
310. HAMMEL, *Alternative Social Structures* (1968).
311. HAMMEL, 'The zadruga as process' (1973).
312. HAMMEL, 'The ethnographer's dilemma' (1970).
313. STEFFLRE, REICH & McCLAREN-STEFFLRE, 'Some eliciting and computational procedures for descriptive semantics' (1971).
314. No published information on this work is yet available. At the Frobenius Institute, Frankfurt, within the 'Atlas Africanus' project, data on African material culture are being put into a computer; this is intended to be the first step in a programme to computerize African materials.

Finally, the analyst must guard against the temptation to ask the computer to do too much. Its virtue lies in its capacity to reduce data to simpler terms; when it produces more output than it receives as input (as for example when in correlational tables it cross-tabulates every variable with every other variable), the tail is wagging the dog.

The most promising use of the computer is in the simulation of social processes, for, given an appropriate model, the computer can move through many cycles of a social process in microseconds to produce results that we could not possibly observe in real time. But in fact the number of simulations performed is small.[315] The difficulties are not merely technical but, more interestingly, anthropological. In constructing models of preferential marriage systems, for example, or in examining the effects of demographic fluctuations of social systems, the analyst must write reasonable rules of marriage, establish reasonable demographic rates, and, in short, provide the rules for the recruitment of members to groups and for their transfer among them. If he uses mechanical rules, the model is limited in its interest. If he uses probabilistic rules, he must decide on the statistical distributions from which he will draw, and their central tendencies, dispersion, and the like. In the end, one may find the model unrealistic [316] or that the same results could have been obtained by the use of pencil and paper.[317]

While much of the work in formal and mathematical thinking to date has done more to identify problems than to solve them, mathematical thinking is potentially of very great importance to the discipline of anthropology in helping it to state a theory without ambiguity, to maintain consistency in argument, and to revise or discard theories that are vague, inconsequential, or merely verbally exhilarating. When mathematical applications work, they will confirm in a conclusive way things about social behaviour that we know, and they will lead us to suspect things about social behaviour that we otherwise would not have imagined.[318]

315. KUNSTADTER, BUHLER, STEPHAN, & WESTOFF, 'Demographic variability and preferential marriage patterns' (1963); KUNSTADTER, 'Computer simulation of preferential marriage systems' (1965) and 'Applications of simulation techniques in social and cultural anthropology' (1968); GILBERT & HAMMEL, 'Computer simulation and analysis of problems of kinship and social structure' (1966).

316. KUNSTADTER *et al.*, 'Demographic variability . . .' (1963).

317. GILBERT & HAMMEL, 'Computer simulation' (1966).

318. For a general exposition of mathematics in relation to the social sciences, see BOUDON, 'Modèles et méthodes mathématiques'/'Mathematical models and methods', in *Main Trends . . . Part I: Social Sciences* (1970).

For some Russian references see GANCKAJA & DEBEC, 'O grafičeskom izobraženii resul'tatov statističeskogo obsledovanija mežnacional'nyh brakov' (= Graphic representation of the results of statistical research into mixed marriages) (1966); PERŠIC, 'O metodike sopostavlenija pokazatelej odnonacional'noj i smešanoj bračnosti' (= A method of comparing indices for uninational and mixed marriages) (1967); and SMIRNOVA, 'Nacional'no smešannye braki u narodov Karačaevo-Čerkesii' (= Mixed marriages among the Karachai Circassian peoples) (1967).

5. *Techniques for the study of complex societies and situations*

'In recent decades social anthropology has explored a wide range of topics: peasant society, community studies, small towns, urban society, national levels of socio-cultural integration, social fields and networks, the culture of poverty, etc.' [319] The characterization is based almost exclusively on the literature in English, but it is none the less true in its broad outlines of anthropology all over the world. Anthropologists have burst the bounds of a self-imposed restriction to the traditional and the small-scale.[320] And by doing so, they have in a sense reverted to an older disciplinary tradition, carried forward into modern times by Kroeber [321] and the evolutionists, in which all humanity is embraced within the sweep of a grand vision. But the tone of nearly all the newer work on the complex is different – it is minutely historical and ethnographic, venturing little into grand schemes of development and change. To that extent it is pedestrian, but the technical innovations and reshaping of methods of enquiry are in themselves interesting and perhaps of promise for the next phase of the discipline.

A number of the relevant developments in method have of course already been mentioned: in ethnohistory, in statistical procedures, in field research by teams, and so on. It remains for us to suggest some other important aspects of the recent study of the complex. They all follow from the radical change in scale, both in time and space, in the facts chosen for observation. The ethnographer ceases to create all his own evidence – he grubs in archives, employs assistants, relies on the findings of his colleagues in other disciplines. He can no longer be the relatively sedentary observer of life in the round – he must specialize, he must travel about, he must often make do with interpreters. But these are merely the surface phenomena of a shift in the underlying programme of the discipline, which is now taking on more than its experience in the past has equipped it for; and we are witnessing the first and clumsy stage of an exercise in re-tooling.

If we start from the older tradition represented by the work of Kroeber, we shall see that the problem involved in tackling large entities is seen primarily as one of conceiving the nature of civilization and the cultural order within it; methods of field study are not in the forefront.[322] But as soon as the question is raised of how precisely to establish the order among social entities interlocked within the frame of a nation-state, then conceptual problems are quickly translated into technical questions of field enquiry. How to

319. KUSHNER, 'The anthropology of complex societies' (1970), p. 80.

320. Of course, by their long and heavy concentration on society and culture within their frontiers, the ethnographers of the Socialist countries of Europe have accumulated great experience in the study of the complex and large-scale.

321. See, e.g., KROEBER, *An Anthropologist Looks at History* (1963).

322. A movement from the older to the more recent point of view is detectable in REDFIELD, *The Little Community. Viewpoints for the Study of a Human Whole* (1955), *Peasant Society and Culture. An Anthropological Approach to Civilization* (1956), and *Human Nature and the Study of Society. The Papers of Robert Redfield*, Vol. 1 (1962), especially pp. 364-391.

discover the links among local communities and between them and the political and economic centres upon which they depend? How to devise methods for studying the englobing social systems? How to provide a coherent account of specialized and differentiated lives and at the same time maintain a vision of the interdependence among all aspects of individual lives? The study of a factory, a voluntary association, a suburb, or a school may be conducted according to the older precepts of field work; but it is scarcely anthropological if it leaves us in ignorance of the relational, institutional, and ideological ties by which the people and groups studied are implicated in lives beyond the limits of the factory, the association, the suburb, or the school. And as these questions are posed, anthropologists shift the focus of their attention from groups to networks, from communities to associations, from highly institutionalized to informal relationships. The newer literature is characteristically full of discussions on networks and friendship. We are in a world of quasi-groups, action-sets, fields, factions, brokers, and patrons. When anthropology has got over its enthusiasm for these and similar novelties, it will be able to settle down to a more balanced treatment of the sorts of society whose complexity has long been understood by other scholars (sociologists and historians in the main). It is not that anthropology has nothing to contribute to the study of the complex − far from it; but its potential contribution may well be masked by the fumbling of some of its pioneers in urban anthropology, network analysis,[323] and the study of informal relationships. The practitioners of older styles of research are slow in being satisfied that an anthropology of the complex has raised the discipline as a whole to a new level of sophistication. One may well ask whether the delay is not due precisely to an element in the new work that the more conventional take for granted: lone ethnography, the one-man job. Teams for field work are formed, but time and again we come back to the solitary ethnographer, now fighting his way through a maze of intricate and dispersed relationships and through a fog of half-formed concepts for their analysis.[324]

Part of the difficulty in making a firm judgment on the success of the new methods lies in the fact that they seem to perform differently in two kinds of context. In the traditional fields of exotic anthropology they often appear indecisive and certainly inelegant by comparison with the work in 'tribal' settings. But when they are applied at home they often seem not only new but fresh, for they introduce into the literature on Europe, the Americas, Asia, and the Middle East a vision of social and cultural life that we are apt to associate more with imaginative writing than with the annals of the social

323. A social network is 'a specific set of linkages among a defined set of persons, with the additional property that the characteristics of these linkages as a whole may be used to interpret the social behaviour of the persons involved' − MITCHELL (ed.), *Social Networks* ... (1969), p. 2.
324. These and many other matters are surveyed in KUSHNER, 'The anthropology of complex societies' (1970). For examples of the technical work and argument in the field of the problems just discussed, see, e.g., BANTON (ed.), *The Social Anthropology of Complex Societies* (1966); and MITCHELL (ed.), *Social Networks* ... (1969).

sciences. Villages, parishes, towns, cities, factories, and hospitals begin to take on a quality of the life lived as they are seen through the professionally alienated eyes of the ethnographers and carefully chronicled. A new world is revealed within what was hitherto thought to be a world well known.[325] It may be a painful lesson for some anthropologists to learn that they may reach a wider intellectual audience more as a result of the practice of their traditional craft of field work than because of the sophisticated techniques by which they seek to improve upon it.

It is a very interesting question, and one which has important implications for the future of the subject, whether the drive to undertake the study of the complex is stronger among the anthropologists of the Third World and is likely to be among them, in the long run, more profitable.[326] There seem to be two underlying reasons why the 'new' anthropologists should be more eager than their colleagues elsewhere to embark upon this more difficult sort of study, and a powerful reason for their being successful in their attempt. In their own countries they are members of very small bodies of social scientists, and they are under a constant challenge to demonstrate, first, that as anthropologists they are not specialists in 'primitives', and, second, that they can make some contribution to nation-building or social and economic development. The smallness of their numbers urges them to diversify their skills; their delicate status encourages them to tackle large problems. So that, whether or not they remuster as sociologists (as many of them do) or cling to the label 'anthropologist', they tend to launch themselves with enthusiasm into the task of describing and analysing the complexities of their milieux.

And they are culturally equipped for the task. They have the language (or at least one of the relevant languages); in an old literate society they have easier access to its literature; they are at home. If they can exploit these advantages without sacrificing their ties with the large world of anthropological scholarship and without becoming intellectual prisoners of their own culture, then they are in a fair way to succeeding handsomely. It would be a piquant paradox to discover at a time when a successor to this chapter has to be written that in the intervening years the anthropologists of the Third World (but what will it then be called?) had become specialists in the complex, leaving the 'old' anthropologists to follow old-fashioned pursuits (and perhaps huddling in a corner into which they have been crowded by the sociologists).

The possibility is perhaps best illustrated from India, where, although the more classical kinds of anthropological research are still pursued, a great

325. To take an example from Eastern Europe, see the remarkable study: FÉL & HOFER, *Proper Peasants. Traditional Life in a Hungarian Village* (1969). A Russian example now accessible to the 'Western' reader is: BENET (ed. and trans.), *The Village of Viriatino* (1970), of which the Russian original was published in Moscow in 1958, edited by P. I. KUŠNER. The 'Western' reader may get some idea of the range of the Soviet studies of Russian life from DUNN & DUNN, *The Peasants of Central Russia. Case Studies in Cultural Anthropology* (1967). For an example from Western Europe, see CUTILEIRO, *A Portuguese Rural Society* (1971).

326. Cf. A above, pp. 15-16.

effort is being made to cope intellectually with the complexities of its civilization. True, the Indian anthropologists are still working at the lower organizational levels of their society (in the villages, small towns, and districts), but
they are attempting to use these 'small' cases to develop an understanding of,
for example, caste, kinship, and cult principles which can be used over a
much wider area of the society as it is and as it was in the past. And it is a
fact that what has been achieved along these lines has been infused into
work done by historians, archaeologists, sociologists, and political scientists.
In India, as in other countries, anthropological investigation serves to weld
together the study of the 'small case' with the study of its total cultural environment to demonstrate that the rural and the popular are intelligible transformations of the 'high civilization' from which, in older views, they were
thought to be much further removed. There of course remains a gap between
these small-scale studies and those mounted by scholars in other social
science disciplines, but it appears to be one which is narrowing.[327]

It would be wrong, on the other hand, to fail to allow for the possibility
that as the seventies mature there may develop a growing disenchantment
with the attempts to apply specifically anthropological methods to the study
of the complex. Already one can hear voices calling for the consolidation of
traditional success in the study of the small-scale and for a clearer division
of labour between anthropology and sociology. The argument runs that anthropologists have specialized and ought to continue to specialize in research
into the modes of life of people who communicate among themselves on a
basis of intimacy, dispensing with the channels and codes of impersonal
communication – 'micro-sociology' once more.

The general discussion has been confined to developments that make the
complex seem no less complex by its being studied. But it must not go un-
noticed that the opposite approach is still alive: the attempt to reduce complexity. Anthropologists still write in the tradition that, seizing upon cultures
and societies holistically (to use the jargon), strives to explain, characterize,
or reduce them by reference to a few principles or themes.[328] In this, anthropology links up with both a certain style of historiography and a kind of
psychology, for what is at stake is the quality of a civilization or the nature
of its people. The key to the individuality of a civilization or to the resemblance among some civilizations may be sought in particular institutions (for
example, kinship) or practices (say, child-rearing). The tradition appears to
have passed its peak, and certainly ought not to figure in an account of
current 'main trends',[329] but it is not in all its forms an intellectually vacuous

327. See, e.g., BÉTEILLE, *Caste, Class and Power* ... (1965) and *Castes, Old and
New* (1969); KOTHARI (ed.), *Caste in Indian Politics* (1970); SHAH, 'Basic Terms ...'
(1964); SRINIVAS, *Social Change* ... (1966), *Caste in Modern India, and Other
Essays* (1962), and 'The cohesive role of Sanskritisation' (1967); SHETH, *The Social
Framework* ... (1968); KARVE, *Hindu Society. An Interpretation* (1961).

328. I.e., in the tradition represented by, among others, BENEDICT, R., *Patterns
of culture* (1949, first published 1934).

329. But it is represented in one of the items in the series, already cited,
'Studies in anthropological method': HSU, *The Study of Literate Civilizations* (1969).

pursuit and could well re-emerge in the near future in a shape that commends itself widely just because the alternative modes of the analysis of the complex leave many anthropologists in general with a feeling of vagueness and indeterminacy. It seems to be an article of faith among structuralists that there is a multiplicity of structures in (or behind and below) any concrete social system; but a super-structuralism could develop in which the contrary was asserted and by means of which civilizations (or cultures or societies) could be shown to transform among themselves as total entities. If the thing happened it would provide a route back to that wholeness of vision and completeness of apprehension from which the present styles of research seem to lead away. Anthropologists are not easily and for long kept with their backs turned to the total.[330]

F.   NATIONAL AND REGIONAL DEVELOPMENTS

Within the straitened circumstances of time in which this chapter has been composed and of the space allotted to it, an attempt has been made to call upon evidence from all over the world. But it is obvious that the research done in some countries dominates the discussion and the bibliographical references. Where the anthropologists are numerous, well organized, and voluble, their voices are more clearly heard. It would therefore be a waste of precious space to undertake here to discuss developments in, say, the U.S.A., the U.S.S.R., Britain, and France. It seems more profitable to glance at the trends of research in those countries which, despite the splendid efforts made in the subject's only supra-national journal, *Current Anthropology*, fail to come fully into view. Alas, the attempt made in this section to redress the balance between the well-known and the neglected must itself be summary and ill-balanced . . .

We may begin with Japan, which, except for a few of its anthropological scholars, seems especially remote. It might be supposed that a language barrier was the chief problem, but on closer examination we can discover that in that country we have an example of how a lack of interest in the exotic hampers a national anthropology in the performance of its rôle in world scholarship. Changed political circumstances have reduced the Japanese interest in Korea, Manchuria, Mongolia, China (including Taiwan), and Micronesia, to the ethnography of which countries important contributions were once made. Since the Second World War a younger generation has begun to concern itself with other areas (South-East Asia, India, Africa, Latin America, and the Arctic region), but their number is tiny, and the greatest scholarly investment has been made in studies of Japan itself. When effort is

---

330. In addition to the works already cited, see ARENSBERG & KIMBALL, *Culture and Community* (1965); ERIXON (ed.), *The Possibilities of Charting Modern Life. A Symposium for Ethnological Research about Modern Times, held in Stockholm, March 1967* (1970).

concentrated on such matters as the ethnogenesis of the Japanese and the rural social organization of Japan, both past and present, then the world wrongly, but understandably, looks away. Indeed, it is part of the argument in favour of maintaining the exotic as an essential ingredient of anthropology that it helps to fashion *intellectual* ties between the student and the studied. But there is certainly a trend in Japan to reverse the process of involution; it needs to be successful in order that the riches of Japanese scholarship may be more widely appreciated.[331]

China in recent years has not been able, except in the archaeological and some folklore fields,[332] to display its anthropological scholarship to the world; its *social* anthropology, which had taken firm root before the Second World War, appears to have languished. In Taiwan, which stands apart from the remainder of China, the Japanese tradition of anthropological scholarship has been added to by Western influences, and research proceeds not only on the aboriginal peoples of the island but, increasingly in the last few years, on the Han (i.e., 'Chinese') people themselves, a trend reinforced by the productive research conducted by foreigners, Americans above all.[333] The politics of China's situation leaves the future of its anthropology in doubt.

When we turn to South and South-East Asia we find the most striking development to have taken place in India, a fact reflected in the allusions to that country already made in several parts of this chapter. What Indian anthropology above all suggests for the future of the subject outside Europe and North America is the possibility that a flourishing discipline may emerge and make its intellectual presence felt very widely, in which, first, a concentration on society and culture at home may be balanced by the maintenance of strong educational and academic ties with international scholarship, and second, a harmonization of anthropology with other disciplines (sociology, history, and so on) may lead to its greater local acceptance, by its contributions to national cultural styles and to the study of pressing national problems. On a smaller scale, what has happened in India is taking place also in Pakistan, Sri Lanka, Thailand, Malaysia, Indonesia, and the Philippines, in all of which, although against different historical and academic backgrounds,

331. To confine the bibliographical references to the bare minimum: ISHIDA, OKA, EGAMI, & YAWATA, *Nihon-minzoku no kigen* (= The Origin of the Japanese People) (1968); *Ethnology in Japan. A Historical Review* (1968); NAKANE, *Kinship . . .* (1967). An earlier survey is to be found in SOFUE, 'Anthropology in Japan. Historical review and current trends' (1962). The dominating interest in Japan itself brings with it the difficulty, known in other countries but here pronounced, of distinguishing between anthropology, folklore, linguistics, archaeology, history, history of religions, and sociology. Of course, in so far as anthropology is touched by ethology, the Japanese studies of primate behaviour are of great international importance.

332. A useful survey is to be found in YEN, 'Folklore research in Communist China' (1967), although it suffers by being written from outside and at a political distance.

333. See, e.g., *Bulletin of the Institute of Ethnology, Academia Sinica*, Nankang, Taipei, Taiwan; and *Bulletin of the Department of Archaeology and Anthropology*. National Taiwan University, Taipei.

small groups of anthropologists in touch with international anthropology, appear to be striving for a balance between national duty and international intellectual attainment.[334] If there is to develop a Third World style of anthropology, then it is in this region of the globe that we can expect to see it first emerge.

In South and South-East Asia, anthropology must, among both local and foreign scholars, confront the achievements and pretensions of oriental studies; these latter have their stimulating and inhibiting effects. But the inhibiting effects seem to be felt most keenly in the Near and Middle East, where on the one hand an earlier generation of foreign anthropologists were not sufficiently alive to the complexities and historical depth of local cultures and, on the other, the present generation of indigenous anthropologists have to fight hard to make their voices heard above those of the Islamists, historians, and others. In a way, a vicious circle operates: the anthropologists, being very few in number and physically incapable of producing great quantities of research of their own, are forced back in their teaching and writing upon the sources created by non-anthropologists, a fact which suggests their intellectual dependence upon 'higher' forms of scholarship. But in Lebanon, Morocco, Iran, and (if it truly belongs in this geographical region) Afghanistan, and to a lesser extent in Turkey and Tunisia, the struggle for a viable anthropology has begun. As it progresses it will almost certainly recapitulate some of the experience of anthropology in India. Because of its strong intellectual ties with the West and as a result of its high development of university education, Israel might have been guessed to have produced a flourishing anthropology. It has not done so under that name because the entrenchment of a powerful school of sociology has led to anthropological achievements being absorbed into that other discipline. That is not necessarily a loss to scholarship, but it may be thought to undermine the international presence of anthropology.

The case of Black Africa is of very special interest, for here were created some of the most astonishing feats of ethnography, on the basis of which a large part of anthropological theory has depended. And its crucial importance as a field of anthropological study has been underlined by the undiminished recourse to it by anthropologists from nearly every non-African country where that subject is well organized. The problem for the African anthropologists themselves is to turn their continent from an anthropologically passive to an active rôle. Their struggle is a moving one, for every effort by their small and scattered group is beset by difficulties, some of which stem from the very success of anthropology in their continent. If they are well trained enough to be anthropologists there is a strong demand for them as public servants and statesmen. (The former Prime Minister of Ghana, Dr. Busia, is a professional anthropologist. President Kenyatta of Kenya has an anthropological qualification.) Minute in number in relation to the scale

334. There can be no question of attempting here to survey the relevant literature. But cf. KOENTJARANINGRAT, 'Anthropology and non-Euro-American anthropologists. The situation in Indonesia' (1964).

of the social problems of their countries, they must turn their hand to many social science jobs (sometimes very practical ones which, as they see the matter, may distract them from fundamental research), and for that reason, as well as because 'anthropology' has often unfortunate connotations among their fellow citizens, they frequently appear in the records as sociologists. The strain upon them is so great and their numbers so small that it is too early to detect any version of an anthropology that might be recognized to be distinctively African. But that is a direction in which, while maintaining themselves within the world community of anthropologists, many of them seem to wish to move; and it is a trend which, if firmly established, is certain to be watched with great interest. Without wishing in any way to diminish their own presence in Africa, non-African anthropologists would view the flowering of an anthropology of Africa by Africans as a necessary complement to their own past work. And it hardly needs pointing out that a much desired African anthropology of the non-African world cannot begin until African anthropologists exist in great numbers.[335]

Before turning to Central and South America, we must mark the individuality of Canada where a flourishing anthropology can be too easily subsumed under the labels 'American', 'British', or (to borrow a splendid joke from Africa) 'Anglo-Saxophone'. For the influence of France is there felt, and not only in the French-speaking areas. Indeed, if American, British, and French styles of anthropology have any chance of being merged, Canada is the country where the feat will be most easily accomplished.

Latin America, like India, the U.S.A., the U.S.S.R., and a number of other areas, enjoys the circumstances in which the two main branches of anthropology, ethnology and home anthropology, or *Völkerkunde* and *Volkskunde,* can flourish together. In Latin America the main concern of all research institutes and university departments of anthropology (under whatever name) has always been to study the Indian populations and their rôle in national heritages. On the other hand, the horizon has expanded to embrace peasants and poor segments of both rural and urban areas. In the course of the latter movement, the line between anthropology and sociology has come to be blurred, especially perhaps in Peru. The heavy concentration on the Indians as a field of study has always provided Latin American scholars with the possibility of fastening upon the exotic without the need to travel outside their own borders, and it is an interesting fact that remarkably little work is done by the anthropologists of one Latin American country in the territory of another. That alone serves to remind us that generalizations about Central and South America are, even if they cannot be avoided, very misleading.

The greatest achievement of Latin American anthropology has lain in its amassing and historical treatment of bodies of data relating both to the Indians in their more or less aboriginal conditions and to the pluri-cultural origins of national (Mexican, Peruvian, Brazilian, etc.) entities. The more recent structural-functional studies, of both Indians and others, some of them

335. The situation in the Republic of South Africa, where anthropology – both liberal and otherwise – survives, calls for a special survey. It cannot be done here.

of a practical nature, have not much deflected the historical bent, and the trend of Latin American anthropology is still towards the production of material from which broader or narrower histories may be written. In fact, there is a sense in which the anthropology of Central and South America, taken as a whole, is the inverted image of that in India: in that latter country a *social* anthropology has widened its dimensions of space and time; Latin American anthropology, already highly conscious of the links between what it studies and its past (a past spread very widely in space), somewhat modifies its work in the direction of small-scale and synchronic studies. In neither India nor Latin America is anthropology merely about 'primitives'.

One group of English-speaking countries remains to be mentioned: Australia and New Zealand. They both have well established anthropological traditions and institutions. Australia today is one of the most successful homes of the subject, in both its ethnographic and theoretical work. Much of it has of course arisen from studies of the Aborigines, but, ethnographically, Australian anthropology has since the Second World War made great advances in the study of New Guinea, while within Australia itself it has provided one of the main inspirations and training grounds for sociological research. If we take note of the fact that anthropology is now being taught in the new universities in New Guinea and Fiji we may guess that, with the weight of Australian and New Zealand scholarship behind them, 'Oceanian' anthropologists may soon be appearing in some numbers (a few already exist); they will have to follow in the footsteps of their Asian and African colleagues when they confront the problem of honouring their obligations to both their countries and their discipline.

This ridiculously cursory review finishes up in Europe, where, apart from British, French, and German scholarship, and that of the Socialist countries,[336] very little has so far been said about its anthropology. Yet extremely important work has been done in a number of other countries, most strikingly in the Netherlands and Belgium, two countries whose former colonies were the inspiration for work now firmly lodged in the history of anthropology. The Dutch seem especially to have built upon their past (which contains some striking theoretical work, especially in the fields of kinship and ritual) and have continued to play a major rôle in anthropological research and innovation. Their field workers appear all over the world, their writings (happily) in many languages. In the Scandinavian countries the older styles of folklore anthropology are still lively, but in places more sociological styles have become established, to the point that they may be looked upon as major centres of newer forms of the discipline. Bergen springs to mind. Once again, we may note the presence of young anthropologists from these countries in

---

336. A useful series of articles appears in the collection 'Anthropology in East-Central and Southeast Europe' (1970), the full details of which will be found in the List of Works Cited, below. The articles cover Bulgarian, Czech, Slovakian, (East) German, Hungarian, Polish, Romanian, and Yugoslavian work. It should not for a moment be imagined that the work done in the Socialist countries falls into one pattern. Far from it; there is great variety.

many parts of the world. The folklore and historical traditions are similarly very much alive in Spain, Italy, and Portugal. The second and third of these countries (the third because until recently it retained substantial overseas territories) conduct some 'exotic' research. In all three, anthropology, by turning to the systematic study of communities and problems at home, merges with or at least takes up residence alongside sociology.[337]

There is a final trend to be noticed in European anthropology as a whole. Not only do anthropologists in Europe study their own societies, but they study one another's. And in recent years, especially in Britain, there has been a tendency to constitute parts of continental Europe as areas where an exotic anthropology may be continued in a different setting. The possibilities of such a trend are interesting, for they include the chance that the countries which send out their anthropologists may stimulate the growth of the subject where the field work is conducted – and they may retrace the steps taken in the more traditional fields by annoying the local intellectuals and their political allies. Even when the exotic is brought closer to home it keeps its profit and its perils.

G. EPILOGUE – REFLECTIONS ON THE CULTURE OF DIVERSITY

It might be supposed that there is an entelechy of surveys of this sort by which their conclusions are lodged in their beginning, and nobody would be wrong in guessing that some final thoughts had been foreseen from the start. But the fact is that the very process of compiling and contemplating the data which have been used has engendered some unexpected reflections, and what is said in this final section is not a mechanical product of a plan. The chapter has in effect turned into an example of the self-interrogation characteristic of the discipline.

What strikes us above all is the disparity between the achievement and the means for achieving it. There are few anthropologists in the world and the resources at their disposal are meagre. As to their numbers, we can be sure that they are small without being able to say precisely what they are – no international census can be accurately made, and in the figures that exist we have the greatest difficulty in isolating the scholars who, distinctively practising a subject dealt with in this chapter, are separate from people who are primarily physical anthropologists, linguists, archaeologists, and historians.

A directory of Anthropologists, in the widest possible sense of the term, is regularly published in *Current Anthropology,* the most recent appearing in Vol. 11, No. 3, June 1970. The analysis of its data is not yet available, but,

---

337. A conveniently compact reference to the co-existence of overseas and home research in one of these countries is DIAS, *Portuguese Contribution to Cultural Anthropology* (1964). Sketches (in some respects now out of date) of anthropology (*ethnologie*) in Britain, Australia and New Zealand, the U.S.A., Germany, Belgium, Netherlands, Italy, Portugal, South America, Japan, the U.S.S.R., and France will be found in POIRIER, 'Histoire de la pensée ethnologique' (1968), pp. 63-157. On Spain now see LISÓN TOLOSANA, *Antropología social en España* (1971).

writing on the basis of material collected in 1967, Tax produces a figure of 4,800. Among a sample of 2,368 'Associates in *Current Anthropology*', 1,848 give ethnology as a main interest, although many of them are also concerned with physical anthropology, archaeology, or linguistics. The 'areas of residence' of this latter number are as follows:

Europe	458
Southern Africa	31
India and South-East Asia	64
Northern Africa	23
North America	1,042
China, Japan, and Korea	82
Australia, New Guinea, and Pacific Islands	47
South and Central America	101

Now, if we were to double Tax's global figure to make it, say, 10,000 and assume on the basis of the sample of 'Associates' that some three-quarters of them are anthropologists in the relatively restricted sense used in this chapter, we shall arrive at a figure of 7,500, the great majority of them living in Europe and North America. With regard to his figure of 4,800 Tax writes: 'They are dense, in proportion to population, in all of Europe, in the whole of the English-speaking world, in Mexico, and in Japan. They are few in the remainder of Latin America and of Asia, and in Africa. The Soviet Union has proportionately fewer than the other Eastern European socialist countries.' [338] It is in fact highly improbable that there are as many as 7,500 fully trained and professionally engaged anthropologists in the world; the figure is more likely to be about 5,000; and we can see that, in relation to their intellectual responsibilities and their productivity, the 'profession' is very small indeed.

It can probably be said of only one national anthropology, the American, that it is well endowed, and it too is now suffering from some financial strain.[339] Elsewhere in the world, even in the economically developed coun-

---

338. TAX, *Anthropological Backgrounds of Adult Education* (1968), p. 5. The data earlier cited are from pp. 5-7. SMITH & FISCHER (eds.), *Anthropology* (1970), p. 102, cite 1968 figures for Associates of *Current Anthropology* as follows:

United States	1,287
Japan	150
Germany (East and West)	138
United Kingdom	99
Czechoslovakia	92
France	83
India	82
Canada	68
Hungary	53
Australia	50
Netherlands	50
Poland	49
U.S.S.R.	47
Others	627
Total	*2,875*

339. There are about 2,000 holders of doctorates in anthropology in the uni-

tries such as the U.S.S.R., Britain, and France, anthropology appears to be sustained more by the devotion of its practitioners than the patronage and support of universities, governments, and foundations. While the natural scientists are provided with their laboratories and equipment and furnished with the resources for their research, the anthropologists are required to put up with cramped quarters, rudimentary equipment, inadequate libraries, and, most damaging of all perhaps, a shortage of funds to finance field work, the central activity by which they live and create.[340]

Of course, to say that despite the struggle the discipline marks up its successes is to invite the reply that it is doing well enough, and might even, if it tried harder, do no worse with even fewer resources. One is always conscious of the perils of appealing to the mean-minded. But the argument is plain for the fair-minded to read: we have done so much, and could do much more if we were given the means to do it. Dare we hope that as the most international of all the social and human sciences – for we do not need conferences and visiting professorships to lure us abroad – we can make an appeal either to that very Unesco which conceived the idea of inviting us to survey ourselves, or to some non-governmental international body, for aid in the promotion of our international work? In *Current Anthropology* a brave effort has been made for some years to institutionalize a world anthropology, and a worldwide organization exists in the International Union of Anthropological and Ethnological Sciences; [341] but we are still very far from a state of affairs in which internationalism fosters the science of the international.

It is not that anthropology can produce peace or make cold wars still cooler. It can produce greater understanding, certainly; but mutual understanding has its perils, as every statesman knows. Anthropology is unlikely to be able to solve any great practical problems. And it is not to be imagined that every discovery made or conclusion drawn by anthropology will give comfort to holders of the received internationalist and meliorist ideas of the day – indeed, anthropology, or some branches of it, may at times be pessimistic about the possibilities of large-scale social and political organization or about the chances of eradicating this or that social ill. But it is in search of a truth about men which they can attain only on the condition that they search together. That is the essence of the case. In anthropology we study ourselves only by studying others. We begin from the fact of the relativity of cultures

---

versities, museums, and institutes of the U.S.A. Some 1,500 of the total membership of the American Anthropological Association of over 7,500 are Fellows. The *Guide to Departments of Anthropology* (1970) lists 217 American college/university departments of Anthropology (72 of them undergraduate only) as well as 47 museums with a major interest in Anthropology (see especially p. iii).

340. In Britain, and perhaps elsewhere too, there is paradoxically more research money than the established professionals can use: money is short to finance the universities in such a way to enable them to release their teachers for the lengthy periods that anthropologists need to be away. But perhaps that paradox will be resolved by the research money being reduced. It is a hard world.

341. Which calls important international congresses; these were until recently held every four years, but are now to be held every five years, the latest in 1973.

in order to arrive, via the culture of the relative, at their unity.

The pursuit of its kind of truth prevents anthropology from declining into academic parochialism, but it brings with it a correlative danger. To put the question brutally, is anthropology as it has been discussed in this chapter a subject at all? Is it not an area in which several subjects overlap? If that is the impression left on the reader it is the outcome of the effort to represent fairly as many aspects of anthropology as possible. If one were writing an account of, say, Soviet or British anthropology, one would certainly be able to produce an outline of a subject which could be seen to have both greater intellectual unity and more organizational coherence. On an international scale the subject is bound to seem vague, its frontiers ill-defined, its aims encyclopaedic, its intellectual efforts dispersed. Between archaeological and sociological interests, between ethology and ethnology, between linguistics and technology there are vast tracts of intellectual ground . . . All that is true, yet behind the heterogeneity there is a basic programme: the pursuit of 'totality' – not the study of everything pertaining to man, but the 'total' study of whatever it is that is chosen for investigation. If anthropology had con-fined itself to the small-scale and the non-literate it would have had a clearer profile, but at the cost of intellectual adventure. When the discipline is next surveyed on an international basis it will probably appear to be composed of different elements or of the same elements differently assembled; but it will still be a science of culture and society that refuses to stop short at narrowly drawn academic frontiers, and by that fact it will be known to be anthro-pology.[342]

It follows that nearly every page of this chapter must show anthropology reaching out to the disciplines which are its fellow citizens of the universities and institutes. In the social sciences as these are generally understood there is not a single one to which anthropology does not look for inspiration and to which it does not hope to contribute. We have touched on sociology, eco-nomics, political science, psychology, and linguistics. In a more leisurely ac-count we should have dealt in addition with, for example, demography, a subject indispensable in studies of such topics as urbanization and changing family structure. Anthropology is linked to the biological sciences through its congener physical anthropology; its relevance to medical science, agriculture, and human ecology hardly needs stressing. It speaks to every one of the humanities; there is not another chapter in this volume that does not overlap with this. True, anthropologists often narrow down their teaching to ensure that they impose a mental discipline upon their pupils; they institutionalize themselves to keep up their *esprit de corps*; but they do not believe that they live in an independent intellectual world. Not everyone who studies man is

---

342. The 'Epilogue', pp. 87-97, to WOLF, *Anthropology* (1964) sets out reflec-tions relevant to this Epilogue. And for a rather sad view of the present state of social anthropology and of its future (which may be used to balance the somewhat more optimistic view taken in this chapter) see NEEDHAM, 'The future of social anthropology: disintegration or metamorphosis?' (1970). For a French view cf. GUIART, *Clefs pour l'ethnologie* (1971), especially pp. 198-265.

an anthropologist, but anthropology listens to all who do. In comparison with the numbers who line up behind each of the authors of the other chapters in this book and its companion, anthropology musters but a small roll; an academic college of heralds could not award it a realistic length of lineage comparable to those of most of the sciences and arts among which it lives; but it has voice enough to speak with confidence. It is by its nature interdisciplinary within itself, and knows on what terms interdisciplinary co-operation is effective: an open but wary attitude to other constructions upon the same reality.

The boundary-making activity by which anthropology marks itself off from its neighbours might be known from its autohistoriography, but although university courses often include instruction in the history of the discipline, the published literature on the subject is surprisingly small. It ought to (and probably will) be increased, and for an additional reason. Not everything that was achieved in the past is fully represented in present work, nor is every important problem tackled by our predecessors of current concern. To read in the history of anthropology is to realize that much that was started remains to be completed and that much that is now neglected might well be revived.

From some points of view, anthropologists are not themselves the best writers of their own history, for they tend to be deeply committed to the present and inclined to see the past in the light of their current preoccupations; and even if they can transcend that limitation they are beset by a further disability: they are competent to deal with the history of the ideas and achievements of their subject, but they are not equipped to relate those ideas and achievements to the general flow of intellectual and institutional change within which they had their being. It is true that historians unlearned in anthropology suffer from the symmetrically opposite handicap, and the conclusion is quickly reached that a satisfactory history will be written only by scholars who are at once anthropologists and historians. Happily, a few such blessed chimeras exist. They are the first sign of an indispensable development whose flowering lies beyond our present horizon.[343]

343. For historical work written by scholars with the necessary equipment in both anthropology and history see, e.g., the book by STOCKING, *Race, Culture and Evolution. Essays in the History of Anthropology* (1968). The advantage enjoyed by the professional historian is also illustrated in BURROW, *Evolution and Society. A Study in Victorian Social Theory* (1966). Recent anthropological autohistoriography is to be found in: MERCIER, *Histoire de l'anthropologie* (1966); TOKAREV, *Istorija russkoj ètnografii, Dooktjabrskij period* (= A History of Russian Ethnography until 1917) (1966); MÜHLMANN, *Geschichte der Anthropologie* (1968); POIRIER, 'Histoire de la pensée ethnologique' (1968); HARRIS, *The Rise of Anthropological Theory* ... (1968); EGGAN, 'One hundred years of ethnology and social anthropology' (1968); LOUNSBURY, 'One hundred years of anthropological linguistics' (1968); PENNIMAN, *A Hundred Years of Anthropology* (3rd edn., 1965); SLOTKIN, *Readings in Early Anthropology* (1965). And see HODGEN, *Early Anthropology in the Sixteenth and Seventeenth Centuries* (1964); KARDINER & PREBLE, *They Studied Man* (1961). Some of the textbooks on anthropology include sections on the history of the subject; for a good example see LIENHARDT, *Social*

However anthropology defines itself in relation to the larger academic world, the discipline has serious problems of organization within its own ranks. Some of these problems can be seen to turn upon the relations among 'museum', 'academy', and 'field', the three chief places where the vocation of anthropology is lived out. It is a sign of the times that the museum features in this list, for (as anybody can see for himself by consulting a textbook of anthropology) it is often held far from the thoughts of the scholars who stand at the head of the discipline. The new generation of anthropologists, their sensibilities perhaps reshaped by their being the first human products of the age of television, are almost certain to be more powerfully attracted by what is to be seen, the concrete manifestations of life in museums and in film.[344]

There are two features of the total difference between the museum and the academy [345] which above all determine their mutual repulsion. The academy is devoted to training and teaching, whatever else it may do; the museum either does not teach at all or does it incidentally. The museum is the palace of the concrete, the academy a temple of the word. In nearly every sector of anthropological endeavour the museum and the academy put many of the same things on display and present them for study, yet treat them in fundamentally different ways.

In the museum the permanent creations of men tend to be placed in artificial isolation from their creators. They may be decontextualized, oversimplified, perversely classified, discoloured, and, in the eyes of the field anthropologist, disconsolately expatriate. The public museum exists to do many things – as G.-H. Rivière succinctly puts it, 'Rassembler, conserver, étudier, exposer, animer'; [346] but the anthropologist often suspects that what it does most is to reinforce in its gawping visitors their conviction of the utter quaintness, foreignness, and backwardness of the peoples whose works are on display.[347] The museum is intended to cultivate; it does it by deculturating, and

Anthropology (1964).

344. Is it significant that during *les événements* in France in the spring of 1968 the students included in their demands 'access to museum collections and introduction to their study'? See STURTEVANT, 'Does anthropology need museums?' (1969), p. 639. In what follows I shall be drawing heavily on that paper; indeed its wise reflections should inspire many more thoughts than can be expressed here. For a majestic survey of ethnographic museums around the world, see RIVIÈRE, G.-H., 'Musées et autres collections publiques d'ethnographie' (1968). Both papers have important bibliographies. On ethnographic films, a topic which for lack of space has not been dealt with in this chapter, see ROUCH, 'Le film ethnographique' (1968) and SORENSON, 'A research film program in the study of changing man' (1967).

345. A shorthand term for the universities, academies, and research institutions.

346. RIVIÈRE, G.-H., 'Musées ...' (1968), p. 488.

347. And it is not only anthropologists unconnected with museums who take this view. Cf. the remarks by Stephan de BORHEGYI (1969) quoted in STURTEVANT, 'Does anthropology need museums?' (1969), p. 644: 'Through exhibits, millions of people can be exposed to the inherent dangers of nationalism, ethnocentrism, and racial and religious prejudice. Yet museum exhibits in general ... instead of stirring the imagination of visitors, tend to perpetuate the visitors' stereotypes of "savages" and "quaint primitive" cultures.'

so defeats its purpose. That, of course, is an exaggeration, for many ethnographic museums try very hard to recreate the total settings to which their objects belong; but the view is just true enough to make the anthropologist more fervent in his efforts to restore things to their native contexts. And there is another sense in which the museum inevitably distorts: by definition it can preserve only the permanent, so that it cannot reproduce the full range of the concrete. Some material works are fleeting, but they are not the less important for being so.

But of course the anthropologist has lost by his distancing from the museum. If he does not collect for it, he has abandoned one responsibility to the culture he has studied. If he develops an antipathy or maintains an indifference towards the techniques for making things, he is not doing the whole job of describing and understanding what he has undertaken to treat. On his side, the museum man is not much given to the field, and when he goes there he is not likely to be equipped to study material things in the round. The gap between the academy and the museum and between the museum and the field was tolerable to anthropologists to the extent that they conceived their study narrowly. That latter is not now the case, or it is decreasingly so; and it is a fair bet that we shall more and more see a salutary intolerance towards the older attitudes to the difference between things seeable and things sayable. Doubtless, a rapprochement between museum and academy will have its own problems in train; every solution has its own inner conflicts and contradictions; but it is better to innovate and take the risks than to put up with what has come to be recognized as stale and unprofitable. But let us leave the museum.

On the relation between the academy and the field much has been said in the course of the chapter. Without the field the academy dies. Without the academy the field is abandoned to the dreadful amateurism that impoverishes, vulgarizes, and trivializes; the colour supplements in newspapers and the coffee-table literature are often a menace to cultural dignity. The effort that anthropologists put into keeping the cultural record straight is their justification, and yet it is that very effort which, if expanded into great schemes of public education, might in the end undermine the discipline. For the rôles of researching and university teaching are already very heavy, and if anthropologists must now expend their energies on ensuring that their subject is taught in the schools, infiltrated into every corner of the instruction of people with public responsibilities, and paraded on television, then the field will recede and research fade into the glory of a lost and golden past. It would be a senseless sort of suicide, motivated by the best of intentions. Let anthropology expand by all means; but let it not increase its burdens before it has the strength to carry them.

It is only by some such act of altruistic suicide that anthropology will come to an end, and that end is, happily, improbable, for the ideal of scholarship weighs heavily against imprudent application. But is is certain that the demands rightly made on the discipline to adjust itself to the changes in the extra-academic world will produce responses that alter, as they already have done, its practitioners' vision. It is in the nature of the subject that it is sensitive not only to the intellectual mutations among its fellow subjects, such that it moves its frontiers back and forth and changes its mind on a score of theoretical issues, but also to the fate of the human material of which it treats. At the humanitarian level it springs to the defence of the persecuted and the harried; at the level of intellectual effort it strives to interpret and analyse the vast transformations of the social and cultural life around it. There is nothing novel about either the impulse to do good or the drive to study change on the grand scale. Anthropology has some of its roots in the nineteenth-century 'protection of aborigines' and others in the old historical and archaeological effort to comprehend the sweep from man's first cultural origins to the industrial era. From time to time it may puff itself up in scientific pride, but its dominant mood is one of deep humility before the facts of human experience and of tenderness towards its sufferings. Men who study men are part and parcel of their own material. And if anthropology has formed a culture of variety, then it is to understand the variousness which rests on that oneness of humanity binding those who study to those who are studied. 'Don't cant in defence of savages', said Dr. Johnson. His exhortation would have been justified if he had known that there were in reality no savages to be sentimental about.

LIST OF WORKS CITED

ABRAMOVA, Z. A., *Izobraženija čeloveka v paleolitičeskom iskusstve Evrazii* (= The Image of Man in Eurasian Palaeolithic Art), Moscow-Leningrad, Nauka, 1966.

AGUIRRE BELTRÁN, Gonzalo, *Medicina y magia: el proceso de aculturación en la estructura colonial*, Mexico City, Instituto Nacional Indigenista, 1963.

ALEKSEEVA, O. B., *Ustnaja poèzija russkih rabočih, Dorevoljucionnyj period* (= Oral Poetry of Russian Workers, Pre-revolutionary Period), Leningrad, Nauka, 1971.

ALLIOT, Michel, 'L'acculturation juridique', in POIRIER (ed.), *Ethnologie générale, op. cit.* (1968), pp. 1180-1236.
[See also *sub* POIRIER (ed.), *Etudes de droit africain et malgache*.]

ANDREEV, E. P. & GAVRILEC, Ju. N. (eds.), *Modelirovanie socialnyh processov* (= The Modelling of Social Processes), Moscow, Nauka, 1970.

'Anthropologie et impérialisme', *Les Temps modernes* 27 (293-294), 1970-71, pp. 1061-1201.

'Anthropology and the problems of society', in SMITH, A. H., & FISCHER, J. L. (eds.), *Anthropology, op. cit.* (1970), pp. 78-93.

'Anthropology in East-Central and Southeast Europe', *East European Quarterly* (University of Colorado), 4 (3), 1970 (Foreword by MADAY; articles by BENET, Poland; DEGH, Hungary; HALPERN, Yugoslavia; LESER, Germany; PODOLÁK and SALZMANN, Czechoslovakia; STAHL, Romania; and TILNEY, Bulgaria; *q.v.* for details).

APRESJAN, Ju. D., *Idei i metody sovremennoj strukturnoj lingvistiki* (= The Ideas and Methods of Present-day Structural Linguistics), Moscow, Izdatel'stvo 'Prosveščenie', 1966.

ARDENER, Edwin, *Divorce and Fertility. An African Study*, Nigerian Institute of Social and Economic Research Study No. 3, London, Oxford University Press, 1962.

——, 'The new anthropology and its critics', *Man*, n.s., 6 (3), Sept. 1971, pp. 449-467.
ARDENER, Edwin (ed.), *Social Anthropology and Language*, A.S.A. Monographs No. 10, London, Tavistock Publications, 1971.
ARENSBERG, Conrad M. & KIMBALL, Solon T., *Culture and Community*, New York, Harcourt, Brace & World, 1965.
[See also POLANYI, ARENSBERG, & PEARSON.]
ARON, Raymond, *Marxismes imaginaires. D'une sainte famille à l'autre*, Paris, Gallimard, 1970.
ARTANOVSKIJ, S. N., 'The Marxist doctrine of social progress and the "cultural evolution" of Leslie White', *Soviet Anthropology and Archeology* 3 (3), Winter 1964-65, pp. 21-30 (translated from *Sovremennaja amerikanskaja ètnografija* (= Present-day American Ethnography), Moscow, 1963).
——, *Istoričeskoe edinstvo čelovečestva i vzaimnoe vlijanie kul'tur. Filosof.-metodol. analiz sovremennyh zarubežnyh koncepcij* (= The Historical Unity of Mankind and the Mutual Influences of Cultures. A Philosophical-Methodological Analysis of Contemporary Foreign Conceptions), Učenye Zapiski Leningradskogo Gosudarstvennogo Pedagogičeskogo Instituta im. Gercena, t. 355, Leningrad, Izd. 'Prosveščenie', 1967.
ARUTJUNOV, S. A., *Sovremennyj byt japoncev* (= Present-day Japanese Way of Life), Moscow, Nauka, 1969.
AVERKIEVA, Ju. P., 'L. G. Morgan i ètnografija SŠA v XX veke' (= L. H. Morgan and ethnography in the U.S.A. in the 20th century), *Voprosy istorii*, 1968, No. 7, pp. 53-66.
AZEVEDO, W. L. d', *The Artist Archetype in Gola Culture*, Desert Research Institute, Preprint No. 14, Reno, University of Nevada, 1966.
——, 'Mask makers and myth in Western Liberia', in FORGE (ed.), *Primitive Art and Society, op. cit.* (1973).

BAILEY, F. G., *Stratagems and Spoils. A Social Anthropology of Politics*, Oxford, Basil Blackwell, 1969 (French translation by Jean Copans, *Les règles du jeu politique. Etude anthropologique*, Paris, Presses Universitaires de France, 1971).
BAJALIEVA, T. B., *Doislamskie verovanija i ih perežitki u Kirgizov* (= Pre-Islamic Beliefs and Their Survivals among the Kirgiz), Leningrad, Nauka, 1969.
BALANDIER, Georges, *Afrique ambiguë*, Paris, Plon, 1957 (English translation by Helen Weaver, *Ambiguous Africa*, London, Chatto & Windus, 1966).
——, *Anthropologie politique*, Paris, Presses Universitaires de France, 1967 (English translation by A. M. Sheridan Smith, *Political Anthropology*, London, Allen Lane The Penguin Press, 1970).
——, *Sens et puissance. Les dynamiques sociales*, Paris, Presses Universitaires de France, 1971.
BANTON, Michael P. (ed.), *The Relevance of Models for Social Anthropology*, A.S.A. Monographs No. 1, London, Tavistock Publications, 1965.
——, *Political Systems and the Distribution of Power*, A.S.A. Monographs No. 2, London, Tavistock Publications, 1965.
——, *Anthropological Approaches to the Study of Religion*, A.S.A. Monographs No. 3, London, Tavistock Publications, 1966.
——, *The Social Anthropology of Complex Societies*, A.S.A. Monographs No. 4, London, Tavistock Publications, 1966.
BARBUT, M., 'Anthropologie et mathématiques', in *The Social Sciences. Problems and Orientations, op. cit.* (1968), pp. 5-14.
BARKUN, Michael, *Law without Sanctions. Order in Primitive Societies and the World Community*, New Haven (Conn.), Yale University Press, 1968.
BARNES, John A., 'Rethinking and rejoining: Leach, Fortes, and filiation', *Journal of the Polynesian Society* 71 (4), 1962, pp. 403-410.
——, 'The frequency of divorce', in EPSTEIN, A. L. (ed.), *The Craft of Social Anthropology, op. cit.* (1967), pp. 47-99.

140   *Maurice Freedman*

——, 'Graph theory and social networks. A technical comment on connections and connectivity', *Sociology* 3 (2), 1969, pp. 215-232.

——, 'Networks and political process', in MITCHELL (ed.), *Social Networks, op. cit.* (1969), pp. 51-76.

——, *Three Styles in the Study of Kinship*, London, Tavistock Publications, 1971.

BARNOUW, Victor, *Culture and Personality*, Homewood (Ill.), Dorsey Press, 1963.

BARTH, Fredrik, 'Segmentary opposition and the theory of games', *Journal of the Royal Anthropological Institute* 89 (1), 1959, pp. 5-21.

——, *Models of Social Organization*, Royal Anthropological Institute Occasional Papers No. 23, London, 1966.

BARTLETT, F. C. *et al.* (eds.), *The Study of Society. Methods and Problems*, London, Kegan Paul, Trench, Trubner, & Co., 1939.

BASANOV, V. G. (ed.), *Ustnaja poèzija rabočih Rossii* (= Oral Poetry of the Workers of Russia), Moscow-Leningrad, Nauka, 1965.

BASCOM, W. R., 'Folklore and anthropology', in DUNDES (ed.), *The Study of Folklore, op. cit.* (1965), pp. 25-33.

BASILOV, V. N., 'Nekotorye perežitki kul'ta predkov u Turkmen' (= Some survivals of ancestor worship among the Turkmens), *Sovetskaja ètnografija*, 1968, No. 5, pp. 53-64.

BASTIDE, Roger, 'La mythologie', in POIRIER (ed.), *Ethnologie générale, op. cit.* (1968), pp. 1037-1090.

——, 'Psychiatrie sociale et ethnologie', in POIRIER (ed.), *Ethnologie générale, op. cit.* (1968), pp. 1655-1679.

——, 'Psychologie et ethnologie', in POIRIER (ed.), *Ethnologie générale, op. cit.* (1968), pp. 1625-1654.

——, *Anthropologie appliquée*, Paris, Petite Bibliothèque Payot, 1971.

BATHGATE, Murray, 'Maori river and ocean-going craft in Southern New Zealand', *Journal of the Polynesian Society* 68 (3), 1959, pp. 334-377.

BEALS, Alan R., 'Food is to eat', *American Anthropologist* 66 (1), 1964, pp. 134-136.

BEATTIE, John, *Other Cultures. Aims, Methods and Achievements in Social Anthropology*, London, Cohen & West, 1964 (French translation by G. Rintzler-Neuburger, *Introduction à l'anthropologie sociale*, Paris, Payot, 1972).

BECKERATH, E. von (ed.), *Handwörterbuch der Sozialwissenschaften*, Stuttgart, G. Fischer, 1961.

BELSHAW, Cyril S., 'Theoretical problems in economic anthropology', in FREEDMAN (ed.), *Social Organization, . . ., op. cit.* (1967), pp. 25-42.

BELTRÁN, Gonzalo AGUIRRE: see AGUIRRE BELTRÁN, Gonzalo.

BENEDICT, Burton, 'The significance of applied anthropology for anthropological theory', *Man*, n.s., 2 (4), 1967, pp. 584-592.

BENEDICT, Ruth, *Patterns of Culture*, London, Routledge & Kegan Paul, 1949 (first published 1934) (French translation by Weill Raphaël, *Echantillons de civilisations*, Paris, Gallimard, 1949-50).

BENET, Sula, 'Ethnographic research in contemporary Poland', in 'Anthropology in East-Central and Southeast Europe', *op. cit.* (1970), pp. 308–318.

BENET, Sula (ed. and transl.), *The Village of Viriatino*, Anchor Books, Garden City (N.Y.), Doubleday & Co., 1970.

BENNETT, John W. & THEISS, Gustav, 'Survey research in anthropological field work', in NAROLL & COHEN, R. (eds.), *A Handbook of Method in Cultural Anthropology, op. cit.* (1970), pp. 316-337.

BENOIST, Jean, 'Du social au biologique. Etude de quelques interactions', *L'homme* 6 (1), 1966, pp. 5-26.

BERLIN, Brent, BREEDLOVE, Dennis E., & RAVEN, Peter H., 'Covert categories and folk taxonomies', *American Anthropologist* 70 (2), 1968, pp. 300-308.

—— & KAY, Paul, *Basic Color Terms*, Berkeley-Los Angeles, University of California Press, 1969.

BERNOVA, A. A., 'Sovremennye ètničeskie processy na Malyh Zondskih ostrovah'

(= Present-day ethnic trends in the Malay Archipelago), *Sovetskaja ètnografija*, No. 2, 1969, pp. 48-59.

BERREMAN, Gerald D., *Behind Many Masks*, Society for Applied Anthropology, Monographs No. 4, Ithaca (N.Y.), 1962.

——, 'Anemic and emetic analyses in social anthropology', *American Anthropologist* 68 (2), Pt. 1, 1966, pp. 346-354.

——, 'Ethnography. Method and product', in CLIFTON (ed.), *Introduction to Cultural Anthropology: . . ., op. cit.* (1968), pp. 336-373.

BÉTEILLE, André, *Caste, Class and Power. Changing Patterns of Stratification in a Tanjore Village*, Berkeley-Los Angeles, University of California Press, 1965.

——, *Castes, Old and New*, Bombay, Asia Publishing House, 1969.

BIAŁOSTOCKI, Jan, *Stil und Ikonographie. Studien zur Kunstwissenschaft*, Dresden, VEB Verlag der Kunst, 1966.

BIEBUYCK, D. P. (ed.), *Tradition and Creativity in Tribal Art*, Berkeley-Los Angeles, University of California Press, 1969.

BIGELOW, Robert, 'Relevance of ethology to human aggressiveness', in *Understanding Aggression, op. cit.* (1971), pp. 18-26 (parallel publication of French translation, 'Ethologie et agressivité humaine', in *Comprendre l'agressivité*, pp. 19-29).

BINFORD, Sally R. & BINFORD, Lewis R. (eds.), *New Perspectives in Archeology*, Chicago, Aldine, 1968.

BIRDWHISTELL, Ray L., 'The kinesic level in the investigation of the emotions', in KNAPP (ed.), *Expression of the Emotions in Man, op. cit.* (1963), pp. 123-139.

——, 'Kinesics', in SILLS (ed.), *International Encyclopedia of the Social Sciences, op. cit.* (1968), Vol. 8, pp. 379-385.

BLALOCK, Hubert M., Jr., 'Correlational analysis and causal inferences', *American Anthropologist* 62 (4), 1960, pp. 624-631.

——, *Causal Inferences in Nonexperimental Research*, Chapel Hill, University of North Carolina, 1961.

BOGATYREV, P. G., *The Functions of Folk Costume in Moravian Slovakia*, Approaches to Semiotics No. 5, The Hague-Paris, Mouton, 1971 (translated by Richard G. Crum; originally published as 'Funkcie kroja na Moravskom Slovensku', in *Spisy Národopisného odboru Matice slovenskej v Turčianskom Sv. Martine*, Sv. 1, 1937).

——, *Voprosy teorii narodnogo iskusstva* (= Theoretical Problems of Folk Art), Moscow, Izdatel'stvo Iskusstvo, 1971.

BOHANNAN, Paul (ed.), *Law and Warfare. Studies in the Anthropology of Conflict*, American Museum Sourcebooks in Anthropology, Garden City (N.Y.), Natural History Press, 1967.

—— & MIDDLETON, John (eds.), *Marriage, Family and Residence*, American Museum Sourcebooks in Anthropology, Garden City (N.Y.), Natural History Press, 1968.

BOSER-SARIVAXEVANIS, T. R., *Aperçus sur la teinture à l'indigo en Afrique occidentale*, Basel, Basler Museum für Völkerkunde, 1968.

BOUDON, Raymond, *A quoi sert la notion de structure?*, Paris, Gallimard, 1968 (English translation by Michalina Vaughan, *The Uses of Structuralism*, London, Heinemann, 1971).

——, 'Modèles et méthodes mathématiques', in *Tendances principales de la recherche dans les sciences sociales et humaines, Partie I: Sciences sociales, op. cit.* (1970), pp. 629-685 (parallel publication of English translation, 'Mathematical models and methods', in *Main Trends of Research in the Social and Human Sciences, Part I: Social Sciences, op. cit.* (1970), pp. 529-577).

BOWEN, Elenore Smith [= Laura BOHANNAN], *Return to Laughter*, London, Gollancz, 1954.

BOWERS, Nancy, 'Permanent bachelorhood in the upper Kaugel Valley of Highland New Guinea', *Oceania* 36 (1), 1965, pp. 27-37.

BOWRA, C. M., *Primitive Song*, London, Weidenfeld & Nicolson, 1962.
BOYD, John Paul, 'Componential analysis and the substitution property', in KAY (ed.), *Explorations in Mathematical Anthropology, op. cit.* (1971), pp. 50-59.
BRANDT, Richard B., *Hopi Ethics. A Theoretical Analysis*, Chicago, University of Chicago Press, 1954.
BREW, J. O. (ed.), *One Hundred Years of Anthropology*, Cambridge (Mass.), Harvard University Press, 1968.
BRIGHT, Jane O. & BRIGHT, William, 'Semantic structures in Northwestern California and the Sapir-Whorf hypothesis', in HAMMEL (ed.), *Formal Semantic Analysis, op. cit.* (1965), pp. 249-258.
BRIGHT, William, 'Language and music. Areas for cooperation', *Ethnomusicology* 7 (1), 1963, pp. 26-32.
BROKENSHA, D. & PEARSALL, M., *The Anthropology of Development in Sub-Saharan Africa*, Society for Applied Anthropology, Monograph No. 10, Ithaca (N.Y.), 1969.
BROMLEI, Iu. V. (= BROMLEJ, Ju. V.), 'Major trends in ethnographic research in the USSR', *Soviet Anthropology and Archeology* 8 (1), Summer 1969, pp. 3-42 (translated from *Voprosy istorii*, 1968, No. 1, pp. 37-56).
BROMLEJ, Ju. V. & ŠKARATAN, O. I., 'O sootnošenii istorii, ètnografii i sociologii' (= The interrelations of history, ethnography, and sociology), *Sovetskaja ètnografija*, 1969, No. 3, pp. 3-19.
BROOKOVER, Linda & BLACK, Kurt W., 'Time sampling as a field technique', *Human Organization* 25 (1), 1966, pp. 64-70.
BROWN, Paula & WINEFIELD, Gillian, 'Some demographic measures applied to Chimbu census and field data', *Oceania* 35 (3), 1965, pp. 175-190.
BRUNSCHWIG, Henry, 'Un faux problème: l'Ethno-histoire', *Annales – Economies, Sociétés, Civilisations*, 20th yr., No. 2, 1965, pp. 291-300.
BUCHLER, Ira R. & SELBY, Henry A., *A Formal Study of Myth*, Center for International Studies in Folklore and Oral History, Monograph Series No. 1, Austin (Tex.), University of Texas, 1968.
——, *Kinship and Social Organization. An Introduction to Theory and Method*, New York, Macmillan Co., 1968.
BUCHLER, Ira R. & NUTINI, H. G. (eds.), *Game Theory in the Behavioral Sciences*, Pittsburgh, University of Pittsburgh Press, 1969.
BULLOUGH, D. A., 'Early medieval social groupings. The terminology of kinship', *Past and Present*, No. 45, 1969, pp. 3-18.
BURGUIÈRE, André *et al.*, *Histoire et structure* = *Annales – Economies, Sociétés, Civilisations*, 26th yr., Nos. 3 & 4 (double issue), 1971, pp. i-vii, 533-888.
BURLING, Robbins, 'Cognition and componential analysis: God's truth or hocus-pocus?', *American Anthropologist* 66 (1), 1964, pp. 20-28.
——, 'Rejoinder', *American Anthropologist* 66 (1), 1964, pp. 120-122.
——, 'Burmese kinship terminology', in HAMMEL (ed.), *Formal Semantic Analysis, op. cit.* (1965), pp. 106-117.
——, 'American kinship terms once more', *Southwestern Journal of Anthropology* 26 (1), 1970, pp. 15-24.
BURRIDGE, Kenelm, *Tangu Traditions*, Oxford, Clarendon Press, 1969.
BURROW, J. W., *Evolution and Society. A Study in Victorian Social Theory*, Cambridge, Cambridge University Press, 1966.

Calcul et formalisation dans les sciences de l'homme (collection of essays), Paris, Editions du Centre National de la Recherche Scientifique, 1968.
CALLAN, Hilary, *Ethology and Society. Towards an Anthropological View*, Oxford Monographs on Social Anthropology, Oxford, Clarendon Press, 1970.
CARNEIRO, Robert L., 'Ascertaining, testing and interpreting sequences of cultural development', *Southwestern Journal of Anthropology* 24 (4), 1968, pp. 354-374.
——, 'Scale analysis, evolutionary sequences, and the rating of cultures', in NAROLL

& COHEN, R. (eds.), *A Handbook of Method in Cultural Anthropology, op. cit.* (1970), pp. 834-871.

CARTER, Gwendolen M. & PADEN, Ann (eds.), *Expanding Horizons in African Studies*, Evanston (Ill.), Northwestern University Press, 1969.

CASAGRANDE, Joseph B. (ed.), *In the Company of Man: Twenty Portraits by Anthropologists*, New York, Harper & Bros., 1960.

CEBOKSAROV, N. N., 'Ètničeskie processy v stranah Južnoj i Jugo-Vostočnoj Azii' (= Ethnic processes in the countries of South and South-East Asia), *Sovetskaja ètnografija*, 1966, No. 2, pp. 50-58.

——, 'Problemy tipologii ètničeskih obščnostej v trudah sovetskih učenyh' (= Problems of the typology of ethnic units in the works of Soviet scholars), *Sovetskaja ètnografija*, 1967, No. 4, pp. 94-109.
[See also PERŠIC & ČEBOKSAROV.]

CHADWICK, Hector Munro & CHADWICK, Nora K., *The Growth of Literature*, Cambridge, Cambridge University Press, 1932-40, 3 vols.

CHADWICK, Nora K. & ZHIRMUNSKY (= ŽIRMUNSKIJ), Victor M., *Oral Epics of Central Asia*, Cambridge, Cambridge University Press, 1969.

CHANCE, Michael & JOLLY, Clifford, *Social Groups of Monkeys, Apes and Men*, London, Cape, 1970.

CHANCE, Norman A., 'Acculturation, self-identification, and personality adjustment', *American Anthropologist* 67 (2), 1965, pp. 372-393.

CHAPPLE, Elliot D., 'Toward a mathematical model of interaction: some preliminary considerations', in KAY (ed.), *Explorations in Mathematical Anthropology, op. cit.* (1971), pp. 141-178.

ČISTOV, K. V., *K voprosu o principah klassifikacii žanrov ustnoj narodnoj prozy* (= On the Classificatory Principles of Varieties of Oral Popular Prose), Moscow, Nauka, 1964.

—— & TUTILOV, B. N. (eds.), *Fol'klor i ètnografija* (= Folklore and Ethnography), Leningrad, Nauka, 1970.

'Classiques africains', series, Paris, Julliard.

CLIFTON, James A. (ed.), *Introduction to Cultural Anthropology. Essays in the Scope and Method of the Science of Man*, Boston, Houghton Mifflin Co., 1968.

COALE, Ansley J., 'Appendix: Estimates of average size of household', in COALE, FALLERS, LEVY, SCHNEIDER, and TOMKINS, *Aspects of the Analysis of Family Structure, op. cit.* (1965), pp. 64-69.

——, FALLERS, Lloyd, LEVY, Marion J., Jr., SCHNEIDER, David M., and TOMKINS, S. S., *Aspects of the Analysis of Family Structure*, Princeton, Princeton University Press, 1965.

COHEN, Abner, *Custom and Politics in Urban Africa. A Study of Hausa Migrants in Yoruba Towns*, London, Routledge & Kegan Paul, 1969.

COHEN, Ronald, 'The political system', in NAROLL & COHEN, R. (eds.), *A Handbook of Method in Cultural Anthropology, op. cit.* (1970), pp. 484-499.

COHEN, RONALD & MIDDLETON, John (eds.), *Comparative Political Systems. Studies in the Politics of Pre-Industrial Societies*, American Museum Sourcebooks in Anthropology, Garden City (N.Y.), Natural History Press, 1967.
[See also NAROLL & COHEN, R. (eds.).]

COHEN, Yehudi A., 'Macroethnology: large-scale comparative studies', in CLIFTON (ed.), *Introduction to Cultural Anthropology: . . ., op. cit.* (1968), pp. 402-449.

COHN, Bernard S., 'Ethnohistory', in SILLS (ed.), *International Encyclopedia of the Social Sciences, op. cit.* (1968), Vol. 6, pp. 440-448.

——, 'History and political science', in VON MERING & KASDAN (eds.), *Anthropology and the Behavioral and Health Sciences, op. cit.* (1970), pp. 89-103 (followed by a 'Commentary' by Lloyd Fallers, Richard L. Park, and Sylvia Thrupp, pp. 103-110, and by a list of references, pp. 110-111).
[See also SINGER & COHN (eds.).]

COLBY, Benjamin N., 'Ethnographic semantics. A preliminary survey', *Current Anthropology* 7 (1), 1966, pp. 3-32.

COLSON, Elizabeth, 'The field', *sub* 'Political anthropology', in SILLS (ed.), *International Encyclopedia of the Social Sciences, op. cit.* (1968), Vol. 12, pp. 189-193.

CONDOMINAS, Georges, *L'exotique est quotidien: Sar Luk, Viet-nam*, Paris, Plon, 1965.

CONKLIN, Harold C., 'The study of shifting agriculture', *Current Anthropology* 2 (1), 1961, pp. 27-61.

——, 'Ethnography', in SILLS (ed.), *International Encyclopedia of the Social Sciences, Anthropology, . . ., op. cit.* (1964), pp. 25-55.

——, 'Ethnography' in SILLS (ed.), *International Encyclopedia of the Social Sciences, op. cit.* (1963), Vol. 5, pp. 172-178.

COOK, S., 'Price and output variability in a peasant-artisan stoneworking industry in Oaxaca, Mexico. An analytical essay in economic anthropology', *American Anthropologist* 72 (4), 1970, pp. 776-801.

COULT, Allan D., 'On the justification of untested componential analyses', *American Anthropologist* 68 (4), 1966, p. 1015.

—— & RANDOLPH, Richard R., 'Computer methods for analyzing genealogical space', *American Anthropologist* 67 (1), 1965, pp. 21-29.

COURRÈGE, Philippe, 'Un modèle mathématique des structures élémentaires de parenté', *L'homme* 5 (3-4), 1965, pp. 248-290; reprinted in RICHARD & JAULIN (eds.), *Anthropologie et calcul, op. cit.* (1971), pp. 126-181.

CROOK, John, 'Social organization and the environment. Aspects of contemporary social ethology', *Animal Behaviour*, Vol. 18, 1970, pp. 197-209.

CUISENIER, Jean, 'Pour une anthropologie sociale de la France contemporaine', *Atomes*, No. 263, Mar. 1969, pp. 140-150.

——, 'Le traitement des données ethnographiques', in *L'informatique, la documentation et les sciences sociales, op. cit.* (1971), pp. 189-203 (parallel publication in English translation, 'The processing of ethnographic data', in *Use of Computers, Documentation, and the Social Sciences, op. cit.* (1971), pp. 175-188).

—— et al., 'La pensée sauvage et le structuralisme', *Esprit* (Paris), n.s., 31st yr., No. 322, 1963, pp. 545-653.

CUISENIER, Jean, SEGALEN, Martine & VIRVILLE, Michel ,de, 'Pour l'étude de la parenté dans les sociétés européennes: le programme d'ordinateur ARCHIV', *L'Homme* 10 (3), 1970, pp. 27-74.

CUTILEIRO, José, *A Portuguese Rural Society*, Oxford Monographs on Social Anthropology, Oxford, Clarendon Press, 1971.

DALTON, George, 'Theoretical issues in economic anthropology', *Current Anthropology* 10 (1), 1969, pp. 63-102.

——, 'The economic system', in NAROLL & COHEN, R. (eds.), *A Handbook of Method in Cultural Anthropology, op. cit.* (1970), pp. 454-483.

DALTON, George (ed.), *Economic Development and Social Change*, American Museum Sourcebooks in Anthropology, Garden City (N.Y.), Natural History Press, 1971.

DAMAS, David (ed.), *Contributions to Anthropology. Band Societies* (Proceedings of a conference on band organization, Ottawa 1965), National Museum of Canada Bulletin No. 228, Anthropological Series No. 84, Ottawa, 1969.

D'ANDRADE, Roy Goodwin, 'Sex differences and cultural institutions', in MACCOBY (ed.), *The Development of Sex Differences, op. cit.* (1967), pp. 173-203.

——, 'Procedures for predicting kinship terminologies from features of social organization', in KAY (ed.), *Explorations in Mathematical Anthropology, op. cit.* (1971), pp. 60-76.
[See also NAROLL & D'ANDRADE; ROMNEY & D'ANDRADE; ROMNEY & D'ANDRADE (eds.).]

DAVYDOV, A. S., 'Tradicionnoe žilišče Tadžikov Verhnego Zeravšana' (= Traditional dwelling houses of the Tadzhiks of Upper Zeravshan), *Sovetskaja ètnografija*, 1969, No. 6, pp. 92-101.

d'AZEVEDO, W. L.: see AZEVEDO, W. L. d'.

DEETZ, James, *Invitation to Archeology*, American Museum Science Books, Garden City (N.Y.), Natural History Press, 1967.

DEGH, Linda, 'Ethnology in Hungary', in 'Anthropology in East-Central and Southeast Europe', *op. cit.* (1970), pp. 293-307.

DE IPOLA, Emilio, 'Ethnologie et histoire', *Cahiers internationaux de sociologie*, Vol. 48, Jan.-June 1970, pp. 37-56.

DE JOSSELIN DE JONG, P. E.: see JOSSELIN DE JONG, P. E. DE.

DENISOV, P. N., *Principy modelirovanija jazyka* (= Principles of Language Modelling), Moscow, Izdatel'stvo Moskovskogo Universiteta, 1965.

DESCHAMPS, Hubert, 'L'ethno-histoire', in POIRIER (ed.), *Ethnologie générale, op. cit.* (1968), pp. 1433-1444.

DEVEREUX, George, *Mohave Ethnopsychiatry and Suicide: The Psychiatric Knowledge and the Psychic Disturbances of an Indian Tribe* = Bureau of American Ethnology Bulletin No. 175, Washington (D.C.), 1961.

——, *From Anxiety to Method in the Behavioral Sciences*, Studies in the Behavioral Sciences No. 3, The Hague-Paris, Mouton. 1967.

——, *Essais d 'ethnopsychiatrie générale*, Paris, Gallimard, 1970.

DEVORE, Irven, 'Primate behavior', *sub* 'Social behavior, animal'', in SILLS (ed.), *International Encyclopedia of the Social Sciences, op. cit.* (1968), Vol. 14, pp. 351-360.
[See also LEE & DEVORE (eds.).]

DIAS, A. Jorge, *Portuguese Contribution to Cultural Anthropology*, Johannesburg, Witwatersrand University Press, 1964.

DOMENACH, Jean-Marie *et al.*, 'Structuralismes: idéologie et méthode', *Esprit* (Paris), n.s., 35th yr., No. 360, 1967, pp. 771-901.

DOUGLAS, Mary, *Purity and Danger. An Analysis of Concepts of Pollution and Taboo*, London, Routledge and Kegan Paul, 1966 (French translation by S. Guérin, *De la souillure. Essais sur les notions de pollution et de tabou*, Paris, Maspero, 1971).

——, 'Is matriliny doomed in Africa?', in DOUGLAS & KABERRY (eds.), *Man in Africa, op. cit.* (1969), pp. 121-136.

——, *Natural Symbols. Explorations in Cosmology*, London, Barrie & Rockliff, The Cresset Press, 1970.

DOUGLAS, Mary (ed.), *Witchcraft Confessions and Accusations*, A.S.A. Monographs No. 9, London, Tavistock Publications, 1970.

——, & KABERRY, Phyllis M. (eds.), *Man in Africa*, London, Tavistock Publications, 1969.

DRIVER, Harold E., 'Ethnology', in SILLS (ed.), *International Encyclopedia of the Social Sciences, op. cit.* (1968), Vol. 5, pp. 178-186.

——, 'Statistical refutation of comparative functional causal models', *Southwestern Journal of Anthropology* 26 (1), 1970, pp. 25-31.

—— & CHANEY, Richard P., 'Cross-cultural sampling and Galton's problem', in NAROLL & COHEN, R. (eds.), *A Handbook of Methods in Cultural Anthropology, op. cit.* (1970), pp. 990-1003.

DUBB, A. A., 'Red and School. A quantitative approach', *Africa* 36 (3), 1966, pp. 292-302.

DUMONT, Louis, *Introduction à deux théories d'anthropologie sociale. Groupes de filiation et alliance de mariage*, Ecole Pratique des Hautes Etudes, Sorbonne, VIe Section, Les textes sociologiques, Paris-The Hague, Mouton, 1971.

DUNDES, Alan, 'Oral literature', in CLIFTON (ed.), *Introduction to Cultural Anthropology: . . ., op. cit.* (1968), pp. 116-129.

DUNDES, Alan (ed.), *The Study of Folklore*, Englewood Cliffs (N.J.), Prentice-Hall, 1965.

DUNN, Stephen P. & DUNN, Ethel, *The Peasants of Central Russia. Case Studies in Cultural Anthropology*, New York, Holt, Rinehart & Winston, 1967.

DURBIN, Mrdula, 'The transformational model of linguistics and its implications for an ethnology of religion. A case study of Jainism', *American Anthropologist* 72 (2), 1970, pp. 334-342

EASTON, David, 'Political anthropology', in SIEGEL (ed.), *Biennial Review of Anthropology 1959, op. cit.* (1959), pp. 210-262.

EDEL, May and EDEL, Abraham, *Anthropology and Ethics. The Quest for Moral Understanding*, rev. edn., Cleveland (Ohio), Press of Case Western Reserve University, 1968.

EGGAN, Fred, 'Cultural drift and social change', *Current Anthropology* 4 (4), 1963, pp. 347-355.

——, *The American Indian. Perspectives for the Study of Social Change*, Chicago, Aldine, 1966.

——, 'Introduction', *sub* 'Kiṇship', in SILLS (ed.), *International Encyclopedia of the Social Sciences, op. cit.* (1968), Vol. 8, pp. 390-401.

——, 'One hundred years of ethnology and social anthropology', in BREW (ed.), *One Hundred Years of Anthropology, op. cit;* (1968), pp. 119-152.

EGGAN, Fred (ed.), *Social Anthropology of North American Tribes*, enl. edn., Chicago, University of Chicago Press, 1955. [See also GLUCKMAN & EGGAN.]

EHRICH, Robert W., 'Current archaeological trends in Europe and America: similarities and differences', *Journal of World History* 12 (4), 1970, pp. 670-681.

EHRMANN, Jacques (ed.), *Structuralism = Yale French Studies* (New Haven, Conn.), Nos. 36-37 (double issue: pp. 1-172), Oct. 1966; republished, with bibliographical additions, Anchor Books, Garden City (N.Y.), Doubleday and Co., 1970.

EIBL-EIBESFELDT, Irenäus, *Ethologie: die Biologie des Verhaltens*, Frankfurt am Main, Akademische Verlaggesellschaft Athenaion, 1966 (English transl. by Erich Klinghammer, *Ethology: The Biology of Behavior*, New York, Holt, 1970).

EISENBERG, John F. & DILLON, Wilton S. (eds.), *Man and Beast. Comparative Social Behavior*, Washington (D.C.), The Smithsonian Institution Press, 1971.

ELDER, J. W., 'Caste and world view. The application of survey methods', in SINGER & COHN (eds.), *Structure and Change in Indian Society, op. cit.* (1968), pp. 173-186.

ELTON, G. R., *The Practice of History*, Fontana Library, London, Collins, 1969 (first published 1967).

EPSTEIN, A. L., 'Urbanization and social change in Africa', *Current Anthropology* 8 (4), 1967, pp. 275-284.

EPSTEIN, A. L., (ed.), *The Craft of Social Anthropology*, London, Tavistock Publications, 1967.

EPSTEIN, T. Scarlett, *Economic Development and Social Change in South India*, Manchester, Manchester University Press, 1962.

——, 'The data of economics in anthropological analysis', in EPSTEIN, A. L. (ed.), *The Craft of Social Anthropology, op. cit.* (1967), pp. 153-180.

EREMEEV, D. E., 'Jazyk kak ètnogenetičeskij istočnik (Iz opyta leksičeskogo analiza tureckogo jazyka)' (= Language as a source for ethnogenesis (On the basis of a lexical analysis of the Turkish language)), *Sovetskaja ètnografija*, No. 4, 1967, pp. 62-74.

——, 'Osobennosti obrazovanija tureckoj nacii' (= The specificity of Turkish national formation), *Sovetskaja ètnografija*, 1969, No. 5, 57-67.

ERIXON, Sigurd (ed.), *The Possibilities of Charting Modern Life. A Symposium for Ethnological Research about Modern Times, held in Stockholm, March 1967*, London, Pergamon Press, 1970.

Ethnology in Japan. A Historical Review, Nihon minzoku-gakkai (= The Japanese Society of Ethnology), Tokyo, 1968.

EVANS-PRITCHARD, E. E., *Witchcraft, Oracles and Magic among the Azande*, Oxford, Clarendon Press, 1937 (French translation by Louis Évrard, *Sorcellerie, oracles et magie chez les Azandé*, Bibliothèque des Sciences Humaines, Paris, Gallimard, 1972).

——, *The Nuer. A Description of the Modes of Livelihood and Political Institutions of a Nilotic People*, Oxford, Clarendon Press, 1940 (French translation by Louis Évrard, *Les Nuer. Description des modes de vie et des institutions politiques d'un peuple nilote*, Bibliothèque des Sciences Humaines, Paris, Gallimard, 1969).

——, *Anthropology and History*, Manchester, Manchester University Press, 1961 (reprinted in EVANS-PRITCHARD, *Essays in Social Anthropology*, London, Faber & Faber, 1962; New York, Free Press of Glencoe, 1963, pp. 46-65).

——. 'Social anthropology: past and present', in EVANS-PRITCHARD, *Essays in Social Anthropology*, London, Faber & Faber, 1962; New York, Free Press of Glencoe, 1963, pp. 13-28.

——, 'The comparative method in social anthropology', in EVANS-PRITCHARD, *The Position of Women in Primitive Societies and Other Essays in Social Anthropology*, London, Faber & Faber, 1965; New York, Free Press, 1965, pp. 37-58 (French translation by Anne & Claude Rivière, 'La méthode comparative en anthropologie sociale', in *La femme dans les sociétés primitives et autres essais d'anthropologie sociale*, Paris, Presses Universitaires de France, 1971, pp. 7-29).

——, *Theories of Primitive Religion*, Oxford, Clarendon Press, 1965 (French translation by M. Matignon, *La religion des primitifs à travers les théories des anthropologues*, Paris, Petite Bibliothèque Payot, No. 186, 1971).
[See also FORTES & EVANS-PRITCHARD (eds.).]

FAGG, William, *Nigerian Images*, London, Lund Humphries, 1963.

FALLERS, Lloyd, 'The range of variation in actual family size. A critique of Marion Levy, Jr.'s argument', in COALE, FALLERS, LEVY, SCHNEIDER, and TOMKINS, *Aspects of the Analysis of Family Structure, op. cit.* (1965), pp. 70-82.

Fältarbetet. Synpunkter på etno-folkloristisk fältforskning (= Field Work. Aspects of Ethno-folkloristic Field Research), Helsingfors, Suomalaisen Kirjallisuuden Seura & Svenska Litteratursällskapet i Finland, 1968.

FÉL, EDIT & HOFER, Tamás, 'Über monographisches Sammeln volkskundlicher Objekte' (= On the monographic collection of folklore objects), *Basler Beiträge zur Geographie und Ethnologie, Ethnologische Reihe*, Vol. 2, 'Festschrift Alfred Bühler', Basel, Pharos Verlag, 1965, pp. 77-92.

——, *Saints, Soldiers, Shepherds: The Human Figure in Hungarian Folk Art*, Budapest, Corvina Press, 1966.

——, *Proper Peasants. Traditional Life in a Hungarian Village*, Viking Fund Publications in Anthropology No. 46, New York, Wenner-Gren Foundation; Budapest, Corvina Press, 1969.

FINLEY, M. I., *The World of Odysseus*, London, Chatto & Windus, 1956 (French translation by Claude Vernant Blanc, *Le monde d'Ulysse*, Petite Collection Maspero, Paris, Maspero, 1969).

FINNEGAN, Ruth, 'How to do things with words: performative utterances among the Limba of Sierra Leone', *Man*, n.s., 4 (4), 1969, pp. 537-552.

——, *Oral Literature in Africa*, Oxford Library of African Literature, Oxford, Clarendon Press, 1970.

FIRTH, Raymond, *Essays on Social Organization and Values*, London School of Economics Monographs on Social Anthropology, No. 28, London, Athlone Press, 1964.

——, *Primitive Polynesian Economy*, 2nd edn., London, Routledge and Kegan Paul, 1965.

——, GREENBERG, J. H. and MANDELBAUM, David G., 'Anthropology', in SILLS (ed.), *International Encyclopedia of the Social Sciences, op. cit.* (1968), Vol. 1, pp. 320-324, 304-313, 313-319.

——, HUBERT, Jane, & FORGE, Anthony, *Families and Their Relatives: Kinship in a Middle-Class Sector of London. An Anthropological Study,* London, Routledge and Kegan Paul, 1969.

FIRTH, Raymond (ed.), *Themes in Economic Anthropology,* A.S.A. Monograph No. 6, London, Tavistock Publications, 1967.

—— & YAMEY, Basil (eds.), *Capital, Saving and Credit in Peasant Societies,* Chicago, Aldine, 1964.

FISCHER, Ann (ed.), *Current Directions in Anthropology* = *Bulletins of the American Anthropological Association* 3 (3), 1970.

FISCHER, E., 'Künstler der Dan: die Bildhauer Tame, Si, Tompieme und Sõn – ihr Wesen und ihr Werk' (= Artists of the Dan: the Sculptors Tame, Si, Tompieme and Sõn – their Nature and their Work), *Baessler-Archiv,* N.F., Vol. 10, 1962, pp. 161-263.

FISCHER, John L., 'Solutions for the Natchez paradox', *Ethnology* 3 (3), 1964, pp. 53-65.

——, 'Psychology and anthropology', in SIEGEL (ed.), *Biennial Review of Anthropology 1965, op. cit.* (1965), pp. 211-261.
[See also SMITH, A. H., & FISCHER, J. L. (eds.).]

FISHMAN, Joshua A. & HERASIMCHUK, Eleanor, 'The multiple prediction of phonological variables in a bilingual speech community', *American Anthropologist* 71 (4), 1969, pp. 648-657.

FORD, Clellan S. (ed.), *Cross-Cultural Approaches. Readings in Comparative Research,* New Haven (Conn.), Human Relations Area Files Press, 1967.

FORGE, Anthony (ed.), *Primitive Art and Society,* London–New York, Oxford *Anthropological Institute of Great Britain and Ireland for 1965,* London, 1966, pp. 23-31.

——, 'The Abelam artist', in FREEDMAN (ed.), *Social Organization, . . ., op. cit.* (1967), pp. 65-84.

——, 'Learning to see in New Guinea', in MAYER, P. (ed.), *Socialization. The Approach from Social Anthropology, op. cit.* (1970), pp. 269-291.

FORGE, Anthony (ed.), *Primitive Art and Society,* London-New York, Oxford University Press, 1973.
[See also FIRTH, HUBERT & FORGE.]

FORTES, Meyer, 'Time and social structure. An Ashanti case study' (first published in 1949) in FORTES, *Time and Social Structure and Other Essays,* London School of Economics Monographs on Social Anthropology No. 40, London, Athlone Press, 1970, pp. 1-32.

——, *Kinship and the Social Order. The Legacy of Lewis Henry Morgan,* Chicago, Aldine, 1969.

FORTES, Meyer (ed.), *Marriage in Tribal Societies,* Cambridge Papers in Social Anthropology No. 3, Cambridge, Cambridge University Press, 1962.

—— & DIETERLEN, Germaine (eds.), *African Systems, of Thought,* London, Oxford University Press, 1965.
[See also GRIAULE & DIETERLEN.]

—— & EVANS-PRITCHARD, E. E. (eds.), *African Political Systems,* London, Oxford University Press, 1940.

FOSTER, George M., *Applied Anthropology,* Boston, Little, Brown & Co., 1969.
[See also POTTER, DIAZ, & FOSTER (eds.).]

FOX, Robin, 'In the beginning: aspects of hominid behavioural evolution', *Man,* n.s., 2 (3), 1967, pp. 415-433.

——, *Kinship and Marriage,* Harmondsworth (Middx.), Penguin Books, 1967 (French translation by Tina Jolas & Simone Dreyfus, *Anthropologie de la parenté. Une analyse de la consanguinité et de l'alliance,* 'Les Essais', Paris, Gallimard, 1972).

——, 'The cultural animal' in EISENBERG & DILLON (eds.), *Man and Beast, op. cit.* (1971), pp. 273-296.

FRAKE, Charles O., 'Further discussion of Burling', *American Anthropologist* 66 (1), 1964, p. 119.

FRANCEV, Ju. P., *U istokov religii i svobodomyslija (*= Origins of Religion and Free Thinking), Leningrad-Moscow, Academy of Sciences Press, 1959.

FRASER, D. *et al., Early Chinese Art and the Pacific Basin,* New York, Intercultural Arts Press, 1968.

FREED, Stanley A., 'An objective method for determining the collective caste hierarchy of an Indian village', *American Anthropologist* 65 (4), 1963, pp. 879-881.

FREEDMAN, Maurice (ed.), *Social Organization. Essays Presented to Raymond Firth,* London, Cass, 1967.

——, *Family and Kinship in Chinese Society,* Stanford (Calif.), Stanford University Press, 1970.

FREILICH, Morris (ed.), *Marginal Natives: Anthropologists at Work,* New York, Harper & Row, 1970.

FRENCH, David, 'The relationship of anthropology to studies in perception and cognition', in KOCH (ed.), *Psychology. A Study of Science,* Vol. 6, *op. cit.* (1963), pp. 388-428.

FRIED, Morton H., *The Evolution of Political Society. An Essay in Political Anthropology,* New York, Random House, 1967.

FRIED, Morton H., *et al.* (eds.), *War. The Anthropology of Armed Conflict and Aggression,* Garden City (N.Y.), Natural History Press, 1967.

FRIEDRICH, Margaret Hardin, 'Design structure and social interaction. Archeological implications of an ethnographic analysis', *American Antiquity* 35 (3), 1970, pp. 332-343.

FÜRER-HAIMENDORF, Christoph von, *Morals and Merit. A Study of the Values and Social Controls in South Asian Societies,* London, Weidenfeld & Nicolson, 1967.

FURNIVALL, J. S., *Netherlands India. A Study of Plural Economy,* Cambridge, Cambridge University Press, 1939.

GAGEN-TORN, N. I., 'Leningradskaja ètnografičeskaja škola v dvadcatye gody (u istokov sovetskoj ètnografii)' (= The Leningrad ethnographic school of the twenties), *Sovetskaja ètnografija,* 1971, No. 2, pp. 134-145.

GANCKAJA, O. A. & DEBEC, G. F., 'O grafičeskom izobraženii resul'tatov statističeskogo obsledovanija mežnacional'nyh brakov' (= Graphic representation of the results of statistical research into mixed marriages), *Sovetskaja ètnografija,* 1966, No. 3, pp. 108-118.

GARCÍA, Antonio, 'Estructura de una hacienda señorial en la Sierra Ecuatoriana: análisis y proyecto de recolonización dentro de un esquema de reforma agraria', *Ciencia Políticas y Sociales* (Mexico), IX (33), July-Sept. 1963, pp. 359-453.

GARDIN, Jean-Claude, 'A typology of computer uses in anthropology', in HYMES (ed.), *The Use of Computers in Anthropology, op. cit.* (1965), pp. 103-118.

GARINE, Igor de, 'Usages alimentaires dans la région de Khombole (Sénégal)', *Cahiers d'Etudes Africaines,* 3 (10), 1962, pp. 218-265.

GAVRILOVA, A. F., 'Svoeobrazie processov urbanizacii v Nigerii' (= Specificity of the processes of urbanization in Nigeria), *Sovetskaja ètnografija,* 1969, No. 3, pp. 74-84.

GEERTZ, Clifford, 'The transition to humanity', in TAX (ed.), *Horizons of Anthropology, op. cit.* (1964), pp. 37-48.

——, 'Anthropological study', *sub* 'Religion', in SILLS (ed.), *International Encyclopedia of the Social Sciences, op. cit.* (1968), Vol. 13, pp. 398-414.

——, *Islam Observed. Religious Development in Morocco and Indonesia*, New Haven (Conn.), Yale University Press, 1968.

GERBRANDS, A. A., *Wow-ipits. Eight Asmat Woodcarvers of New Guinea*, The Hague, Mouton, 1967.

——, 'The study of art in anthropology', in *The Social Sciences, Problems and Orientations, op. cit.* (1968), pp. 15-21 (reprinted in the present work as 'The anthropological approach' (to art), in Mikel Dufrenne's first chapter on 'Aesthetics and the sciences of art', Ch. IV, pp. 652-658).

GILBERT, John P., 'Computer methods in kinship studies', in KAY (ed.), *Explorations in Mathematical Anthropology, op. cit.* (1971), pp. 127-138.

—— & HAMMEL, Eugene A., 'Computer simulation and analysis of problems of kinship and social structure', *American Anthropologist* 68 (1), 1966, pp. 71-93.

GINSBERG, Morris, 'On the diversity of morals', in GINSBERG, *Essays in Sociology and Social Philosophy*, Vol. 1: *On the Diversity of Morals*, London, Heine-.mann, 1956, pp. 97-129.

[See also HOBHOUSE, WHEELER, & GINSBERG.]

GLADWIN, Thomas & STURTEVANT, William C. (eds.), *Anthropology and Human Behavior*, Washington (D.C.), The Anthropological Society of Washington, 1962.

GLUCKMAN, Max, *Politics, Law and Ritual in Tribal Society*, Oxford, Basil Blackwell, 1965.

——, *The Judicial Process among the Barotse of Northern Rhodesia*, 2nd edn., Manchester, Manchester University Press, 1967.

—— & EGGAN, Fred, 'Introduction', in BANTON (ed.), *Political Systems and the Distribution of Power, op. cit.* (1965), pp. xi-xiii.

GLUCKMAN, Max (ed.), *Ideas and Procedures in African Customary Law*, London, Oxford University Press, 1969.

GODELIER, Maurice, 'Objet et méthodes de l'anthropologie économique', *L'Homme* 5 (2), 1965, pp. 32-91 (republished in a slightly augmented version as Pt. III, 'Rationalité des systèmes économiques', of the same author's *Rationalité et irrationalité en économie*, 2 vols., Petite collection Maspero, Paris, Maspero, 1971, Vol. 2, pp. 125-209).

GOFFMAN, Erving, *Behavior in Public Places*, New York, Free Press of Glencoe, 1963.

GOLDE, Peggy (ed.), *Women in the Field: Anthropological Experiences*, Chicago, Aldine, 1970.

GOLDSCHMIDT, Walter, *Man's Way*, New York, Holt, Rinehart & Winston, 1959.

GOODENOUGH, Ward H., *Cooperation in Change. An Anthropological Approach to Community Development*, New York, Russell Sage Foundation, 1963.

——, 'Rethinking "status" and "role": toward a general model of the cultural organization of social relationships', in BANTON (ed.), *The Relevance of Models for Social Anthropology, op. cit.* (1965), pp. 1-24.

——, *Description and Comparison in Cultural Anthropology*, Chicago, Aldine, 1970.

GOODENOUGH, Ward H. (ed.), *Explorations in Cultural Anthropology. Essays in Honor of George Peter Murdock*, New York, McGraw-Hill, 1964.

GOODY, Jack, 'Descent groups', in SILLS (ed.), *International Encyclopedia of the Social Sciences, op. cit.* (1968), Vol. 8, pp. 401-408.

——, 'Economy and feudalism in Africa', *Economic History Review*, 2nd ser., 22 (3), 1969, pp. 393-405.

GOODY, Jack (ed.), *The Developmental Cycle in Domestic Groups*, Cambridge Papers in Social Anthropology No. 1, Cambridge, Cambridge University Press, 1958.

——, *Literacy in Traditional Societies*, Cambridge, Cambridge University Press, 1968.

GORSKIJ, D. P. (ed.), *Gnoseologičeskie problemy formalizacii* (= Gnoseological Problems of Formalization), Minsk, Izdatel'stvo 'Nauka i Tehnika', 1969.

GRANT, Ewan C., 'Human facial expression', *Man,* n.s., 4 (4), 1969, pp. 525-536.

GRAVES, Theodore D., 'Psychological acculturation in a tri-ethnic community', *Southwestern Journal of Anthropology* 23 (4), 1967, pp. 337-350.

—— & ARSDALE, Minor van, 'Values, expectations and relocation: the Navaho migrant to Denver', *Human Organization* 25 (4), 1966, pp. 300-307.
[See also WATSON, O. M. & GRAVES.]

GRAY, Charles Edward, 'A measurement of creativity in Western civilization', *American Anthropologist* 68 (6), 1966, pp. 1384-1417.

GREENBERG, Joseph H., *Anthropological Linguistics,* New York, Random House, 1968.

——, 'Culture history', in SILLS (ed.), *International Encyclopedia of the Social Sciences, op. cit.* (1968), Vol. 6, pp. 448-455.

GREENFIELD, Sidney M., 'More on the study of subsistence agriculture', *American Anthropologist* 67 (3), 1965, pp. 737-744.

GREIMAS, Algirdas Julien, 'Structure et histoire', in POUILLON *et al., Problèmes du structuralisme, op. cit.* (*Les Temps modernes,* 1966), pp. 815-827; republished in GREIMAS, *Du sens. Essais sémiotiques,* Paris, Seuil, 1970, pp. 103-115.

GRIAULE, Marcel, *Méthode de l'ethnographie,* Publications de la Faculté des Lettres de Paris, Paris, Presses Universitaires de France, 1957.

—— & DIETERLEN, Germaine, *Le renard pâle,* tome 1, *Le mythe cosmogonique,* fasc. 1, *La création du monde,* Université de Paris, Travaux et Mémoires de l'Institut d'Ethnologie, no. 72, Paris, Institut d'Ethnologie, 1965.
[See also FORTES & DIETERLEN (eds.).]

GUIART, Jean, 'L'enquête d'ethnologie de la parenté', in POIRIER (ed.), *Ethnologie générale, op. cit.* (1968), pp. 200-213.

——, *Clefs pour l'ethnologie,* Paris, Seghers, 1971.

Guide to Departments of Anthropology = *Bulletins of the American Anthropological Association* 3 (2), 1970.

GUILLAUMIN, Jean, 'Des modèles statistiques pour l'ethnologue', in POIRIER (ed.), *Ethnologie générale, op. cit.* (1968), pp. 385-428.

GUMPERZ, John J. & HYMES, Dell H. (eds.), *The Ethnography of Communication* =*American Anthropologist* 66 (6), Pt. 2, 1964.

——, *Directions in Sociolinguistics,* New York, Holt, Rinehart & Winston, 1970.

GUNDLACH, Rolf, 'Zur maschinellen Erschliessung historischer Museumbestände' (= On making historical museum collections accessible by use of mechanical methods), *Museumskunde* 37 (3), 1968, pp. 135-146.

GURVIČ, I. S. & DOLGIH, B. O. (eds.), *Obščestvennyj stroj u narodov Severnoj Sibiri* (= Social Structure of North Siberian Peoples), Moscow, Nauka, 1970.

HACKENBERG, Robert A., 'The parameters of an ethnic group: a method for studying the total tribe', *American Anthropologist* 69 (5), 1967, pp. 478-492.

HAGE, Per, 'A Guttman scale analysis of Tikopia speech taboos', *Southwestern Journal of Anthropology* 25 (1), 1969, pp. 96-104.

HÄGERSTRAND, Torsten, *Innovation Diffusion as a Spatial Process,* Chicago, Chicago University Press, 1968.

HAJNAL, John, 'Concepts of random mating and the frequency of consanguineous marriages', *Proceedings of the Royal Society* (London), B, Vol. 159, 1963, pp. 125-177.

HAJTUN, D. E., *Totemizm, ego suščnost' i proishoždenie* (= Totemism. Its meaning and Origin), Dushanbe, Tadjik University Press, 1958.

HALL, Edward T., 'Proxemics', *Current Anthropology* 9 (2-3), 1968, pp. 83-95.

HALPERN, Joel M., 'Ethnology in Yugoslavia since World War II. A review of research and publications', in 'Anthropology in East-Central and Southeast Europe', *op. cit.* (1970), pp. 328-342.

HAMMEL, Eugene A., 'Further comments on componential analysis', *American Anthropologist* 66 (5), 1964, pp. 1167-1171.

——, *Alternative Social Structures and Ritual Relations in the Balkans*, Englewood Cliffs (N.J.), Prentice-Hall, 1968.

——, 'Anthropological explanations: style in discourse', *Southwestern Journal of Anthropology* 24 (2), 1968, pp. 155-169.

——, *The Pink Yoyo. Occupational Mobility in Belgrade ca. 1915-1965*, Institute of International Studies, Research Monograph Series No. 13, Berkeley (Calif.), 1969.

——, 'The ethnographers dilemma: alternative models of occupational prestige in Belgrade', Man, n.s., 5 (4), 1970, pp. 652-670.

——, 'The zadruga as process', in LASLETT (ed.), *Household and Family in Past Time, op. cit.* (1973).

HAMMEL, Eugene A. (ed.), *Formal Semantic Analysis = American Anthropologist* 67 (5), Pt. 2, 1965.
   [See also GILBERT & HAMMEL.]

HAMMER, Muriel, 'Some comments on formal analysis of grammatical and semantic systems', *American Anthropologist* 68 (2), Pt. 1, 1966, pp. 362-373.

HAMMOND-TOOKE, W. D., 'Urbanization and the interpretation of misfortune. A quantitative analysis', *Africa* 40 (1), 1970, pp. 25-38.

HARRIES-JONES, P., '"Home-boy" ties and political organization in a copperbelt township', in MITCHELL (ed.), *Social Networks in Urban Situations, . . ., op. cit.* (1969), pp. 297-347.

HARRIS, Marvin, *The Rise of Anthropological Theory. A History of Theories of Culture*, New York, Thomas Y. Crowell and Co., 1968; London, Routledge & Kegan Paul, 1969.

HARRISON, Frank Ll., HOOD, Mantle, and PALISCA, Claude V., *Musicology*, 'Humanistic Scholarship in America. The Princeton Studies' series, Englewood Cliffs (N.J.), Prentice-Hall, 1963.

HAUCK, Gerhard, 'Die "strukturale Anthropologie" von C. Lévi-Strauss', *Sociologus*, n.s., 18 (1), 1968, pp. 63-74.

HAUDRICOURT, André-G., 'Linguistique et ethnologie', in POIRIER (ed.), *Ethnologie générale, op. cit.* (1968), pp. 288-316.

——, 'La technologie culturelle. Essai de méthodologie', in POIRIER (ed.), *Ethnologie générale, op. cit.* (1968), pp. 731-822.

HAYES, E. Nelson & HAYES, Tanya (eds.), *Claude Lévi-Strauss: The Anthropologist as Hero*, Cambridge (Mass.), M.I.T. Press, 1970.

HEINE-GELDERN, Robert, 'Introduction', *Bulletin of the International Committee on Urgent Anthropological and Ethnological Research*, Vol. 1, 1958, pp. 5-9.

——, 'Cultural diffusion', in SILLS (ed.), *International Encyclopedia of the Social Sciences, op. cit.* (1968), Vol. 4, pp. 169-173.

HEIZER, Robert F., 'Domestic fuel in primitive society', *Journal of the Royal Anthropological Institute*, Vol. 93, Pt. 2, 1963, pp. 186-194.

HELM, J. (ed.), *Essays on the Verbal and Visual Arts*, Proceedings of the 1966 Annual Spring Meeting, Seattle (Wash.), American Ethnological Society, 1967.

HENIN, R. A., 'Marriage patterns and trends in the nomadic and settled populations of the Sudan', *Africa* 39 (3), 1969, pp. 238-259.

HEUSCH, Luc de, 'Les points de vue structuralistes en anthropologie et leurs principaux champs d'application', in *The Social Sciences. Problems and Orientations, op. cit.* (1968), pp. 33-46.

HEYERDAHL, T., *Sea Routes to Polynesia*, London, Allen & Unwin, 1968.

HIATT, Betty, 'The food quest and economy of the Tasmanian aborigines', *Oceania* 38 (2), 1967, pp. 99-133.

HIMMELHEBER, H., *Negerkünstler*, Stuttgart, Strecker & Schröder, 1935.

——, *Negerkunst und Negerkünstler*, Braunschweig, Klinkhardt & Bierman, 1960.

HIRSCHBERG, W., 'Kulturhistorie und Ethnohistorie. Eine Gegenüberstellung', *Paideuma* 12, 1966, pp. 61-69.

—— & Janata, A., *Technologie und Ergologie in der Völkerkunde*, Mannheim, Bibliographisches Institut, 1966.

'The historical relations of science and technology', *Technology and Culture* 6 (4), Wayne State University Press, 1965.

Hobhouse, L. T., Wheeler, G. C., & Ginsberg, M., *The Material Culture and Social Institutions of the Simpler Peoples*, London, Routledge & Kegan Paul, 1965 (first published 1915).

Hodgen, Margaret T., *Early Anthropology in the Sixteenth and Seventeenth Centuries*, Philadelphia, University of Pennsylvania Press, 1964.

Hofer, Tamás, 'Anthropologists and native ethnographers in Central European villages. Comparative notes on the professional personality of two disciplines', *Current Anthropology* 9 (4), 1968, pp. 311-315.
[See also Fél & Hofer.]

Hoffmann, Hans, 'Formal versus informal estimates of cultural stability', *American Anthropologist* 67 (1), 1965, pp. 110-115.

——, 'Mathematical anthropology', in Siegel (ed.), *Biennial Review of Anthropology 1969, op. cit.* (1970), pp. 41-79.

——. 'Markov chains in Ethiopia', in Kay (ed.), *Explorations in Mathematical Anthropology, op. cit.* (1971), pp. 181-190.

Hoggart, Richard, *The Uses of Literacy. Aspects of Working Class Life with Special Reference to Publications and Entertainments*, London, Chatto & Windus, 1957 (French translation by Françoise & Jean-Claude Garcias & Jean-Claude Passeron, *La culture du pauvre*, Paris, Editions de Minuit, 1970).

Holm, B., *Northwest Coast Indian. An Analysis of Form*, Seattle-London, University of Washington Press, 1965.

Homans, George C. & Schneider, David M., *Marriage, Authority, and Final Causes. A Study of Unilateral Cross-Cousin Marriage*, Glencoe (Ill.), Free Press, 1955.

Honigmann, John J., 'Sampling in ethnographic field work', in Naroll & Cohen, R. (eds.), *A Handbook of Method in Cultural Anthropology, op. cit.* (1970), pp. 266-281.

Hood, Mantle, 'Music, the unknown', in Harrison, Hood, and Palisca, *Musicology, op. cit.* (1963), pp. 215-326.

Hoppál, Mihály, *Egy falu kommunikációs rendszere* (= Systems of Communication in a Hungarian Village), Budapest, Magyar Rádió és Televizió Tömekommunikációs Kutatóközpontja, 1970.

—— & Voigt, Vilmos, 'Kultura és kommunikáció' (= Culture and communication), *Ethnographia* (Budapest), Vol. 80, 1969, pp. 579-591.

——, 'Models in the research of forms of social mind', *Acta Ethnographica* (Budapest), Vol. 18, 1969, pp. 384-388.

Hsu, Francis L. K., *The Study of Literate Civilizations*, Studies in Anthropological Method, New York, Holt, Rinehart & Winston, 1969.

Hsu, Francis L. K. (ed.), *Psychological Anthropology. Approaches to Culture and Personality*, Homewood (Ill.), Dorsey Press, 1961.

Hunt, Robert (ed.), *Personalities and Cultures*, American Museum Sourcebooks in Anthropology, Garden City (N.Y.), Natural History Press, 1967.

Huxley, Julian S. (ed.), *Ritualizaiton of Behaviour in Animals and Man = Philosophical Transactions of the Royal Society* (London), 251 (772), 1966 (French translation by Paulette Vielhomme, *Le comportement rituel chez l'homme et l'animal*, Bibliothèque des Sciences humaines, Paris, Gallimard, 1971).

Hymes, Dell H., 'On Hammel on componential analysis', *American Anthropologist* 67 (5), Pt. 1, 1965, p. 1285.

——, 'Reply to Coult', *American Anthropologist* 68 (4), 1966, p. 1015.

——, 'Linguistic models in archaeology', in *Archéologie et calculateurs, Problèmes sémiologiques et mathématiques*, Colloques internationaux du Centre National

154 *Maurice Freedman*

de la Recherche Scientifiques (CNRS), Paris, Editions du Centre National de la Recherche Scientifique, 1970, pp. 91-118.

Hymes, Dell H. (ed.), *Language in Culture and Society*, New York, Harper & Row, 1964.

—, *The Use of Computers in Anthropology*, The Hague, Mouton, 1965.

—, *Pidgenization and Creolization of Languages*, Cambridge, Cambridge University Press, 1970.

[See also Gumperz & Hymes (eds.).]

L'informatique, la documentation et les sciences sociales: see *Use of Computers, Documentation, and the Social Sciences*.

International Congresses of Anthropological and Ethnological Sciences: see *VIIe* [Septième] *Congrès international des Sciences Anthropologiques et Ethnologiques (Moscou, 1964); Proceedings, VIIIth International Congress of Anthropological and Ethnological Sciences (Tokyo and Kyoto, 1968)*.

International Journal of Psychology/Journal international de psychologie (Paris), founded in 1966.

Ipola, Emilio de: see de Ipola, Emilio.

Ishida, E., Oka, M., Egami, N., & Yawata, I., *Nihon-minzoku no kigen* (= The Origin of the Japanese People), Tokyo, Heibonsha, 1968.

Ivanov, S. V., *Materialy po izobraziteľnomu iskusstvu narodov Sibiri XIX-načala XX v.* (= Materials of the Art of Siberian Peoples, 19th and Early 20th Centuries), Moscow-Leningrad, Izdatel'stvo Akademii Nauk SSSR, 1954.

—, *Skuľptura narodov Severa Sibiri XIX-pervoj poloviny XX v.* (= Sculpture of North Siberian Peoples 1800-1950), Leningrad, Nauka, 1970.

Ivanov, V. V., 'Dvoičnaja simboličeskaja klassifikacija v afrikanskih i aziatskih tradicijah' (= Dual symbolic classification in African and Asian traditions), *Narody Azii i Afriki*, 1969, No. 5, pp. 105-115.

— & Toporov, V. I., *Slavjanskie jazykovye model irujuščie sistemy* (= Slavic Language Model Systems), Moscow, Nauka, 1965.

Izard, Françoise & Izard, Michel, 'L'enquête ethno-démographique', in Poirier (ed.), *Ethnologie générale, op. cit.* (1968), pp. 257-287.

Jakobson, Roman, 'Linguistics' in *Main Trends of Research in the Social and Human Sciences, Part I: Social Sciences, op. cit.* (1970), pp. 418-463 (parallel publication of French translation, 'La linguistique', in *Tendances principales de la recherche dans les sciences sociales et humaines, Partie I: Sciences sociales, op. cit.* (1970), pp. 504-556).

— & Lévi-Strauss, Claude, '"Les Chats" de Charles Baudelaire', *L'Homme* II (1), 1962, pp. 5-21; republished in Roman Jakobson, *Questions de poétique*, Paris, Seuil, 1973, pp. 401-419.

Jason, Heda, 'A multidimensional approach to oral literature', *Current Anthropology* X (4), Pt. 2, 1969, pp. 413-420.

Jaulin, Robert, *La géomancie. Analyse formelle*, Paris-The Hague, Mouton, 1966, 'Cahiers de l'Homme', n.s., No. 4; and, in a shorter version, as 'Analyse formelle de la géomancie', in Richard & Jaulin (eds.), *Anthropologie et calcul, op. cit.* (1971), pp. 185-215.

—, *La paix blanche. Introduction à l'ethnocide*, Paris, Seuil, 1970.

[See also Richard & Jaulin (eds.).]

Johnston, Francis E. et al., 'Culture and genetics' (a symposium and discussion), *Bulletins of the American Anthropological Association* III (3), 1970, pp. 67-107.

Jongmans, D. G. & Gutkind, P. C. W. (eds.), *Anthropologists in the Field*, Assen, Van Gorcum & Co., 1967.

Jopling, Carol F. (ed.), *Art and Aesthetics in Primitive Societies. A Critical Anthology*, New York, E. P. Dutton & Co., 1971.

JOSSELIN DE JONG, P. E. DE, 'A new approach to kinship studies, being a discussion of F. G. G. ROSE, *Kin, Age Structure and Marriage'*, *Bijdragen tot de taal-, land- en volkenkunde*, No. 118, Pt. 1, 1962, pp. 42-67.

——, *Contact der continenten. Bijdrage tot het begrijpen van niet-westerse samenlevingen*, Leiden, Universitaire Pers, 1969; 2nd edn., 1972.

Journal of Cross-Cultural Psychology, West Washington State College, Washington (D.C.).

JOY, Leonard, 'An economic homologue of Barth's presentation of economic spheres in Darfur', in FIRTH (ed.), *Themes in Economic Anthropology, op. cit.* (1967), pp. 175-189.

KAPFERER, B., *The Population of a Zambian Municipal Township*, Institute for Social Research, Communication No. 1, Lusaka, University of Zambia, 1966.

KAPLAN, Bert (ed.), *Studying Personality Cross-Culturally*, Evanston (Ill.)-Elmsford (N.Y.), Row, Peterson & Co., 1961.

KARDINER, Abram & PREBLE, Edward, *They Studied Man*, Cleveland (Ohio), The World Publishing Co.; London, Secker & Warburg, 1961 (French translation by Anne Guérin, *Introduction à l'ethnologie*, Idées series, Paris, Gallimard, 1966).

KARVE, Irawati, *Hindu Society. An Interpretation*, Poona, Deccan College, 1961 (2nd edn., Poona, Deshmukh Prakashan, 1968).

KATZ, Ruth, 'Mannerism and cultural change. An ethnomusicological example', *Current Anthropology* 11 (4-5), 1970, pp. 465-469.

KAY, Paul, 'Comment on Colby', *Current Anthropology* 7 (1), 1966, pp. 20-23.

——, 'On the multiplicity of cross/parallel distinctions', *American Anthropologist* 69 (1), 1967, pp. 83-85.

——, 'Some theoretical implications of ethnographic semantics', in FISCHER, Ann (ed.), *Current Directions in Anthropology, op. cit.* (1970), pp. 19-30.

KAY, Paul (ed.), *Explorations in Mathematical Anthropology*, Cambridge (Mass.)-London, The M.I.T. Press, 1971.
[See also BERLIN & KAY.]

KEESING, Roger M., 'Statistical models and decision models of social structure: a Kwaio case', *Ethnology* 6 (1), 1967, pp. 1-16.

KEMENY, John G., SNELL, J. Laurie, & THOMPSON, Gerald L., *Introduction to Finite Mathematics*, 2nd edn., Englewood Cliffs (N.J.), Prentice-Hall, 1966 French translation by M. C. Loyau & M. Didier, *Algèbre moderne et activités humaines*, 3rd edn., Paris, Dunod, 1969).

KIRK, G. S., *Myth. Its Meaning and Functions in Ancient and Other Cultures*, Cambridge, Cambridge University Press, 1970.

KISLJAKOV, A. A., 'Problemy sem'i i braka v rabotah sovetskih ètnografov (po materialam Srednej Azii i Kazahstana)' (= Problems of marriage and the family in the works of Soviet ethnographers (from materials on Central Asia and Kazakhstan)), *Sovetskaja ètnografija*, 1967, No. 5, pp. 92-104.

KLUCKHOHN, Clyde, *Navaho Witchcraft*, Peabody Museums Papers 22, Cambridge (Mass.), Harvard University, 1944.

——, *Anthropology and the Classics*, Providence (R.I.), Brown University Press, 1961.

KNAPP, P. H. (ed.), *Expression of the Emotions in Man*, New York, International Universities Press, 1963.

KNYŠENKO, Ju. V., *Istorija pervobytnogo obščestva i osnovy ètnografii* (= The History of Primitive Society and the Bases of Ethnography), Rostov. Izdatel'stvo Rostovkogo Universiteta, 1965.

KÖBBEN, André J., 'New ways of presenting an old idea: the statistical method in social anthropology', in MOORE, F. W. (ed.), *Readings in Cross-Cultural Methodology, op. cit.* (1961), pp. 175-192 (first published 1952).

——, 'Why exceptions? The logic of cross-cultural analysis', *Current Anthropology* 8 (1-2), 1967, pp. 3-19.

KOCH, Sigmund (ed.), *Psychology. A Study of Science*, Vol. 6, New York, McGraw-Hill, 1963.

KOENTJARANINGRAT. 'Anthropology and non-Euro-American anthropologist. The situation in Indonesia', in GOODENOUGH (ed.), *Explorations in Cultural Anthropology ...*, *op. cit.* (1964), pp. 293-308.

KOLINSKI, Mieczyslaw, 'Recent trends in ethnomusicology', *Ethnomusicology* 11 (1), 1967, pp. 1-24.

KORN, Francis & NEEDHAM, Rodney, 'Permutation models and prescriptive systems. The Tarau case', *Man*, n.s., 5 (3), 1970, pp. 393-420.

KOTHARI, R. (ed.), *Caste in Indian Politics*, New Delhi, Orient Longman, 1970.

KOZELKA, Robert M. & ROBERTS, John M., 'A new approach to nonzero concordance', in KAY (ed.), *Explorations in Mathematical Anthropology, op. cit.* (1971), pp. 214-225.

KOZLOV, V. I., 'Nekotorye problemy teorii nacii" (= Some problems of the theory of the nation), *Voprosy istorii*, 1967, No. 1, pp. 88-99.

——, 'O ponjatii ètničeskoj obščnosti' (= The concept of the ethnic unit), *Sovetskaja ètnografija*, 1967, No. 2, pp. 100-111.

KRADER, Lawrence, 'Recent trends in Soviet anthropology', in SIEGEL (ed.), *Biennial Review of Anthropology 1959, op. cit.* (1959), pp. 155-184.

KROEBER, A. L., *An Anthropologist Looks at History*, Berkeley-Los Angeles, University of California Press, 1963.

——, *Configurations of Culture Growth*, Berkeley-Los Angeles, University of California Press, 1969 (first published 1944).

KROEBER, A. L. (ed.), *Anthropology Today. An Encyclopedic Inventory*, Chicago, University of Chicago Press, 1953.

KRONENBERG, A. & KRONENBERG, W., 'Soziale Struktur und religiöse Antinomien', *Anthropos* 63-64, 1968-69, pp. 497-520.

KRYVELEV, I. A., 'K harakteristike suščnosti i značenija religioznogo povedenija' (= Features of the essence and meaning of religious behaviour), *Sovetskaja ètnografija*, 1967, No. 6, pp. 21-31.

——, *Religioznaja kartina mira i ee bogoslovskaja modernizacija* (= The Religious Picture of the World and Its Theological Modernization), Moscow, Nauka, 1968.

KUBBEL', L. E., 'Voprosy razvitija sovremennoj kul'tury stran Afriki v svete leninskogo učenija o kul'turnoj preemstvennosti' (= Questions of cultural development in African countries today in the light of the Leninist teaching on cultural continuity), *Sovetskaja ètnografija*, 1970, No. 2, pp. 47-56.

KULA, Witold, 'On the typology of economic systems', in *The Social Sciences. Problems and Orientations, op. cit.* (1968), pp. 108-144.

KULCSÁR, Kálmán, *A jogszociológia problémái* (= Problems of Legal Sociology), Budapest, Kózgazdasági és Jogi Kőnyvkiadó, 1960.

KUNST, Jaap, *Ethnomusicology*, 3rd edn., The Hague, Martinus Nijhoff, 1959.

KUNSTADTER, Peter, 'Computer simulation of preferential marriage systems', in HYMES (ed.), *The Use of Computers in Anthropology, op. cit.* (1965), pp. 520-521.

——, 'Applications of simulation techniques in social and cultural anthropology', in *The Social Sciences. Problems and Orientations, op. cit.* (1968), pp. 423-431.

——, BUHLER, R., STEPHAN, F., & WESTOFF, C., 'Demographic variability and preferential marriage patterns', *American Journal of Physical Anthropology* 21 (4), 1963, pp. 511-519.

KUPER, Leo & SMITH, M. G. (eds.), *Pluralism in Africa*, Berkeley-Los Angeles, University of California Press, 1969.

KUSHNER, Gilbert, 'The anthropology of complex societies', in SIEGEL (ed.), *Biennial Review of Anthropology 1969, op. cit.* (1970), pp. 80-131.

KUTUKDJIAN, Georges, 'A propos de l'étude formelle du mythe', *L'Homme* 10 (3), 1970, pp. 84-103.

LAADE, W., *Die Situation von Musikleben und Musikforschung in den Ländern Afrikas und Asiens und die neuen Aufgaben der Musikethnologie*, Tutzing, Hans Schneider, 1969.

LABOV, William, 'Phonological correlates of social stratification', *American Anthropologist* 66 (6), Pt. 2, 1964, pp. 164-176.

——, *The Social Stratification of English in New York City*, Washington (D.C.), Center for Applied Linguistics, 1966.

LADD, John, *The Structure of a Moral Code. A philosophical Analysis of Ethical Discourse Applied to the Ethics of the Navaho Indians*, Cambridge (Mass.), Harvard University Press, 1957.

LAMB, Sidney & ROMNEY, A. Kimball, 'An anthropologist's introduction to the computer', in HYMES (ed.), *The Use of Computers in Anthropology, op. cit.* (1965), pp. 37-90.

LANCASTER, Lorraine, 'Kinship in Anglo-Saxon society', *The British Journal of Sociology* 9 (3), pp. 230-250; (4), pp. 359-377, 1958.

LANE, Michael, 'Introduction', in LANE (ed.), *Structuralism. A Reader, op. cit.* (1970), pp. 11-39.

LANE, Michael (ed.), *Structuralism. A Reader*, London, Cape, 1970.

'Langues et littératures de l'Afrique noire', series, Paris, Klinksieck.

LASLETT, Peter (ed.), *Household and Family in Past Time*, Cambridge, Cambridge University Press, 1973.

LÁSZLÓ, Gyula, *Az ősember művészete* (= The Art of Ancient Man), Budapest, Corvina Press, 1968.

LAWRENCE, Roger, *Aboriginal Habitat and Economy*, Canberra, Australian National University Press, 1968.

LAZARSFELD, Paul F., 'Sociology', in *Main Trends of Research in the Social and Human Sciences, Part I: Social Sciences, op. cit.* (1970), pp. 61-165 (parallel publication of French translation, 'La sociologie', in *Tendances principales de la recherche dans les sciences sociales et humaines, Partie I: Sciences sociales, op. cit.* (1970), pp. 70-197).

LEACH, Edmund R., *Rethinking Anthropology*, London School of Economics Monographs on Social Anthropology No. 22, London, Athlone Press, 1961 (French translation by Dan Sperber & Serge Thion, *Critique de l'anthropologie*, SUP 'Le sociologue' series, Paris, Presses Universitaires de France, 1968).

——, 'The structural implications of matrilateral cross-cousin marriage', in LEACH, *Rethinking Anthropology, op. cit.* (1961), pp. 54-104.

——, 'The legitimacy of Solomon', *European Journal of Sociology/Archives européennes de Sociologie*, Vol. 7, 1966, pp. 58-101 (reprinted in LANE (ed.), *Structuralism. A Reader, op. cit.* (1970), pp. 248-292, and in LEACH, *Genesis as Myth, and Other Essays, op. cit.* (1969), pp. 25-83).

——, 'The comparative method in anthropology', in SILLS (ed.), *International Encyclopedia of the Social Sciences, op. cit.* (1968), Vol. 1, pp. 339-345.

——, *Genesis as Myth, and Other Essays*, London, Cape, 1969.

——, *Lévi-Strauss*, Fontana Modern Masters Series, London, Collins, 1970 (French translation by Denis Verguin, Les maîtres modernes series, Paris, Seghers, 1970).

——, 'Language and anthropology', in MINNIS (ed.), *Linguistics at Large, op. cit.* (1971), pp. 137-158.

LEACH, Edmund R. (ed.), *The Structural Study of Myth and Totemism*, A.S.A. Monographs No. 5, London, Tavistock Publications, 1967.

——, *Dialectic in Practical Religion*, Cambridge Papers in Social Anthropology No. 5, Cambridge, Cambridge University Press, 1968.

LEBEUF, Jean-Paul, 'L'enquête orale en ethnographie', in POIRIER (ed.), *Ethnologie générale, op. cit.* (1968), pp. 180-199.

—, 'Ethnologie et coopération technique', in POIRIER (ed.), *Ethnologie générale, op. cit.* (1968), pp. 494-522.

LECLAIR, EWARD & SCHNEIDER, Harold K. (eds.), *Economic Anthropology. Readings in Theory and Analysis*, New York, Holt, Rinehart and Winston, 1968.

LEE, Richard B., '!Kung Bushman subsistence. An input-output analysis', in VAYDA (ed.), *Environment and Cultural Behavior. Ecological Studies in Cultural Anthropology, op. cit.* (1969), pp. 47-79.

LEE, Richard B. & DEVORE, Irven (eds.), *Man the Hunter*, Chicago, Aldine Publishing Co., 1968.

LEEDS, Anthony & VAYDA, Andrew P. (eds.), *Man, Culture, and Animals: The Role of Animals in Human Ecological Adjustments*, American Association for the Advancement of Science Publications No. 78, Washington (D.C.), 1965.

LEFEBVRE, Henri, *Le langage et la société*, Paris, Gallimard, 1966.

Leninskie idei v izučenii istorii pervobytnogo obščestva, rabovladenija i feodalizma (= Leninist Ideas on the Study of the History of Primitive Society, Slavery, and Feudalism), Moscow, Nauka, 1970.

LEROI-GOURHAN, André, *Evolution et techniques – L'homme et la matière*, 'Sciences d'aujourd'hui' ser., Paris, Albin Michel, 1943, 2nd edn. 1971; *Evolution et techniques – Miliieu et techniques, id.*, 1945; *Le geste et la parole – Technique et langage, id.*, 1964; *Le geste et la parole – La mémoire et les rythmes, id.*, 1965.

—, *Préhistoire de l'art occidental*, Paris, Mazenod, 1965.

—, 'L'expérience ethnographique', in POIRIER (ed.), *Ethnologie générale, op. cit.* (1968), pp. 1816-1825.

LESER, Paul, 'Ethnology in Germany', in 'Anthropology in East-Central and Southeast Europe', *op. cit.* (1970), pp. 275-292.

LEVIN, Ju. I., 'Ob opisanii sistemy terminov rodstva' (= On the description of systems of kinship nomenclature), *Sovetskaja ètnografija*, 1970, No. 4, pp. 18-30.

LEVIN, M. G., & POTAPOV, L. P. (eds.), *Istoriko-ètnografičeskij atlas Sibiri* (= Historico-ethnographic Atlas of Siberia), Moscow-Leningrad, Nauka, 1961.

LÉVI-STRAUSS, Claude, 'Le dédoublement de la représentation dans les arts de l'Asie et de l'Amérique', *Renaissance* (quarterly journal published by the Ecole libre des Hautes Etudes in New York), Vol. 2-3, 1944-45, pp. 168-186; reprinted in LÉVI-STRAUSS, *Anthropologie structurale, op. cit.* (1958), pp. 269-294 (Chap. XIII) (English translation, 'Split representation in the art of Asia and America', in *Structural Anthropology, op. cit.* (1963), pp. 245-268).

—, *Les structures élémentaires de la parenté*, Paris, Presses Universitaires de France, 1949; 2nd edn. rev., with new preface, Paris-The Hague, Mouton, 1967 (English translation by J. H. Bell, J. R. von Sturmer, & R. Needham, *The Elementary Structures of Kinship*, London, Eyre & Spottiswoode, 1969).

—, *Race et histoire*, Paris, Unesco, 1952, 'La question raciale devant la science moderne' series (parallel publication of English version, *Race and History*, same ref., 'The Race Question in Modern Science' series); original French text republished (with a Preface by Jean POUILLON, op. cit.), Paris, Gontier, 1967, Bibliothèque 'Méditations'; also included in *Le racisme devant la science*, Paris, Unesco, new edn., 1973, pp. 9-49 (English version, *Race, Science and Society*, Paris, Unesco, 1975) and, in a revised version, in LÉVI-STRAUSS, *Anthropologie structurale deux, op. cit.* (1973), pp. 377-422.

—, *Tristes Tropiques*, Paris, Plon, 1955 (English translation by John Russell, *World on the Wane*, London, Hutchinson, 1961).

—, *Anthropologie structurale* (collection of essays), Paris, Plon, 1958 (English translation by Claire Jacobson & Brooke Grundfest Schoepf, *Structural Anthropology*, New York-London, Basic Books, 1963).

——, *Leçon inaugurale* (Chaire d'Anthropologie sociale, Collège de France), Paris, Collège de France, 1960 (the lecture was delivered 5 Jan. 1960) (English translation by Sherry Ortner & Robert A. Paul, *The Scope of Anthropology*, London, Cape, 1967); original French text republished as 'Le champ de l'anthropologie' in LÉVI-STRAUSS, *Anthropologie structurale deux, op. cit.* (1973), pp. 11-44.

——, *La pensée sauvage*, Paris, Plon, 1962 (English translation, *The Savage Mind*, London, Weidenfeld & Nicolson, 1966).

——, *Le totémisme aujourd'hui*, Paris, Presses Universitaires de France, 1962 (English translation by Rodney Needham, *Totemism*, Boston (Mass.), Beacon Press, 1963; another edn., Harmondsworth (Middx.), Penguin Books, 1969).

——, 'Critères scientifiques dans les disciplines sociales et humaines', *Revue internationale des Sciences sociales* XVI (4), 1964 ('Problèmes posés par une étude des sciences sociales et humaines'), pp. 579-597 (parallel publication of English version, 'Criteria of science in the social and human disciplines', *International Social Science Journal*, same ref. ('Problems of surveying the social sciences and the humanities'), pp. 534-552); original French text republished in LÉVI-STRAUSS, *Anthropologie structurale deux, op. cit.* (1973), pp. 339-364.

——, *Mythologiques*. Le cru et le cuit*, Paris, Plon, 1964 (English translation by John & Doreen Weightman, *The Raw and the Cooked. An Introduction to a Science of Mythology: I*, New York, Harper & Row, 1969; London, Jonathan Cape, 1970).

——, 'Anthropology. Its achievements and future' (Remarks at the bicentennial celebration commemorating the birth of James Smithson, Smithsonian Institution, Washington, D.C., 17 Sept. 1965), *Current Anthropology* VII (2), 1966, pp. 124-127, and in *Knowledge among Men*, New York, Simon & Schuster, 1966; freely translated into French by the author as 'L'œuvre du *Bureau of American Ethnology* et ses leçons', in LÉVI-STRAUSS, *Anthropologie structurale deux, op. cit.* (1973), pp. 63-75.

——, *Mythologiques**. Du miel aux cendres,* Paris, Plon, 1966 (English translation by John & Doreen Weightman, *From Honey to Ashes. An Introduction to a Science of Mythology: II*, New York, Harper & Row, 1973).

——, *The Scope of Anthropology* (1967): see *Leçon inaugurale* (1960).

——, *Mythologiques***. L'origine des manières de table*, Paris, Plon, 1968.

——, *Mythologiques****. L'homme nu*, Paris, Plon, 1971.

——, *Anthropologie structurale deux* (collection of essays), Paris, Plon, 1973. [See also JAKOBSON & LÉVI-STRAUSS.]

LÉVY-BRUHL, Henri, 'L'ethnologie juridique', in POIRIER (ed.), *Ethnologie générale, op. cit.* (1968), pp. 1111-1179.

LEWIS, I. M., *Ecstatic Religion*, Harmondsworth (Middx.), Penguin Books, 1971.

LEWIS, I. M. (ed.), *History and Social Anthropology*, A.S.A. Monographs No. 7, London, Tavistock Publications, 1968.

LIENHARDT, Godfrey, *Social Anthropology*, London, Oxford University Press, 1964.

LINTON, Ralph, *Culture and Mental Disorders*, ed. by George DEVEREUX, Springfield (Ill.), Charles C. Thomas, 1956.

LIPINSKAJA, V. A., 'Nekotorye čerty sovremennoj material'noj kul'tury russkogo naselenija Altajskogo kraja' (= Some features of the present-day material culture of the Russian population in the Altai region), *Sovetskaja ètnografija*, 1968, No. 2, pp. 96-105.

LISÓN TOLOSANA, Carmelo, *Antropología social en España*, Madrid, Siglo XXI de España Editores, 1971.

LITTLE, Kenneth, *West African Urbanization*, Cambridge, Cambridge University Press, 1965.

LIVINGSTONE, F. B., 'Physical anthropology and cultural evolution', in *The Social Sciences. Problems and Orientations, op. cit.* (1968), pp. 47-53.

——, 'The application of structural models to marriage systems in anthropology', in BUCHLER & NUTINI (eds.), *Game Theology in the Behavioral Sciences, op. cit.* (1969), pp. 235-252.

LLOYD, Dennis, *The Idea of Law*, Harmondsworth (Middx.), Penguin Books, 1964.

LLOYD, P. C., *The New Elites of Tropical Africa*, London, Oxford University Press, 1966.

——, *Africa in Social Change, Harmondsworth* (Middx.), Penguin Books, 1967.

LOMAX, Alan *et al., Folk Song Style and Culture*, American Association for the Advancement of Science, Washington (D.C.), 1968.

LONGACRE, William A., *Archeology as Anthropology. A Case Study*, Anthropological Papers of the University of Arizona No. 17, Tucson, University of Arizona Press, 1970.

LORD, A. B., *The Singer of Tales*, Harvard Studies in Comparative Literature, Cambridge (Mass.), 1960.

LOUNSBURY, Floyd, 'The structure of the Latin kinship system and its relation to Roman social organization', in *VIIe Congrès des Sciences Anthropologiques et Ethnologiques*, Vol. 4, *op. cit.* (1967), pp. 261-270.

——, 'One hundred years of anthropological linguistics', in BREW (ed.), *One Hundred Years of Anthropology, op. cit.* (1968), pp. 153-226.

MACBEATH, A., *Experiments in Living. A Study of the Nature and Foundation of Ethics or Morals in the Light of Recent Work in Social Anthropology*, London, Macmillan, 1952.

MACCOBY, E. E. (ed.), *The Development of Sex Differences*, Stanford (Calif.), Stanford University Press, 1967.

McGINN, Noel F., HARBURG, Ernest, & GINSBURG, Gerald P., 'Responses to interpersonal conflict by middle-class males in Guadalajara and Michigan', *American Anthropologist* 67 (6), Pt. 1, 1965, pp. 1483-1494.

MACKENZIE, W. J. M., *Politics and Social Science*, Harmondsworth (Middx.), Penguin Books, 1967.

MACLEAN, Catherine M. U., 'Hospitals or healers? An attitude survey in Ibadan', *Human Organization* 25 (2), 1966, pp. 131-139.

MADAN, T. N., 'Political pressures and ethical constraints upon Indian sociologists', in SJOBERG (ed.), *Ethics, Politics, and Social Research, op. cit.* (1967), pp. 162-179.

MADAY, Béla C., 'Hungarian anthropology. The problem of communication', *Current Anthropology* 9 (2-3), 1968, pp. 180-184.

——, 'Foreword', in 'Anthropology in East-Central and Southeast Europe', *op. cit.* (1970), pp. 237-241.

MAGET, Marcel, 'Problèmes d'ethnographie européenne', in POIRIER (ed.), *Ethnologie générale, op. cit.* (1968), pp. 1247-1338.

Main Trends of Research in the Social and Human Sciences, Part I: Social Sciences, Paris-The Hague, Mouton/Unesco, 1970 (parallel publication in French, *Tendances principales de la recherche dans les sciences sociales et humaines, Partie I: Sciences sociales*, same reference).

MAIR, Lucy, *Primitive Government*, Harmondsworth (Middx.), Penguin Books, 1962.

——, 'Applied anthropology', in SILLS (ed.), *International Encyclopedia of the Social Sciences, op. cit.* (1968), Vol. 1, pp. 325-379.

——, *Anthropology and Social Change*, London School of Economics Monographs on Social Anthropology No. 38, London, Athlone Press, 1969.

——, *Witchcraft*, World University Library, London, Weidenfeld & Nicolson, 1969.

——, *Marriage*, Harmondsworth (Middx.), Penguin Books, 1971.

MALINOWSKI, Bronislaw, *A Diary in the Strict Sense of the Term*, London, Routledge & Kegan Paul, 1967.

MANNERS, Robert A. & KAPLAN, David (eds.), *Theory in Anthropology. A Sourcebook*, Chicago, Aldine, 1968.

MARANDA, Pierre, 'L'ordinateur et l'analyse des mythes', in *L'informatique, la documentation et les sciences sociales, op. cit.* (1971), pp. 244-251 (parallel publication of English translation, 'The computer and the analysis of myths', in *Computers, Documentation, and the Social Sciences, op. cit.* (1971), pp. 228-235).
[See also POUILLON & MARANDA (eds.).]

MARIN, Louis, 'Présentation' in Françoise & Louis Marin, translators, RADCLIFFE-BROWN, A. R., *Structure et fonction dans la société primitive*, Paris, Editions de Minuit, 1970, pp. 15-64.

MARKARJAN, E. S., *Očerki teorii kul'tury* (= Essays on the theory of culture), Yerevan, Izdatel'stvo AN Armjanskoj SSR, 1969.

MARTINDALE, Don (ed.), *Functionalism in the Social Sciences*, American Academy of Political and Social Sciences, Monograph No. 5, Philadelphia, 1965.

MARWICK, Max (ed.), *Witchcraft and Sorcery. Selected Readings*, Harmondsworth (Middx.), Penguin Books, 1970.

MASON, Philip (ed.), *India and Ceylon: Unity and Diversity*, London, Oxford University Press, 1967.

MAUSS, Marcel, 'Essai sur le don. Forme et raison de l'échange dans les sociétés archaïques', *L'Année sociologique*, nouvelle série, Vol. 1, Fasc. 1, 1923-24, pp. 30-186; republished in MAUSS, *Sociologie et anthropologie*, Paris, Presses Universitaires de France, 1950, 2nd edn., 1960, pp. 143-279 (English translation by I. Cunnison, *The Gift*, London, Cohen & West, 1954).

——, *Manuel d'ethnographie*, ed. by Denise Paulme, Paris, Payot, 1947; 2nd edn., Paris, Petite Bibliothèque Payot, 1967.

MAYBURY-LEWIS, David, *The Savage and the Innocent*, London, Evans Bros., 1965.

MAYER, Adrian C., 'The significance of quasi-groups in the study of complex societies', in BANTON (ed.), *The Social Anthropology of Complex Societies, op. cit.* (1966), pp. 97-122.

MAYER, Philip (ed.), *Socialization. The Approach from Social Anthropology*, A.S.A. Monographs No. 8, London, Tavistock Publications, 1970.

MAZUR, Allan, 'Game theory and Pathan segmentary opposition', *Man*, n.s., 2 (3), 1967, pp. 465-466.

MEAD, Margaret, *Continuities in Cultural Evolution*, New Haven (Conn.)-London, Yale University Press, 1964.

MEILLASSOUX, Claude, *Anthropologie économique des Gouro de Côte-d'Ivoire*, Paris-The Hague, Mouton, 1965.

MELETINSKIJ, Elizar M., *Proishoždenie geroičeskogo eposa. Rannie formy i arhaičeskie pamjatniki* (= The Origin of the Heroic Epic . . .), Moscow, Izdatel'stvo Vostočnoj Literatury, 1963 (English summary, 'Primitive heritage in archaic epics', in *VIIe Congrès International des Sciences Anthropologiques et Ethnologiques*, Vol. 6, Moscow, Nauka, 1970, pp. 187-193).

——, *Edda i rannie formy eposa* (= The Edda and Archaic Forms of Epic), Moscow, Nauka, 1968.

——, 'Die Ehe im Zaubermärchen' (= Marriage in fairy tales), *Acta Ethnographica Academiae Scientiarum Hungaricae* 19 (1-4), 1970, 'Gyula Ortutay sexagenario', pp. 281-292.

——, 'Mif i skazka' (= Myth and folk tale), in PUTILOV (ed.), *Fol'klor i ètnografija, op. cit.* (1970).

——, 'Klod Levi-Stross i strukturnaja tipologija mifa', *Voprosy filosofii*, 1970, No. 7, pp. 165-173 (English version, 'Claude Lévi-Strauss and the structural typology of myth', *Soviet Anthropology and Archeology* IX (3), Winter 1970-71, pp. 179-203).

——, 'Structural typological study of folklore', *Social Sciences* (USSR Academy of Sciences, Moscow), No. 3, 1971, pp. 64-81.

——, 'Klod Levi-Stross. Tol'ko ètnologija? (= Claude Lévi-Strauss. Is it only ethnology?), *Voprosy literatury*, 15 (4), Apr. 1971, pp. 115-134.

——, NEKLJUDOV, S. Ju., NOVIK, E. S., & SEGAL, D. M., 'Problemy strukturnogo opisanija volšebnoj skazki' (= The problems of the structural description of fairy tales) and 'Eščë raz o probleme strukturnogo opisanija volšebnoj skazki' (= Further thoughts on the problem . . .), *Trudy po znakovym sistemam*, Nos. 4 and 5, Tartu, Učenye Zapiski Tartuskogo Gosudarstvennogo Universiteta, Vol. 236, 1969, pp. 86-135 and Vol. 284, 1971, pp. 63-91. [See also *sub* PROPP, *Morfologija skazki*, 2nd edn.]

MERCIER, Paul, *Histoire de l'anthropologie*, Paris, Presses Universitaires de France, Paris 1966.

——, 'Anthropologie sociale et culturelle', in POIRIER (ed.), *Ethnologie générale, op. cit.* (1968), pp. 881-1036.

MERING, Otto von & KASDAN, Leonard (eds.), *Anthropology and the Behavioral and Health Sciences*, Pittsburgh, University of Pittsburgh Press, 1970.

MERRIAM, Alan P., *The Anthropology of Music*, Evanston (Ill.), Northwestern University Press, 1964.

——, *Ethnomusicology of the Flathead Indians*, Chicago, Aldine, 1964.

——, 'The anthropology of music: CA book review', *Current Anthropology* 7 (2), 1966, pp. 217-230.

——, 'Ethnomusicology', in SILLS (ed.), *International Encyclopedia of the Social Sciences, op. cit.* (1968), Vol. 10, pp. 562-566.

——, 'Ethnomusicology revisited', *Ethnomusicology* 13 (2), 1969, pp. 213-229.

MERRILL, Robert S., 'The study of technology', in SILLS (ed.), *International Encyclopedia of the Social Sciences, op. cit.* (1968), Vol. 15, pp. 576-589.

MICHÉA, Jean, 'La technologie culturelle. Essai de systématique, in POIRIER (ed.), *Ethnologie générale, op. cit.* (1968), pp. 823-880.

MIDDLETON, John, 'The religious system', in NAROLL & COHEN, R. (eds.), *A Handbook of Methods in Cultural Anthropology, op. cit.* (1970), pp. 500-508.

MIDDLETON, John (ed.), *Gods and Rituals. Readings in Religious Beliefs and Practices*, American Museum Sourcebooks in Anthropology, Garden City (N.Y.), Natural History Press, 1967.

——, *Magic, Witchcraft and Curing*, American Museum Sourcebooks in Anthropology, Garden City (N.Y.), Natural History Press, 1967.

——, *Myth and Cosmos. Readings in Mythology and Symbolism*, American Museum Sourcebooks in Anthropology, Garden City (N.Y.), Natural History Press, 1967. [See also BOHANNAN & MIDDLETON (eds.); COHEN, R. & MIDDLETON (eds.).]

MILLER, Wick R., 'Language', in SIEGEL (ed.), *Biennial Review of Anthropology 1969, op. cit.* (1970), pp. 1-40.

MINNIS, Noel (ed.), *Linguistics at Large*, London, Gollancz, 1971.

MINTURN, Leigh & LAMBERT, William W., *Mothers of Six Cultures. Antecedents of Child Rearing*, New York, Wiley & Sons, 1964.

MITCHELL, J. Clyde, 'On quantification in social anthropology', in EPSTEIN, A. L. (ed.), *The Craft of Social Anthropology, op. cit.* (1967), pp. 17-54.

——, 'The concept and use of social networks', in MITCHELL (ed.), *Social Networks in Urban Situations . . ., op. cit.* (1969), pp. 1-50.

MITCHELL, J. Clyde (ed.), *Social Networks in Urban Situations. Analyses of Personal Relationships in Central African Towns*, Manchester, Manchester University Press, 1969.

MKRTUMJAN, Ju. I., 'Formy skotovodstva i byt naselenija v armjanskoj derevne vtoroj poloviny XIX veka' (= Cattle-raising and daily life of Armenian villagers in the second half of the 19th century), *Sovetskaja ètnografija*, 1968, No. 4, pp. 14-29.

'Modellálás a folklorisztikában' (= Modelling in folklore studies), *Ethnographia* (Budapest), Vol. 80, 1969, pp. 347-430.

MOLOŠNAJA, T. N. (ed.), *Strukturno-tipologičeskie issledovanija. Sbornik statej* (= Papers on Structural-Typological Investigations), Moscow, Izdatel'stvo Akademii Nauk SSR, 1962.

MONBERG, Torben, 'Determinants of choice in adoption and fosterage on Bellona Island', *Ethnology* 9 (2), 1970, pp. 99-136.

MONOGAROVA, L., On the journal *Sovetskaja ètnografija* (= *Sovetskaja ètnografija*), *Social Sciences*, Moscow, USSR Academy) of Sciences, 2, 1970, pp. 205-207.

MONTAGU, Ashley (ed.), *The Concept of the Primitive*, New York, The Free Press, 1968.

MOORE, Frank W., 'Current trends in cross-cultural research', in *The Social Sciences, Problems and Orientations, op. cit.* (1968), pp. 469-474.

——, 'The human relations area files', in NAROLL & COHEN, R. (eds.), *A Handbook of Method in Cultural Anthropology, op. cit.* (1970), pp. 640-648.

MOORE, Frank W. (ed.), *Readings in Cross-Cultural Methodology*, New Haven (Conn.), Human Relations Area Files Press, 1961.

MOORE, Sally Falk, 'Law and anthropology', in SIEGEL (ed.), *Biennial Review of Anthropology 1969, op. cit.* (1970), pp. 252-300.

MOULOUD, Noël *et al., Structuralisme et marxisme* = *La Pensée* (Paris), No. 135, Oct. 1967 (special number), pp. 1-192.

MUENSTERBERGER, Werner (ed.). *Man and his Culture. Psychoanalytic Anthropology after 'Totem and Taboo'*, London, Rapp & Whiting, 1969.

MÜHLMANN, Wilhelm E., 'Ethnologie und Völkerpsychologie', in VON BECKERATH (ed.), *Handwörterbuch der Sozialwissenschaften, op. cit.* (1961), pp. 348-353.

——, *Geschichte der Anthropologie*, Frankfurt am Main, Athenäum Verlag, 1968.

MÜHLMANN, Wilhelm E. (ed.), *Chiliasmus und Nativismus. Studien zur Psychologie, Soziologie und historischen Kasuistik der Umsturzbewegungen*, Berlin, Dietrich Reimer, 1961.

MÜLLER, Ernst Wilhelm, *Der Begriff 'Verwandtschaft' in der modernen Ethnosoziologie* (= The concept of 'kinship' in modern social anthropology), Studia Ethnologica, Vol. 4, Meisenheim am Glan, Verlag Anton Hain (in press – 1973).

MUNN, Nancy D., 'Walbiri graphic signs. An analysis', *American Anthropologist* 64 (5), Pt. 1, 1962, pp. 972-984.

——, 'The spatial representation of cosmic order in Walbiri iconography', in FORGE (ed.), *Primitive Art and Society, op. cit.* (1973).

MURDOCK, George P., *Social Structure*, New York, Macmillan Co., 1949 (French translation by S. Laroche & M. Giacometti, with a foreword by Michel PANOFF, *De la structure sociale*, Paris, Payot, 1972).

——, *Culture and Society*, Pittsburgh, University of Pittsburgh, 1965.

MURDOCK, George P. (ed.), *Social Structure in Southeast Asia*, Viking Fund Publ. in Anthrop. 29, Chicago, Quadrangle Books, 1960.

MURPHY, Robert F., 'Cultural change', in SIEGEL & BEALS (eds.), *Biennial Review of Anthropology 1967, op. cit.* (1967), pp. 1-45.

'Le mythe aujourd'hui', *Esprit* (Paris), 39 (402), Apr. 1971, pp. 609-833.

NACHT, Sacha, 'Psychanalyse et ethnologie', in POIRIER (ed.), *Ethnologie générale, op. cit.* (1968), pp. 1680-1705.

NADEL, S. F., *The Foundations of Social Anthropology*, London, Cohen & West, 1951.

——, 'Applied anthropology', Section III of 'Anthropology', in *Encyclopaedia Britannica*, Vol. 2, 1963 (but written in the early fifties).

NADER, Laura (ed.), *The Ethnography of Law* = *American Anthropologist* 67 (6), Pt. 2, 1965.

——, *Law in Culture and Society*, Chicago, Aldine, 1969.

NAKANE, Chie, *Kinship and Economic Organization in Rural Japan*, London School of Economics Monographs on Social Anthropology No. 32, London, Athlone Press, 1967.

——, *Japanese Society*, London, Weidenfeld & Nicolson/Berkeley-Los Angeles, University of California Press, 1970.

NAROLL, Raoul, 'A preliminary index of social development', *American Anthropologist* 58 (4), 1956, pp. 687-715.

——, 'Galton's problem', in NAROLL & COHEN, R. (eds.), *A Handbook of Method in Cultural Anthropology, op. cit.* (1970), pp. 974-989.

——, 'What have we learned from cross-cultural surveys?', *American Anthropologist* 72 (6), 1970, pp. 1227-1288.

—— & D'ANDRADE, Roy G., 'Two further solutions to Galton's problem', *American Anthropologist* 65 (6), 1963, pp. 1053-1067.

NAROLL, Raoul & COHEN, Ronald (eds.), *A Handbook of Method in Cultural Anthropology*, Garden City (N.Y.), The Natural History Press, for the American Museum of Natural History, 1970.

NASH, Manning, 'Economic anthropology', in SIEGEL (ed.), *Biennial Review of Anthropology 1965, op. cit.* (1965), pp. 121-138.

——, *Primitive and Peasant Economic Systems*, San Francisco, Chandler Publishing Co., 1966.

NATHHORST, Bertel, *Formal or Structural Studies of Traditional Tales. The Usefulness of Some Methodological Advances by Vladimir Propp, Alan Dundes, Claude Lévi-Strauss, and Edmund Leach*, Acta Universitatis Stockholmiensis, Stockholm Studies in Comparative Religion No. 9, Stockholm, 1969.

NEEDHAM, Rodney, *Structure and Sentiment. A Test Case in Social Anthropology*, Chicago, University of Chicago Press, 1962.

——, 'Percussion and transition', *Man*, n.s., 2 (4), 1967, pp. 606-614.

——, 'The future of social anthropology: disintegration or metamorphosis?', in *Anniversary Contributions to Anthropology. Twelve Essays Published on the Occasion of the 40th Anniversary of the Leiden Ethnological Society W.D.O.*, Leiden, Brill, 1970, pp. 34-46.

NEEDHAM, Rodney (ed.), *Rethinking Kinship and Marriage*, A.S.A. Monograph No. 11, London, Tavistock Publications, 1971.
[See also KORN & NEEDHAM.]

NEEL, J. V., 'Lessons from a "primitive" people', *Science* 170 (3960), 1970, pp. 815-822.

NERLOVE, Sara & ROMNEY, A. Kimball, 'Sibling terminology and cross-sex behavior', *American Anthropologist* 69 (2), 1967, pp. 179-187.

NETTL, Bruno, *Theory and Method in Ethnomusicology*, Glencoe (Ill.), Free Press of Glencoe/London, Collier-Macmillan, 1964.

——, 'Biography of a Blackfoot Indian singer', *Musical Quarterly* (New York), 54 (2), 1968, pp. 199-207.

NEUMANN, P., *Wirtschaft und materielle Kultur der Buschneger Surinams*, Berlin, Akademie Verlag, 1967.

OBEYESEKERE, Gananath, *Land Tenure in Village Ceylon. A Sociological and Historical Study*, Cambridge, Cambridge University Press, 1967.

OKLADNIKOV, A. P., *Utro iskusstva* (= The Dawn of Art), Leningrad, Izdatel'stvo Iskusstvo, 1967.

OKOT p'BITEK, *African Religions in Western Scholarship*, Kampala-Nairobi-Dar es Salaam, East African Literature Bureau [1971?].

OL'DEROGGE, D. A., 'Osnovnye čerty razvitija sistem rodstva' (= Main evolutionary features of kinship systems), *Sovetskaja ètnografija*, 1960, No. 6, pp. 24-30.

——, 'Several problems in the study of kinship', *Current Anthropology* 2 (2), 1961, pp. 103-107.

O'LEARY, Timothy, 'Ethnographic bibliographies', in NARROLL & COHEN, R. (eds.), *A Handbook of Method in Cultural Anthropology, op. cit.* (1970), pp. 128-146.

OLIVER, Roland, 'The problem of Bantu expansion', *The Journal of African History* 7 (3), 1966, pp. 361-376.

'On Hungarian Anthropology', *Current Anthropology* 11 (1), 1970, pp. 61-65.

OPLER, Marvin K. (ed.), *Culture and Mental Health. Cross-Cultural Studies*, New York, Macmillan, 1959.

OPLER, Morris E., 'The human being in culture theory', *American Anthropologist* 66 (3), Pt. 1, 1964, pp. 507-528.

ORANS, Martin, 'Social organization', in SIEGEL (ed.), *Biennial Review of Anthropology 1969, op. cit.* (1970), pp. 132-190.

ORTIZ, Sutti, 'Colombian rural market organization. An exploratory model', *Man*, n.s. 2 (3), 1967, pp. 393-414.

OSGOOD, Charles E., 'Semantic differential technique in the comparative study of cultures', in ROMNEY & D'ANDRADE (eds.), *Transcultural Studies in Cognition, op. cit.* (1964), pp. 171-200.

——, 'On the strategy of cross-national research into subjective culture', in *The Social Sciences. Problems and Orientations, op. cit.* (1968), pp. 475-507.

PANJAN, A. E., 'Izmenenija v strukture i čislennosti sel'skoj sem'i u armjan za gody sovetskoj vlasti' (= Changes in the structure and size of the Armenian rural family in the years of Soviet rule), *Sovetskaja ètnografija*, 1968, No. 4, pp. 93-103.

PANOFF, Michel, 'Ethnologie et économie', *Esprit*, Sept. 1970, pp. 336-354.

—— & PANOFF, Françoise, *L'ethnologue et son ombre*, Paris, Payot, 1968. [See also *sub* MURDOCK, *Social Structure.*]

PARRACK, D. W., 'An approach to the bio-energetics of rural West Bengal', in VAYDA (ed.), *Environment and Cultural Behavior. Ecological Studies in Cultural Anthropology, op. cit.* (1969), pp. 29-46.

PAUL, Benjamin D. & MILLER, Walter B. (eds.), *Health, Culture and Community*, New York, Russell Sage Foundation, 1955.

PAUW, Berthold Adolf, *The Second Generation. A Study of the Family among Urbanized Bantu in East London*, Rhodes University Institute of Social and Economic Research, 'Xhosa in Town', No. 3, Cape Town, Oxford University Press, 1963.

PAWLOWSKA, Harriet M., *Merrily We Sing. 105 Polish Folksongs*, Detroit (Mich.), Wayne State University Press, 1961.

PELTO, Pertti J., 'Psychological anthropology', in SIEGEL and BEALS (eds.), *Biennial Review of Anthropology 1967, op. cit.* (1967), pp. 140-208.

——, *Anthropological Research. The Structure of Inquiry*, New York-Evanstone (Ill.)-London, Harper & Row, 1970.

PENNIMAN, T. K., *A Hundred Years of Anthropology*, 3rd edn., London, Duckworth, 1965.

PENTIKÄINEN, Juha, 'Depth research', *Acta Ethnographica Academiae Hungaricae*, Vol. 21, 1972 (in press).

PEREIRA DE QUEIROZ, Maria Isaura, *O mesianismo no Brasil e no mundo*, São Paulo, Dominus, 1965.

PERŠIC, A. I., 'Aktual'nye problemy sovetskoj ètnografii' (= Current problems of Soviet ethnography), *Sovetskaja ètnografija*, 1964, No. 4, pp. 5-21.

PERSHITZ (= PERŠIC), A. I. (ed.), 'Symposium: La théorie de L. H. Morgan de périodisation de l'histoire de la société primitive et l'ethnographie moderne', in *VIIe Congrès International des Sciences Anthropologiques et Ethnologiques*. Vol. 8, *op. cit.* (1970), pp. 439-511.

PERŠIC, A. I. & ČEBOKSAROV, N. N., 'Polveka sovetskoj ètnografii' (= Half a

166   Maurice Freedman

century of Soviet ethnography), *Sovetskaja ètnografija*, 1967, No. 5, pp. 3-24.

——, MONGAJT, A. L., & ALEKSEEV, V. P., *Istorija pervobytnogo obščestva* (= A history of primitive society), Moscow, Izdatel'stvo 'Vysšaja Škola', 1968.

PERŠIC, Ju. I., 'O metodike sopostavlenija pokazatelej odnonacional'noj i smešannoj bračnosti' (= A method of comparing indices for uninational and mixed marriages), *Sovetskaja ètnografija*, 1967, No. 4, pp. 129-136.

PIAGET, Jean, 'La psychologie', in *Tendances principales de la recherche dans les sciences sociales et humaines, Partie I: Sciences sociales, op. cit.* (1970), pp. 274-339 (parallel publication of English translation, 'Psychology', in *Main Trends of Research in the Social and Human Sciences, Part I: Social Sciences, op. cit.* (1970), pp. 225-282).

——, *Le Structuralisme*, 'Que sais-je?', No. 1311, Paris, Presses Universitaires de France, 1970 (English translation by Chaninah Maschler, *Structuralism*, London, Routledge & Kegan Paul, 1971).

PINGAUD, Bernard *et al., Claude Lévi-Strauss* = *L'Arc* (Aix-en-Provence), No. 65, 1965, 87 pp.

PODOLÁK, Jan, 'Ethnology in Slovakia', in 'Anthropology in East-Central and Southeast Europe', *op. cit.* (1970), pp. 265-274.

POIRIER, Jean, 'Dépendance et aliénation: de la situation coloniale à la situation condominiale', *Cahiers Internationaux de Sociologie*, No. 40, 1966, pp. 73-88.

——, 'Ethnologie diachronique et histoire culturelle', in POIRIER (ed.), *Ethnologie générale, op. cit.* (1968), pp. 1444-1464.

——, 'Histoire de la pensée ethnologique', in POIRIER (ed.), *Ethnologie générale, op. cit.* (1968), pp. 3-179.

——, 'Introduction à l'ethnologie de l'appareil juridique', in POIRIER (ed.), *Ethnologie générale, op. cit.* (1968), pp. 1091-1110.

——, 'Problèmes d'ethnologie économique', in POIRIER (ed.), *Ethnologie générale, op. cit.* (1968), pp. 1546-1624.

——, 'Situation actuelle et programme de travail de l'ethnologie juridique', *Revue internationale des Sciences sociales* XXII (3), 1970 ('Tendances de la science juridique'), pp. 509-527 (parallel publication of English translation, 'The current state of legal ethnology and its future tasks', *International Social Science Journal*, same ref. ('Trends in legal learning'), pp. 476-494).

POIRIER, Jean (ed.), series 'Economie, Ethnologie, Sociologie', Cahiers de l'Institut de Science Economique Appliquée, Paris, 1959.

——, *Etudes de droit africain et malgache* (contributions by Michel ALLIOT, Anthony ALLOTT, R. BALARD, and J. BINET), Paris, Editions Cujas, 1965, Université de Madagascar, Faculté des Lettres et des Sciences humaines, Etudes malgaches.

——, *Ethnologie générale*, Encyclopédie de la Pléiade, Paris, Gallimard, 1968.

POLANYI, K. K., ARENSBERG, C. M., & PEARSON, H. W., *Trade and Markets in the Early Empires*, Glencoe (Ill.), Free Press, 1957.

PORSHNEV (= PORŠNEV), B. F., 'Attempts at synthesis in the field of the history of religion', *Soviet Anthropology and Archeology* 7 (3), Winter 1968-69, pp. 20-36 (translated from *Voprosy istorii*, 1965, No. 7).

POSNANSKY, Merrick, 'Bantu genesis', *The Uganda Journal* 25 (1), 1961, pp. 86-93.

POSPISIL, Leopold, 'A formal analysis of substantive law: Kapauku Papuan laws of land tenure', in HAMMEL (ed.), *Formal Semantic Analysis, op. cit.* (1965), pp. 186-214.

——, 'Law and order', in CLIFTON (ed.), *Introduction to Cultural Anthropology ...*, *op. cit.* (1968), pp. 200-223.

POTTER, Jack M., DIAZ, May N., & FOSTER, George M. (eds.), *Peasant Society. A Reader*, Boston, Little, Brown and Co., 1967.

POUILLON, Jean, 'L'œuvre de Claude Lévi-Strauss', in LÉVI-STRAUSS, *Race et histoire, op. cit.* (2nd edn., 1967), pp. 87-128.

—— *et al., Problèmes du structuralisme = Les Temps modernes* (Paris), 22nd yr., No. 246, Nov. 1966 (special number: pp. 769-960).

POUILLON, Jean & MARANDA, Pierre (eds.), *Echanges et communications. Mélanges offerts à Claude Lévi-Strauss*, The Hague-Paris, Mouton, 1970, 2 vols.

POWDERMAKER, Hortense, *Stranger and Friend*, New York, Norton and Co., 1966.

——, 'Fieldwork', in SILLS (ed.), *International Encyclopedia of the Social Sciences, op. cit.* (1968), Vol. 5, pp. 418-424.

PRICE, Richard, 'Saramaka woodcarving. The development of an Afroamerican art', *Man*, n.s., 5 (3), 1970, pp. 363-378.

PRICE-WILLIAMS, Douglass R., 'Ethnopsychology I: Comparative psychological processes' and 'Ethnopsychology II: Comparative personality processes', in CLIFTON (ed.), *Introduction to Cultural Anthropology ..., op. cit.* (1968), pp. 304-318, 319-335.

PRICE-WILLIAMS, Douglass R. (ed.), *Cross-Cultural Studies*, Penguin Modern Psychology Readings, Harmondsworth (Middx.), Penguin Books, 1969.

Proceedings, VIIIth International Congress of Anthropological and Ethnological Sciences (Tokyo and Kyoto, 1968), Tokyo, Science Council of Japan, 1969, 1970, 3 vols.

PROPP, Vladimir Ja., *Morfologija skazki* (= Morphology of the Folk Tale), Leningrad, Akademija, 1928, 2nd edn., Moscow, Nauka, 1969, with postface by E. M. MELETINSKIJ (French translation of 2nd edn. by Marguerite Derrida, *Morphologie du conte*, Paris, Editions du Seuil, 1970).

PROPP, Vladimir Ja. (ed.), *Metodičeskaja zapiska po arhivnomu hraneniju i sistemitazacii fol'klornyh materialov* (= Handbook of Methods for the Archiving an Cataloguing of Folklore Materials), Institut Litovskogo Jazyka i Literatury, Akademija Nauk Litovskoj SSR, Vilnius, 1964.

PUTILOV, B. N. (ed.), *Fol'klor i ètnografija*, Moscow-Leningrad, Nauka, 1970.

RADCLIFFE-BROWN, A. R., *A Natural Science of Society*, Glencoe (Ill.), Free Press, 1957.

RADCLIFFE-BROWN, A. R. & FORDE, Daryll (eds.), *African Systems of Kinship and Marriage*, London, Oxford University Press, 1950 (French translation by M. Griaule, *Systèmes familiaux et matrimoniaux en Afrique*, Paris, Presses Universitaires de France, 1953).
[See also *sub* MARIN, Louis.]

RAPPOPORT, Roy A., *Pigs for the Ancestors*, New Haven (Conn.)-London, Yale University Press, 1967.

Razloženie rodovogo obščestva i formirovanie klassovogo obščestva (= The Break-up of the Patrimonial System and the Formation of Class Society), Moscow, Nauka, 1968.

READ, Kenneth E., *The High Valley*, New York, Scribner, 1965.

READER, Desmond Harold, *The Black Man's Portion. History, Demography, and Living Conditions in the Native Locations of East London, Cape Province*, Rhodes University Institute of Social and Economic Research, 'Xhosa in Town', No. 1, Cape Town, Oxford University Press, 1961.

REDFIELD, Robert, *The Little Community. Viewpoints for the Study of a Human Whole*, Chicago, University of Chicago Press, 1955.

——, *Peasant Society and Culture. An Anthropological Approach to Civilization*, Chicago, University of Chicago Press, 1956.

——, *Human Nature and the Study of Society. The Papers of Robert Redfield* (ed. Margaret Park REDFIELD), Vol. 1, Chicago, University of Chicago Press, 1962.

REICHEL-DOLMATOFF, Gerardo, *Desana. Simbolismo de los Indios Tukano del Vaupés*, Bogotá, Universidad de los Andes, 1968 (English translation by the author, *Amazonian Cosmos. The Sexual and Religious Symbolism of the Tukano Indians*, Chicago, Chicago University Press, 1971).

REINFUSS, Roman, *Malarstwo Iudowe* (= Folk Painting), Cracow, Wydawnictwo Literackie, 1962.

REVZIN, I. I., *Modeli jazyka* (= Language Models), Moscow, Izdatel'stvo Akademii Nauk SSR, 1962.

RICHARD, Philippe & JAULIN, Robert (eds.) ('Textes choisis et présentés par ...'), *Anthropologie et calcul*, Collection 10/18, Série '7' edited by Robert Jaulin, Paris, Union Générale d'Editions, 1971.

RICHARDS, Audrey I., 'The development of field work methods in social anthropology, in BARTLETT *et al.* (eds.), *The study of Society. Methods and Problems, op. cit.* (1939), pp. 272-316.

RIVIÈRE, Georges-Henri, 'Musées et autres collections publiques d'ethnographie', in POIRIER (ed.), *Ethnologie générale, op. cit.* (1968), pp. 472-493.

ROBERTS, John M., STRAND, Richard F., & BURMEISTER, Edwin, 'Preferential pattern analysis', in KAY (ed.), *Explorations in Mathematical Anthropology, op. cit.* (1971), pp. 242-268.
[See also KOZELKA & ROBERTS.]

RODGERS, William B., 'Household atomism and change in the Out Island Bahamas', *Southwestern Journal of Anthropology* 23 (3), 1967, pp. 244-260.

ROKKAN, Stein, 'Cross-cultural, cross-societal ad cross-national research', in *Main Trends of Research in the Social and Human Sciences, Part I: Social Sciences, op cit.* (1970), pp. 645-689 (parallel publication of French translation, 'Recherche trans-culturelle, trans-sociétale et trans-nationale', in *Tendances principales de la recherche dans les sciences sociales et humaines, Partie I: Sciences sociales, op. cit.* (1970), pp. 765-821).

ROMNEY, A. Kimball, 'Measuring endogamy', in KAY (ed.), *Explorations in Mathematical Anthropology, op. cit.* (1971), pp. 191-213.

—— & D'ANDRADE, Roy G., 'Cognitive aspects of English kin terms', in ROMNEY & D'ANDRADE (eds.), *Transcultural Studies in Cognition, op. cit.* (1964), pp. 146-170.

ROMNEY, A. Kimball & D'ANDRADE, Roy G. (eds.), *Transcultural Studies in Cognition = American Anthropologist* 66 (3), Pt. 2, June 1964.
[See also LAMB & ROMNEY; NERLOVE & ROMNEY.]

RÖPKE, J., *Primitive Wirtschaft, Kulturwandel und die Diffusion von Neuerungen* (= Primitive Economy, Cultural Change, and the Diffusion of Innovations), Tübingen, J. C. B. Mohr, 1970.

ROSMAN, Abraham, 'Structuralism as a conceptual framework', *African Studies Review* 13 (1), 1970, pp. 69-74.

ROSTWOROSKI DE DIEZ CANSECO, María, 'Succession, coöption to kingship and royal incest among the Inca', *Southwestern Journal of Anthropology* 16 (4), 1960, pp. 417-427.

ROUCH, Jean, 'Le film ethnographique', in POIRIER (ed.), *Ethnologie générale, op. cit.* (1968), pp. 429-471.

ROUGET, Gilbert, 'L'ethnomusicologie', in POIRIER (ed.), *Ethnologie générale, op. cit.* (1968), pp. 1339-1390.

RUDOLPH, W., 'Entwicklungshilfe und Sozialwissenschaften' (= Development aid and the social sciences), *Sociologus*, Vol. 11, 1961, pp. 4-19.

——, ' "Akkulturation" und Akkulturationsforschung', *Sociologus*, n.s., 14 (2), 1964, pp. 97-113.

SAHLINS, Marshall D. & SERVICE, Elman R. (eds.), *Evolution and Culture*, Ann Arbor, University of Michigan, 1960.

SALISBURY, Richard, *From Stone to Steel: Economic Consequences of a Technological Change in New Guinea*, Melbourne, Melbourne University Press, 1962.

——, 'Formal analysis in anthropological economics. The Rossel Island case', in

BUCHLER & NUTINI (eds.), *Game Theory in the Behavioral Sciences, op. cit.* (1969), pp. 75-94.

——, 'Economics', in von MERING & KASDAN (eds.), *Anthropology and the Behavioral and Health Sciences, op. cit.* (1970), pp. 62-72 (followed by a' Commentary' by George Dalton, Cyril S. Belshaw, and Leonard Kasdan, pp. 72-84, and by a list of references, pp. 85-88).

SALZMÁNN, Zděněk, 'Czech ethnography since World War II', in 'Anthropology in East-Central and Southeast Europe', *op. cit.* (1970), pp. 252-264.

ŠAREVSKAJA, B. I., *Starye i novye religii Tropičeskoj i Južnoj Afriki* (= Old and New Religions in Tropical and South Africa), Moscow, Nauka, 1964.

SARLES, Harvey B., 'Communication and ethology', in von MERING & KASDAN (eds.), *Anthropology and the Behavioral and Health Sciences, op. cit.* (1970), pp. 149-162 (followed by a 'Commentary' by C. R. Carpenter, Henry W. Brosin, and Suzanne Ripley, pp. 162-172, and by a list of references, pp. 172-175).

SARMELA, Matti, *Perinneaineiston kvantitatiivisesta tutkimuksesta* (= On Quantitative Methods in Research on Folk Tradition), Helsinki, Suomalaisen Kirjallisuuden Seura, 1970.

SCHAPERA, I., *Tribal Legislation among the Tswana of the Bechuanaland Protectorate*, London School of Economics Monographs on Social Anthropology No. 9, London, 1943.

——, *Government and Politics in Tribal Societies*, London, Watts, 1956.

——, *Tribal Innovators: Tswana Chiefs and Social Change 1795-1940*, London School of Economics Monographs on Social Anthropology No. 43, London, Athlone Press, 1970.

SCHAPERA, I. (ed.), *Studies in Kinship and Marriage Dedicated to Brenda Z. Seligman on her 80th Birthday*, Royal Anthropological Institute, Occasional Papers No. 16, London, 1963.

SCHEANS, Daniel J., 'A new view of Philippines pottery manufacture', *Southwestern Journal of Anthropology* 22 (3), 1966, pp. 206-219.

SCHEFFLER, Harold W., 'Structuralism in anthropology', in EHRMANN (ed.), *Structuralism, op. cit.* (1966), pp. 66-88; republication, *op. cit.* (1970), pp. 56-79.

SCHEFLEN, A. E., 'The significance of posture in communication systems', *Psychiatry* (Washington, D.C.), 27 (4), 1964, pp. 316-332.

SCHEFOLD, Reimar, *Versuch einer Stilanalyse der Aufhängehaken vom Mittleren Sepik in Neu-Guinea* (= Towards a Stylistic Analysis of the Suspension Hooks of the Middle Sepik River Region in New Guinea) = *Basler Beiträge zur Ethnologie*, Vol. IV, 1966.

SCHIRMUNSKI, Viktor: see ŽIRMUNSKIJ, Viktor Maksimovič.

SCHLESIER, E., 'Sippen-Diagramme und lokale Ethnohistorie' (= Kinship diagrams and local ethnohistory), *Paideuma*, Vol. 12, 1966, pp. 70-72.

SCHMITZ, Carl August, *Wantoat. Art and Religion of the Northeast New Guinea Papuans* (translated by Mrs. G. E. van Baaren-Pape), The Hague, Mouton, 1963.

——, *Grundformen der Verwandtschaft* (= Basic forms of kinship), *Basler Beiträge zur Geographie und Ethnologie*, Ethnol. R., H. 1, Basel, 1964.

SCHNEIDER, David M., *American Kinship. A Cultural Account*, Anthropology of Modern Society Series, Englewood Cliffs (N.J.), Prentice-Hall, 1968.

SCHNEIDER, David M. & GOUGH, Kathleen (eds.), *Matrilineal Kinship*, Berkeley-Los Angeles, University of California Press, 1961.

[See also COALE, FALLERS, LEVY, SCHNEIDER, and TOMKINS; HOMANS & SCHNEIDER.]

SCHOTT, R., 'Die Funktionen des Rechts in primitiven Gesellschaften', *Jahrbuch für Rechtssoziologie und Rechtstheorie* (Gütersloh), Vol. 1, 1970, pp. 108-174.

SEGALL, N. H., CAMPBELL, D. T., & HERSKOVITS, M. J., *The Influence of Culture on Visual Perception*, Indianapolis, Bobbs-Merrill, 1966.

SELLNOW, Irmgard, *Grundprinzipien einer Periodisierung der Urgeschichte* (Deutsche Akademie der Wissenschaften zu Berlin, Bd. 4), Berlin, Akademie-Verlag, 1961.

SELLNOW, Werner, *Gesellschaft, Staat, Recht*, Berlin, Rütten & Loening, 1963.

SEMENOV, Ju. I., 'The doctrine of Morgan, Marxism and contemporary ethnography', *Soviet Anthropology and Archeology* 4 (2), Fall 1965, pp. 3-15 (translated from 'Učenie Morgana, marksizm i sovremennaja ètnografija', *Sovetskaja ètnografija*, 1964, No. 4, pp. 170-185).

SEMENOV, S. A., 'Izučenie pervobytnoj tehniki metodom èksperimenta' (= A study of primitive technology by experimental method), in C. I. RUDENKO (ed.), *Novye metody v arheologičeskih issledovanijah* (= New Methods in Archaeological Research), Moscow-Leningrad, Nauka, 1963.

—, *Prehistoric Technology. An Experimental Study of the Oldest Tools and Artefacts from Traces of Manufacture and Wear*, translated and with a preface by M. W. Thompson, New York, Barnes & Noble/London, Cory, Adams & Mackay, 1964.

—, *Razvitie tehniki v kamennom veke* (= The Development of Technology in the Stone Age), Leningrad, Nauka, 1968.

VIIe Congrès international des Sciences anthropologiques et ethnologiques (Moscou, 1964) (Russian title: *Trudy VII Meždunarodnogo Kongressa Antropologičeskih i Ètnografičeskih Nauk*), Moscow, Nauka, Vol. 4, 1967; Vols. 6, 7 and 8, 1970.

SERGEEV, M. A., *Nekapitalističeskij put' razvitija malyh narodov severa* (= The Non-capitalist Development of the Small Peoples of the North), Moscow-Leningrad, Izdatel'stvo Akademii Nauk, 1955.

SERVICE, Elman R., *Primitive Social Organization. An Evolutionary Perspective*, New York, Random House, 1962.

—, *The Hunters*, Foundations of Modern Anthropology Series, Englewood Cliffs (N.J.), Prentice-Hall, 1966.
[See also SAHLINS & SERVICE (eds.).]

SHAH, A. M., 'Basic terms and concepts in the study of family in India', *Indian Economic and Social History Review* 1 (3), 1964, pp. 1-36.
[See also SRINIVAS & SHAH.]

SHARP, Andrew, *Ancient Voyagers in the Pacific*, Harmondsworth (Middx.), Penguin Books, 1957.

SHETH, N. R., *The Social Framework of an Indian Factory*, Manchester, Manchester University Press, 1968.

SIEGEL, Bernard J. (ed.), *Biennial Review of Anthropology 1959*, Stanford (Calif.), Stanford University Press, 1959.

—, *Biennial Review of Anthropology 1961*, Stanford (Calif.), Stanford University Press, 1962.

—, *Biennial Review of Anthropology 1965*, Stanford (Calif.), Stanford University Press, 1965.

—, *Biennial Review of Anthropology 1969*, Stanford (Calif.), Stanford University Press, 1970.

— & BEALS, Alan R. (eds.), *Biennial Review of Anthropology 1967*, Stanford (Calif.), Stanford University Press, 1967.

SIGRIST, Christian, *Regulierte Anarchie. Untersuchungen zum Fehlen und zur Entstehung politischer Herrschaft in segmentären Gesellschaften Afrikas* (= Regulated Anarchy. Investigations into the Absence and the Beginnings of Political Authority in Segmentary Societies of Africa), Olten-Freiburg im Breisgau, Walter-Verlag, 1967.

SILLS, David L. (ed.), *International Encyclopedia of the Social Sciences*, New York, Macmillan Co./Free Press, 1968, 17 vols.

SIMONIS, Yvan, *Claude Lévi-Strauss ou la 'Passion de l'inceste'. Introduction au structuralisme*, Paris, Aubier-Montaigne, 1968.

SINGER, Milton, 'The concept of culture', in SILLS (ed.), *International Encyclopedia of the Social Sciences, op. cit.* (1968), Vol. 3, pp. 527-543.

SINGER, Milton & COHN, Bernard S. (eds.), *Structure and Change in Indian Society*, Viking Fund Publ. in Anthrop. 47, Chicago, Aldine, 1968.

SINHA, D. P., *Culture Change in an Inter-Tribal Market*, Bombay, Asia Publishing House, 1968.

SIXEL, F. W., 'Inkonsistenzen in Transkulturations-Prozessen', *Sociologus*, n.s. 19 (2), 1969, pp. 166-177.

SJOBERG, Gideon (ed.), *Ethics, Politics, and Social Research*, Cambridge (Mass.), Schenkman Publishing Co., 1967.

SLOTKIN, J. S., *Readings in Early Anthropology*, Viking Fund Publ. in Anthrop. 40, New York, Wenner-Gren Foundation/Chicago, Aldine, 1965.

SMIRNOVA, JA. S., 'Nacional'no smešannye braki u narodov Karačaevo-Čerkesii' (= Mixed marriages among the Karachai Circassian peoples), *Sovetskaja ètnografija*, 1967, No. 4, pp. 137-142.

SMITH, Allan H. & FISCHER, John L. (eds.), *Anthropology* (Behavioral and Social Sciences Survey), Englewood Cliffs (N.J.), Prentice-Hall, 1970.

SMITH, M. G., 'Political organization', in SILLS (ed.), *International Encyclopedia of the Social Sciences, op. cit.* (1968), Vol. 12, pp. 103-202.
[See also KUPER & SMITH, M. G. (eds.).]

SMITH, Raymond T., 'Comparative structure', *sub* 'Family', in SILLS (ed.), *International Encyclopedia of the Social Sciences, op. cit.* (1968), Vol. 5, pp. 301-313.

SNESAREV, G. P., *Relikty domusul'manskih verovanij i obrajadov u Uzbekov Horezma* (= Survivals of Pre-Muslim Beliefs and Rituals among the Uzbeks of Khoresm), Moscow, Nauka, 1969.

Social Science Research Council, *Research in Social Anthropology*, London, Heinemann, 1968.

The Social Sciences. Problems and Orientations/Les sciences sociales. Problèmes et orientations, The Hague-Paris, Mouton/Unesco, 1968.

SOFUE, Takao, 'Anthropology in Japan. Historical review and current trends', in SIEGEL (ed.), *Biennial Review of Anthropology 1961, op. cit.* (1962), pp. 173-214.

SOKOLOVA, V. K., 'Sovetskaja fol'kloristika k 50-letiju Oktjabrja' (= Soviet folklore studies to the 50th anniversary of the October Revolution), *Sovetskaja ètnografija*, 1967, No. 5, pp. 44-61.

SORENSON, E. Richard, 'A research film program in the study of changing man', *Current Anthropology* 8 (5), 1967, pp. 443-469.

SPECKMAN, J. D., 'Social surveys in non-Western areas', in JONGMANS & GUTKIND (eds.), *Anthropologists in the Field, op. cit.* (1967), pp. 56-74.

SPERBER, Dan, 'Le structuralisme en anthropologie', in WAHL (ed.), *Qu'est-ce que le structuralisme?, op. cit.* (1968), pp. 167-238.

SPINDLER, George D. (ed.), *Being an Anthropologist. Fieldwork in Eleven Cultures*, New York, Holt, Rinehart & Winston, 1970.

—— & SPINDLER, Louise (eds.), 'Studies in Anthropological Methods' series, New York, Holt, Rinehart & Winston.

SPIRO, Melford E., 'Culture and personality', in SILLS (ed.), *International Encyclopedia of the Social Sciences, op. cit.* (1968), Vol. 3, pp. 558-563.

SRINIVAS, M. N., *Caste in Modern India, and Other Essays*, Bombay, Asia Publishing House, 1962.

——, *Social Change in Modern India*, Berkeley-Los Angeles, University of California Press, 1966.

——, 'The cohesive role of Sanskritisation', in MASON (ed.), *India and Ceylon: Unity and Diversity, op. cit.* (1967), pp. 67-82.

172   *Maurice Freedman*

—, 'Sociology and sociologists in India today', *Sociological Bulletin, Journal of the Indian Sociological Society* 19 (1), 1970, pp. 1-10.
— & SHAH, A. M., 'Hinduism', in SILLS (ed.), *International Encyclopedia of the Social Sciences, op. cit.* (1968), Vol. 6, pp. 358-366.
STAHL, Paul Henri, 'Cultural anthropology in Romania', in 'Anthropology in East-Central and Southeast Europe', *op. cit.* (1970), pp. 319-327.
STANNER, W. E. H., *On Aboriginal Religion*, 'Oceania' Monograph No. 11, Sydney (N.S.W.), University of Sydney, 1964.
STEFFLRE, Volney, REICH, Peter, & MCCLAREN-STEFFLRE, Marlys, 'Some eliciting and computational procedures for descriptive semantics', in KAY (ed.), *Explorations in Mathematical Anthropology, op. cit.* (1971), pp. 79-116.
STENNING, D. J., *Documentary Survey of Crime in Kampala, Uganda*, United Nations Economic Commission for Africa, Workshop on Urbanization in Africa, Addis Ababa, 1962.
STEWARD, Julian H., 'Introduction' to Julian H. STEWARD *et al., Irrigation Civilizations. A Comparative Study, A Symposium on Method and Result in Cross-Cultural Regularities*, Social Science Monographs No. 1, Social Science Section, Washington (D.C.), Dept. of Cultural Affairs, Pan American Union, 1955, pp. 1-5.
—, *Theory of Culture Change*, Urbana, University of Illinois Press, 1955.
STEWARD, Julian H. (ed.), *Contemporary Change in Traditional Societies*, Urbana, University of Illinois Press, 1967, 3 vols.
STOCKING, George W., Jr., 'Matthew Arnold, E. B. Tylor, and the uses of invention', *American Anthropologist* 65 (4), 1963, pp. 783-799 (reprinted in the same authors *Race, Culture and Evolution. Essays in the History of Anthropology, op. cit.* (1968), Chap. 4).
—, *Race, Culture and Evolution. Essays in the History of Anthropology*, New York, Free Press, 1968.
STOCKMANN, Doris, 'Das Problem der Transkription in der musikethnologischen Forschung', *Deutsches Jahrbuch für Volkskunde* (Berlin), Vol. 12, 1966, pp. 207-242.
STOCKMANN, Erich & STROBACH, Hermann (Berlin) in collab. with CHISTOV (= ČISTOV), Kirill (Leningrad) & HIPPIUS, Eugen (Moscow) (eds.), *Sowjetische Volkslied- und Volksmusikforschung. Augewählte Studien* (= Soviet Research on Folk Song and Folk Music. Selected Studies), Berlin, Akademie Verlag, 1967 (in particular, essays by Z. V. EVALD, A. N. AKSENOV, V. S. VINOGRADOV, and K. V. KVITKA).
ŠTOFF, V. A., *Modelirovanie i filosofija* (= Models and Philosophy), Moscow-Leningrad, Nauka, 1966.
STRATHERN, A. & STRATHERN, M., *Self-Decoration in Mount Hagen*, London, Duckworth, 1971.
Studia Musicologica Academiae Scientiarum Hungaricae (Budapest), Vol. 7, 1965.
STURTEVANT, William C., 'Studies in ethnoscience', in ROMNEY & D'ANDRADE (eds.), *Transcultural Studies in Cognition, op. cit.* (1964), pp. 99-131.
—, 'Anthropology, history and ethnohistory', *Ethnohistory* 13 (1-2), 1966 (published 1967), pp. 1-51 and in a slightly different version in CLIFTON (ed.), *Introduction to Cultural Anthropology ..., op. cit.* (1968), pp. 450-475.
—, 'Seminole men's clothing', in HELM (ed.), *Essays on the Verbal and Visual Arts, op. cit.* (1967), pp. 160-174.
—, 'Does anthropology need museums?', *Proceedings of the Biological Society of Washington*, Vol. 82, 17 Nov. 1969, pp. 619-650.
[See also GLADWIN & STURTEVANT (eds.).]
SUCHOFF, Benjamin, 'Computer applications to Bartok's Serbo-Croatian material', *Tempo* (London), Vol. 80, 1967, pp. 15-19.
—, 'Computerized folk song research and the problem of variants', *Computers*

and the Humanities (Queen's College, New York) 2 (4), 1968, pp. 155-158.
SWARTZ, Marc J., TURNER, Victor W., & TUDEN, Arthur (eds.), *Political Anthropology*, Chicago, Aldine, 1966.

TAMBIAH, S. J., 'The magical power of words', *Man*, n.s., 3 (2), 1968, pp. 175-208.
TÁRKÁNY-SZŰCS, Ernő, 'Results and task of legal ethnology in Europe', *Ethnologia Europaea* 1 (3), 1967, pp. 195-217.
TAX, Sol, 'The uses of anthropology', in TAX (ed.), *Horizons of Anthropology, op. cit.* (1964), pp. 248-253.
——, *Anthropological Backgrounds for Adult Education*, Center for Study of Liberal Education for Adults, Boston, Boston University, 1968.
——, 'Letter to Associates' No. 49, *Current Anthropology* 10 (4), Oct. 1969.
TAX, Sol (ed.), *Horizons of Anthropology*, Chicago, Aldine, 1964.
TAYLOR, Archer, 'Folklore and the study of literature', in DUNDES (ed.), *The Study of Folklore, op. cit.* (1965), pp. 34-42.
Tendances principales de la recherche dans les sciences sociales et humaines, Partie I: Sciences sociales: see *Main Trends of Research in the Social and Human Sciences, Part I: Social Sciences.*
TERRAY, Emmanuel, *Le marxisme devant les sociétés 'primitives'. Deux études*, Paris, Maspero, 1969 (English translation by Mary Klopper, *Marxism and 'Primitive' Societies. Two Studies*, New York-London, Monthly Review Press, 1972).
——, 'Morgan et l'anthropologie contemporaine', in TERRAY, *Le marxisme devant les sociétés 'primitives', op. cit.* (1969) (English translation, 'Morgan and contemporary anthropology', in TERRAY, *Marxism and 'Primitive' Societies, op. cit.*, 1972).
THOMAS, Keith, 'History and anthropology', *Past and Present*, No. 24, 1963, pp. 3-24.
THOMPSON, R., 'Àbátàn: a master potter of the Ègbádò Yorùba', in BIEBUYCK (ed.), *Tradition and Creativity in Tribal Art, op. cit.* (1969), pp. 120-182.
TIGER, Lionel, *Men in Groups*, London, Nelson, 1969.
——, 'Introduction' [to *Understanding Aggression, op. cit.* (1971), pp. 9-17] (parrallel publication of French translation. 'Introduction' to *Comprendre l'agressivité*, pp. 9-18).
TILNEY, Philip V. R., 'Ethnographic research in Bulgaria', in 'Anthropology in East-Central and Southeast Europe', *op. cit.* (1970), pp. 242-251.
TIPPET, A. R., *Fijian Material Culture* = *Bernice P. Bishop Museum Bulletin*, No. 232, Honolulu (Haw.), 1968, 193 pp.
TOKAREV, S. A., 'K postanovke problem ètnogeneza' (= On the position of the problems of ethnogenesis), *Sovetskaja ètnografija*, 1949, No. 3, pp. 12-36.
——, *Rannie formy religii i ih razvitie* (= Early Forms of Religion and Their Development), Moscow, Nauka, 1964 (the Introduction to this book is translated in *Soviet Anthropology and Archeology* 4 (4), Spring 1966, pp. 3-10, and 5 (1), Summer 1966, pp. 11-25).
——, *Religija v istorii narodov mira* (= Religion in the History of the Peoples of the World), Moscow, Izdatel'stvo Političeskoj Literatury, 1964.
——, *Istorija russkoj ètnografii, Dooktjabrskij period* (= A History of Russian Ethnography until 1917), Moscow, Nauka, 1966.
——, 'The problem of totemism as seen by Soviet scholars', *Current Anthropology* 7 (2), 1966, pp. 185-188.
——, 'Die Grenzen der ethnologischen Erforschung der Völker industrieller Länder', *Ethnologia Europaea* 1 (1), 1967, pp. 12-36.
——, '50 Jahre sowjetische Ethnographie', *Ethnographisch-Archäologische Zeitschrift (EAZ)* (Berlin), 10 (1), 1969, pp. 15-32.
——, 'Probleme der Forschung der frühen Religionen', *Ethnographisch-Archäologische Zeitschrift (EAZ)* 10 (2), 1969, pp. 151-165.

174   Maurice Freedman

——, 'K metodike ètnografičeskogo izučenija material'noj kul'tury' (= On methods for the ethnographical investigation of material culture), *Sovetskaja ètnografija*, 1970, No. 4, pp. 3-17.

TOLSTOV, S. P., 'Nekotorye problemy vsemirnoj istorii v svete dannyh sovremennoj istoričeskoj ètnografii' (= Some problems of world history in the light of present-day ethnohistorical data), *Voprosy istorii*, 1961, No. 11, pp. 107-118.

—— & ZHDANKO (= ŽDANKO), T. A., 'Directions and problems of Soviet ethnography', *Soviet Anthropology and Archeology* 3 (3), Winter 1964-65, pp. 3-20 (translated from *Voprosy istorii*, 1964, No. 7).

TOLSTOV, S. P. (ed.), *Russkie, Istoriko-ètnografičeskij atlas* (= The Russians, Historico-Ethnographic Atlas), Moscow, Nauka, 1967.

'Toward a philosophy of technology', *Technology and Culture* (Wayne State Univ. Press), 7 (3), 1966.

TRACEY, Andrew, 'The Mbira music of Jeje Tapero', *African Music* (African Music Society, Roodepoort, Transvaal), 2 (4), 1961, pp. 44-63.

TRIGGER, Bruce G., *Beyond History. The Methods of Prehistory*, Studies in Anthropological Method, New York-London, Holt, Rinehart & Winston, 1968.

TURNER, Victor W., *The Forest of Symbols. Aspects of Ndembu Ritual*, Ithaca (N.Y.), Cornell University Press, 1967.

——, *The Ritual Process. Structure and Anti-Structure*, Chicago, Aldine, 1969.
[See also SWARTZ, TURNER, & TUDEN (eds.).]

TYLER, Stephen A., 'Parallel/cross. An evaluation of definitions', *Southwestern Journal of Anthropology* 22 (4), 1966, pp. 416-432.

TYLER, Stephen A. (ed.), *Cognitive Anthropology*, New York, Holt, Rinehart and Winston, 1969.

UBEROI, J. P. Singh, 'Science and Swaraj', *Contributions to Indian Sociology*, n.s., No. 2, 1968, pp. 119-123.

UCHENDU, Victor C., 'Priority issues for social anthropological research in Africa in the next two decades', in CARTER & PADEN (eds.), *Expanding Horizons in African Studies, op. cit.* (1969), pp. 3-23.

UDY, Stanley H., *Organization of Work,* New Haven (Conn.), Human Relations Area Files, 1959.

Understanding Aggression (publication arising from an interdisciplinary meeting on the implications of recent scientific research on the understanding of human aggressiveness, held at Unesco Headquarters from 19 to 23 May 1970) = *International Social Science Journal* XXIII (1), 1971, pp. 5-110 (parallel publication in French, *Comprendre l'agressivité* = *Revue internationale des Sciences sociales*, same ref., pp. 5-126).

'Urgent anthropology: Associates 'views on the definition of "urgency" ', *Current Anthropology* 12 (2), 1971, pp. 243-254.

Use of Computers, Documentation, and the Social Sciences = *International Social Science Journal* XXIII (2), 1971, pp. 161-292 (parallel publication in French, *L'informatique, la documentation et les sciences sociales* = *Revue internationale des Sciences sociales*, same ref., pp. 173-315).

VÁCLAVÍK, Antonín, *Výroční obyčeje a lidové uměni* (= Calendar Customs and Folk Art), Prague, Nakladatelství Československé Akademie Věd, 1959.

VAJNŠTEJN, S. I., 'Ornament v narodnom iskusstve tuvincev (= Ornament in the folk art of the people of Tuva), *Sovetskaja ètnografija*, 1967, No. 2, pp. 45-61.

VANSINA, Jan, *De la tradition orale. Essai de méthode historique,* Annales du Musée Royal de l'Afrique centrale, Tervuren, 1961 (English translation by H. M. Wright, *The Oral Tradition. A Study in Historical Methodology*, Chicago, The University of Chicago Press/London, Routledge & Kegan Paul, 1965.

——, 'Cultures through time', in NAROLL & COHEN, R. (eds.), *A Handbook of Methods in Cultural Anthropology, op. cit.* (1970), pp. 165-179.

VASILYEV (= VASIL'EV), V., 'Institute of Ethnography', *Social Sciences* (USSR Academy of Sciences, Moscow), Vol. 2, 1970, pp. 201-204.

VATUK, V. P., 'Protest songs of East Indians in British Guiana', *Journal of American Folklore* 77 (305), 1964, pp. 220-236.

——, 'Let's dig up some dirt. The idea of humour in children's folklore in India', in *Proceedings of the VIIIth International Congress of Anthropological and Ethnological Sciences, Tokyo and Kyoto, 1968*, Vol. 2, Tokyo, Science Council of Japan, 1969, pp. 274-277.

VAYDA, Andrew P., 'Anthropologists and ecological problems', in LEEDS & VAYDA (eds.), *Man, Culture, and Animals ..., op. cit.* (1965), pp. 1-6.

VAYDA, Andrew P. (ed.), *Environment and Cultural Behavior. Ecological Studies in Cultural Anthropology*, American Museum Sourcebooks in Anthropology, Garden City (N.Y.), Natural History Press, 1969.

VIDYARTHI, Lalita P., 'Conference on urgent social research in India', *Current Anthropology* 10 (4), 1969, pp. 377-379.

VILLONES, Luis, *Introducción al proceso de aculturación religiosa indígena*, Instituto Indigenista Peruano, Serie Monográfica no. 18, Lima, 1967.

VINNIKOV, Ja. R., 'Novoe v semejnom bytu kolhoznikov Turkmenistana' (= New aspects of the family life of collective-farm workers in Turkmenistan), *Sovetskaja ètnografija*, 1967, No. 6, pp. 32-41.

VINOGRADOV, V. S., *Muzyka Gvinei* (= Music of Guinea), Moscow, Sovetskij Kompozitor, 1969.

[See also *sub* STOCKMANN, E. & STROBACH with CHISTOV & HIPPIUS.]

VOGT, Evon Z., 'Culture change', in SILLS (ed.), *International Encyclopedia of the Social Sciences, op. cit.* (1968), Vol. 3, pp. 554-558.

VOIGT, Vilmos, 'As epikus néphagomány strukturális-tipológikus elemzésének lehetőségei' (= Possibilities for structural-typological analysis of epic folk traditions), *Ethnographia* (Budapest), Vol. 75, 1964, pp. 36-46.

——, 'A néprajztudomány elméleti-terminologiai kérdései' (= Theoretical and methodological problems in recent East European ethnology, ethnography, and folklore), *Ethnographia* (Budapest), Vol. 76, 1965, pp. 481-500.

——, 'Modellalási kisérletek a folklorisztikában' (= Research in folklore models), *Studia Ethnographica* (Budapest), No. 5, 1969, pp. 355-392, 419-420, 426.

——, 'Structural definition of oral (folk)´literature', in *Proceedings of the Vth Congress of the International Comparative Literature Association*, University of Belgrade/Amsterdam, Swets & Zeitlinger, 1969, pp. 461-467.

——, 'Towards balancing of folklore structuralism', *Acta Ethnographica* (Budapest), Vol. 18, 1969, pp. 247-255.

[See also HOPPÁL & VOIGT.]

WAHL, François (ed.), *Qu'est-ce que le structuralisme?*, Paris, Editions du Seuil, 1968.

WALLACE, Anthony F. C., *Culture and Personality*, New York, Random House, 1961.

——, *Religion. An Anthropological View*, New York, Random House, 1966.

WANE, Yaya, 'Réflexions sur la recherche sociologique en milieu africain', *Cahiers d'Etudes africaines* X/3 (39), 1970, pp. 384-406.

WARMAN, Arturo, NOLASCO ARMAS, Margarita, BONFIL, Guillermo, OLIVERA DE VÁZQUEZ, Mercedes, and VALENCIA, Enrique, *De eso que llaman antropología mexicana* (= On So-called Mexican Anthropology), 'La Cultura al Pueblo' series, Mexico City, Editorial Nuestro Tiempo, 1970.

WATSON, James B., 'Pueraria: names and traditions of a lesser crop in the Central Highlands, New Guinea', *Ethnology* 7 (3), 1968, pp. 268-279.

WATSON, O. Michael, *Proxemic Behavior. A Cross-Cultural Study,* The Hague-Paris, Mouton, 1970.

—— & GRAVES, Theodore D., 'Quantitative research in proxemic behavior', *American Anthropologist* 68 (4), 1966, pp. 971-985.

WATT, W., *Morphology of the Nevada Cattlebrands and Their Blasons,* Pt. 1, US Dept. of Commerce, National Bureau of Standards Report No. 9050, Washington (D.C.), 1966; Pt. 2, Pittsburgh, Carnegie-Mellon University, 1967.

WEIL, André, 'Sur l'étude algébrique de certains types de lois de mariage (Système Murngin)', in LÉVI-STRAUSS, *Les structures élémentaires de la parenté, op. cit.* (1940, 1967) (Ch. X, Appendix to Part One) (English translation, 'On the algebraic study of certain types of marriage laws (Murngin system)', in LÉVI-STRAUSS, *The Elementary Structures of Kinship,* translated by J. H. *et al., op. cit.,* 1969).

WEMAN, Henry, *African Music and the Church in Africa,* Uppsala, Svenska Institutet för Missionsforskning, 1960.

WHITE, Leslie A., *The Evolution of Culture. The Development of Civilization to the Fall of Rome,* New York, McGraw-Hill, 1959.

WHITELEY, W. H., *A Selection of African Prose: I. Traditional Oral Texts,* Oxford Library of African Literature, Oxford, Clarendon Press, 1964.

WHITING, Beatrice (ed.), *Six Cultures. Studies of Child Rearing,* New York, Wiley & Sons, 1963.

WHITING, John W. M., 'Socialization process and personality', in HSU (ed.), *Psychological Anthropology. Approaches to Culture and Personality, op. cit.* (1961), pp. 355-380.

Who's Who of Indian Musicians, New Delhi, Sangeet Natak Academy, 1968.

WINCKLER, Edwin A., 'Political anthropology', in SIEGEL, *Biennial Review of Anthropology 1969, op. cit.* (1970), pp. 301-392.

WOLF, Eric R., *Anthropology,* 'Humanistic scholarship in America. The Princeton Studies' Series, Englewood Cliffs (N.J.), Prentice-Hall, 1964.

——, *Peasants,* Foundations of Modern Anthropology Series, Englewood Cliffs (N.J.), Prentice-Hall, 1966.

WOODBURN, James, 'Stability and flexibility in Hadza residential groupings', in LEE & DEVORE (eds.), *Man the Hunter, op. cit.* (1968), pp. 103-109.

WRIGLEY, Christopher, 'Speculations on the economic prehistory of Africa', *The Journal of African History* 2 (3), 1960, pp. 189-203.

YEN, Chun-chiang, 'Folklore research in Communist China', *Asian Folklore Studies* (Tokyo), 26 (2), 1967, pp. 1-62.

YEN, Douglas E. & WHEELER, Jocelyn M., 'Introduction of Taro into the Pacific. The indications of chromosome numbers', *Ethnology* 7 (3), 1968, pp. 229-267.

ŽIRMUNSKIJ (SCHIRMUNSKI), Viktor Maksimovič, *Vergleichende Epenforschung,* Vol. 1, Berlin, Akademie Verlag, 1961.
[See also CHADWICK, N. K. & ZHIRMUNSKY, V. M.]

301.2
F853

82483

LINCOLN CHRISTIAN COLLEGE AND SEMINARY